RESHAPING GENDER
AND CLASS IN RURAL SPACES

Gender in a Global/Local World

Series Editors: Jane Parpart, Pauline Gardiner Barber
and Marianne H. Marchand

Gender in a Global/Local World critically explores the uneven and often contradictory ways in which global processes and local identities come together. Much has been and is being written about globalization and responses to it but rarely from a critical, historical, gendered perspective. Yet, these processes are profoundly gendered albeit in different ways in particular contexts and times. The changes in social, cultural, economic and political institutions and practices alter the conditions under which women and men make and remake their lives. New spaces have been created – economic, political, social – and previously silent voices are being heard. North-South dichotomies are being undermined as increasing numbers of people and communities are exposed to international processes through migration, travel, and communication, even as marginalization and poverty intensify for many in all parts of the world. The series features monographs and collections which explore the tensions in a 'global/local world', and includes contributions from all disciplines in recognition that no single approach can capture these complex processes.

Previous titles are listed at the back of the book

Reshaping Gender and Class in Rural Spaces

Edited by

BARBARA PINI
Curtin University of Technology, Australia

BELINDA LEACH
University of Guelph, Canada

ASHGATE

Published by
Ashgate Publishing Limited
Wey Court East
Union Road
Farnham
Surrey, GU9 7PT
England

Ashgate Publishing Company
Suite 420
101 Cherry Street
Burlington
VT 05401-4405
USA

www.ashgate.com

British Library Cataloguing in Publication Data
Reshaping gender and class in rural spaces. -- (Gender in a
    global/local world)
    1. Sociology, Rural. 2. Social classes--Cross-cultural
    studies. 3. Rural conditions. 4. Manpower policy, Rural--
    Case studies. 5. Rural women--Social conditions--Case
    studies. 6. Rural women--Employment--Case studies.
    7. Social change--Cross-cultural studies.
    I. Series II. Pini, Barbara. III. Leach, Belinda, 1954-
    307.7'2-dc22

Library of Congress Cataloging-in-Publication Data
Reshaping gender and class in rural spaces / [edited] by Barbara Pini and Belinda Leach.
    p. cm. -- (Gender in a global/local world)
    Includes bibliographical references and index.
    ISBN 978-1-4094-0291-6 (hardback) -- ISBN 978-1-4094-0292-3 (ebook) 1. Sociology,
Rural. 2. Rural women--Social conditions. 3. Gender-based analysis. 4. Social classes. I.
Pini, Barbara. II. Leach, Belinda, 1954-
    HT421.R377 2011
    305.3--dc22

2011004230

ISBN 978 1 4094 0291 6 (hbk)
ISBN 978 1 4094 0292 3 (ebk)

Printed and bound in Great Britain by the
MPG Books Group, UK

Contents

List of Figures

List of Tables

Notes on Contributors

Debra Davidson is Associate Professor of Environmental Sociology, with a joint appointment between the Departments of Rural Economy and Renewable Resources at the University of Alberta, where she has been for 10 years. Over the past three years she has also served as the Director of the Environmental Research and Studies Centre, a non-profit, outreach organization the mandate of which is to breach the barriers between academic research in environmental sciences and civil society. She received her training in environmental sciences at the undergraduate level from UC-Berkeley, then went on to receive an MSc from the Institute of Environmental Studies at the University of Wisconsin-Madison. She remained at UW-Madison for her PhD in Sociology, working under the mentorship of Frederick Buttel and William Freudenburg. Recent publications have been featured in *Canadian Review of Sociology*; *Society and Natural Resources*; and *Sociological Inquiry*. She is also the co-editor of *Consuming Sustainability: Critical Social Analyses of Ecological Change* (Fernwood Publishing, 2005) for which she worked closely with Mike Gismondi.

Rae Dufty is a Lecturer in Human Geography at the University of Western Sydney. Her research interests revolve around the political-economic geographies of neoliberal policy approaches in both rural and urban settings. This has resulted in a wide range of research projects from the archival analysis of housing policy in Australia, to investigating the causes and actual migration pathways of Australian rural youth. She has recently published articles in the *Journal of Rural Studies* (2008), *Australian Geographer* (2009) and has a chapter in the book *Welfare Reform in Rural Places* (2010) edited by Paul Milbourne.

Evelyn Encalada Grez is a Chilean born community organiser, educator and researcher completing a doctoral degree at the Ontario Institute for Studies in Education of the University of Toronto. Evelyn is a founding member of Justice for Migrant Workers, a grassroots collective that promotes the rights of migrant farm workers and their families in rural Canada and rural Mexico. As a result of her affiliation with 'Rural Women Making Change' she was invited to speak at the UN about her work with Mexican migrant women in observance of the first International Day of Rural Women.

Annie Hughes is a Principal Lecturer in the School of Geography, Geology and the Environment at Kingston University, London. Annie has worked on several projects relating to gender and rural environments; including an ESRC project entitled 'Lone parents and paid work: evidence from rural England'. She has published several articles on issues relating to rurality, gender and mothering, as well as work on lone parenthood, paid work and social policy. However she is currently working on a Higher Education Academy funded project 'Ethnic identities and positioning in the field: identifying key issues for the GEES subjects' which relates to her other research interest in pedagogy and geographical education. She is a regular reviewer for journals such as *Culture, Place and Society, Journal of Rural Studies* and *Sociologia Ruralis*; as well as funding bodies such as the ESRC.

Belinda Leach is a Professor in the Department of Sociology and Anthropology at the University of Guelph. She held a University Research Chair in Rural Gender Studies between 2004 and 2009. Her research investigates gender, livelihoods and economic restructuring in Canada and has been published in *Critique of Anthropology, Identities, Labour-Le Travail* and *Signs*. She is coeditor with Winnie Lem of *Culture, Economy, Power: Anthropology as Critique, Anthropology as Praxis* (State University of New York Press, 2002), and co-author with Tony Winson of *Contingent Work, Disrupted Lives: Labour and Community in the New Rural Economy* (University of Toronto Press, 2002) which was awarded the John Porter Award of the Canadian Sociology and Anthropology Association. She is currently a co-editor of *Identities: Global Studies in Culture and Power*.

Edgar Liu is a Research Associate at the City Futures Research Centre, UNSW. His research interests span cultural and urban geographies as well as urban and housing studies. He successfully completed his PhD on the relationships between gender, sexuality and space at UNSW in 2008 and continues his research into identity performatives in alternative spaces, including graffiti and latrinalia. His other research includes social aspects of housing and urban policies, particularly transitions in people's housing careers and pathways and their wider socioeconomic implications. He is currently collaborating with several early career researchers on an edited book on geographic research practices.

Susan Machum holds a Canada Research Chair in Rural Social Justice and is an Associate Professor of Sociology at St. Thomas University in Fredericton, New Brunswick, Canada. She received her BA (Hons.) from St. Thomas in 1987, her MA from Dalhousie in 1992 and her PhD from Edinburgh University in 1999. Her major research interests are women's work in the primary sector, rural-urban relations, economic and social development, and environmental issues. She has been Executive Director of the Conservation Council of New Brunswick, and worked for Canada World Youth, an international development education and exchange programme. Dr. Machum grew up in rural New Brunswick and has watched her community shift the productive farming to urban housing.

Robyn Mayes is a Research Fellow at the John Curtin Institute of Public Policy. Her current research examines the social and cultural dimensions of mining, with particular attention to relationships between communities and corporate social responsibility agendas and practices, community and family dimensions of industrial relations, and changing senses of rural community and place.

Edward Morris is an Assistant Professor of Sociology at the University of Kentucky. His research interests include the intersections of race, class, and gender; rural and urban education; and white privilege. His research has won awards and been featured in the popular press. His publications include articles in *Symbolic Interaction, Youth and Society, Sociology of Education* and *Gender and Society*, and a book entitled *An Unexpected Minority: White Kids in an Urban School* (Rutgers University Press, 2006). Currently, Dr. Morris is analysing data from a comparative ethnography of two high schools – one urban and one rural. This analysis focuses on (1) reasons behind the 'gender gap' in achievement favouring girls among disadvantaged students, (2) the 'stop snitching' code and distrust of formal authorities in conflict resolution among students, and (3) micro-level processes of exclusion, boundary maintenance, and differentiation among students.

Martin Phillips is a Reader in Social and Cultural Geography at the University of Leicester. His research interests include work on rural social and cultural geographies, in relation to which he has published widely. He has written extensively on issues of rural genrification and rural class analysis. Much of his current work focuses on issues of social and environmental change in the countryside. He has co-authored *Writing the Rural* (1994) and *Society and Exploitation through Nature* (2000), as well as editing and contributing to *Contested Worlds* (2005). Forthcoming publications include an edited book entitled *Gentrification and the Countryside*.

Barbara Pini is a Professor in the John Curtin Institute of Public Policy. She has an extensive publication in the fields of gender and rurality including the book *Masculinities and Management in Agricultural Organizations Worldwide* (2008) published by Ashgate and *Gender and Rurality* (Routledge, 2011) (with Lia Bryant). She is currently undertaking a large project investigating disability in rural Australia.

Kerry Preibisch is an Associate Professor in the Department of Sociology and Anthropology at the University of Guelph. Specializing in international migration and rural development, her research focuses on gender and migration, labour migration and global agro-food systems, and im/migrant communities in rural Canada. Current projects include examining the new social relations of agriculture in the Global North, temporary migration programs, im/migrant farm workers' health, and immigration in rural Canada. She has published in *International Migration Review, Signs*, the *Journal of Ethnic and Migration Studies*, and the *Journal of International Development*.

Maureen Reed is Professor in the School of Environment and Sustainability and the Department of Geography and Planning at the University of Saskatchewan. She is interested in how, and with what effects, rural people become involved in conservation and environmental governance. More specifically, she studies how participatory conservation and decision-making approaches, working conditions, gender relations, and socio-cultural changes affect the capacity of rural communities to advance sustainability. She undertakes research with people living in or near biosphere reserves, national parks, model forests and forestry communities. Her favourite holidays involve exploring the continent and appreciating other people's gardens.

Suzanne E. Tallichet is a professor of sociology in the Department of Sociology, Social Work and Criminology at Morehead State University in Kentucky, USA. Her research interests include gender and work, animals and society and Appalachian studies. She has published in *Gender and Society*, *Rural Sociology*, *Criminal Justice Review*, *Criminal Justice Studies*, *International Journal of Offender Therapy and Comparative Criminology*, *Society and Animals* and the *Journal of Interpersonal Violence*. Her book, *Daughters of the Mountain: Women Coal Miners in Central Appalachia*, was published in 2006 by Pennsylvania State University Press. In 2007, she received Morehead State University's Distinguished Researcher Award.

Yvette Taylor is a Senior Lecturer in Sociology at Newcastle University and held the Lillian S. Robinson Scholarship at Concordia University, Montreal. Her publications include *Working-class Lesbian Life: Classed Outsiders* (Palgrave, 2007), *Lesbian and Gay Parenting: Securing Social and Educational Capitals* (Palgrave, 2009) and an edited collection *Classed Intersections: Spaces, Selves, Knowledges* (Ashgate, 2010). She has articles in a range of journals including *British Journal of the Sociology of Education*, *Women's Studies International Forum*, *Sexualities* and *Feminism and Psychology*. Yvette is working on a forthcoming book *Fitting into Place?* (Ashgate) from ESRC-funded research (2007-9) and is beginning a new ESRC grant 'Making space for queer identifying religious youth'.

Series Editors' Preface

The city and the countryside are mutually interdependent in the geographies and political economies of contemporary capitalism, but we seldom read about rural social change, or rural poverty. *Reshaping Gender and Class in Rural Spaces* addresses a series of interlinked silences surrounding rurality. First of all, we are reminded that class matters now as much as it always did. It configures and reconfigures social life and livelihoods everywhere. Yet rural spaces are typically conceptualized, sometimes romantically, as classless. Similarly, rural gender relations, certainly in western industrial countries, are often reductively transposed to the concerns of 'rural women' who are seldom viewed through a class and gender lens. Contributors to *Reshaping Gender and Class in Rural Spaces* identify the complex and changing articulations of gender and class in rural localities. They write against the grain of neoliberal policy discourses such as 'social inclusion' and/or 'social well being' to address the remarkable academic (and policy) silence about rural social disparities. By situating rural lives within the analytical purview of globalization, the volume tackles important questions about the contradictions and complexities of rural economies. How do class and gender matter in rural spaces: to what effect, for whom, and how? How does social justice apply to disadvantaged people in rural areas?

Many readers will be interested in Pini and Leach's cogent introductory chapter which lays out the conceptual framework and political agenda for the volume. They demonstrate why it is important for researchers and policy makers to also pay careful attention to the material conditions of life in rural localities. In so doing they provide a compelling overview of the literature on class theory and gender. Chapter by chapter, authors then offer a powerful set of case studies from Australia, North America, and the United Kingdom. The volume is a welcome edition to the academic and policy literature on economic restructuring, gender, geography, and social justice, and we are excited to include it in our series. It provides an important compliment to the burgeoning literature on gender and development which primarily remains focused upon those countries which are recipients of development aid. In this volume's case studies the categories of global north and south merge as we see how immigrant workers are scripted into vulnerable slots in rural agricultural labour markets. In keeping with the volume's emphasis on how capitalism shapes rural spaces, authors examine the nuances of gender, ethnicity and class within the agricultural labour force. We also see how economic restructuring in the countryside produces unemployment for rural factory workers. Further, the volume broaches new understandings of the gendered political economy of rurality by examining other non-agricultural topics such as rural tourism and the classed politics of rural masculinities and sexualities. In sum, in their thorough-going analyses of how 'regimes of gender and class intersect change and ramify' in rural contexts, contributors to *Reshaping Gender and Class in Rural Spaces* provide an exemplary study of gender in a global/local world.

Pauline Gardiner Barber
Marianne Marchand
Jane Parpart

Acknowledgments

We are grateful to Rebecca Rees for her work editing the manuscript. Belinda Leach would like to thank the Rural Women Making Change research alliance and the Social Sciences and Humanties Research Council of Canada for funding her research.

Chapter 1

Transformations of Class and Gender in the Globalized Countryside: An Introduction

Barbara Pini and Belinda Leach

As the title suggests, this book addresses how regimes of gender and class intersect, change and ramify in the context of rurality. The premise for such a book is multilayered. Primarily our concern is with a term that today is so little used in academic discourse, that is, social justice. Indeed, its virtual disappearance from the vocabularies of academics and policy makers mirrors the erasure of the nomenclature of class in favour of what may be seen as more politically palatable notions such as 'social inclusion' or 'social wellbeing'. Yet class matters. It is a key determining factor in terms of poverty as well as mediates material access to all aspects of life from housing and education to transport and health. Thus, to talk of the growing income disparities between urban and rural areas, the lower levels of education, the higher mortality rates or the increasing unemployment in non-metropolitan communities is to talk about class. This is, however, an increasingly uncommon link for scholars and governments to make.

The disconnect between ruminations about social disadvantage and the notion of class in contemporary times is, as we explain in more detail below, related to a number of factors, but has particular implications in terms of social justice in rural areas. As any student of rurality will know, rural spaces have typically been imagined and constructed as classless. This perspective has been evident in scholarly as well as popular knowledges, practices and discourses. What is important to those of us concerned with contributing to more equitable rural communities is that it has been politically advantageous for particular groups to claim rural environments as classless so that they could position their interests and experiences as legitimate, imperative and, ultimately, shared by all. To give prominence to class based differences in rural areas disrupts this hegemony and suggests that aspects of one's class position such as financial status, employment status or ownership of property will render the claims you make on the state quite distinct. The category 'rural woman', for example, has been mobilized for political gain in recent decades across a range of western industrial nations, yet it has rarely been named as a classed position whether it be in terms of the possession of capital or the involvement in specific forms of agricultural produce (Bryant and Pini 2011). Muting the very distinct middle-class location of this identity category has meant that it is middle-class concerns which have been addressed by government as part of the so-called 'rural women's movement', such as, for example, a concern with women's leadership on agricultural organizations and a concern with state funding for farmers as a result of factors like drought or restructuring. We are not, of course, suggesting that these are unimportant issues, but merely emphasizing that they are unlikely to be the central concerns of the larger population of 'rural women' who are not property owning agriculturalists involved in higher status commodities. To identify agendas around 'rural women' as narrowly classed, is to open up space for other non-metropolitan women with different class biographies to have their voices heard. This, as we explore more fully below, is of increasing importance given the radical changes occurring in rural spaces.

Change and Rurality

Rural areas reshape themselves, and are reshaped, through the vagaries of the global economy, layering on to existing social and economic relations and cultural meanings that have particular contours and tenacity in the rural. Rural areas have been seriously affected by global shifts over the past several decades. Economic change, as capital more deeply penetrates some rural areas and withdraws to a greater or lesser extent from others, has, we argue, major implications for how class and gender are lived and experienced in those areas. These dynamics are considerably different from their manifestations in urban places, leading the contributors to this book to begin from the premise that 'place matters;' in this case that the reshaping taking place in rural regions deserves specific attention.

Globally, rural areas have been subjected in recent decades to change taking place at an unprecedented pace and with dramatic consequences for reshaping the rural. These changes are important in two ways. First, they alter rural economies in material ways that eliminate historically entrenched aspects of rural life while introducing new ones. Second, they challenge rural myths and meanings in ways that destabilize but also potentially reconstitute rural ideologies.

The agriculture sector has been restructured through growing capitalization and commercialization, throwing many farms that adhere to a family owned and operated model into tailspins of debt (Gray and Lawrence 2002, Lobao 1990, Ghorayshi 2008) and leading them to consider new ways to address their sustainability. As smaller farms have become increasingly difficult to maintain, farmers have turned to new ways to generate income, from farm gate sales to bed and breakfast, to off farm work; what analysts have termed pluriactivity (Fuller 1990, Salmi 2005, Evans and Ilbery 1993). Attention to pluriactivity, dating from the 1980s, raised new and challenging questions for both gender and class analysts (Whatmore 1991), as farm household divisions of labour stretched beyond the farm enterprise and into wage labour and new forms of commodity production. The inverse of farmers move out from the farm towards alternative sources of income is their strategy of attempting to put the family farm on a firmer footing by pulling in lower cost labour from new sources, most especially low wage countries. In a more immediate way than other industries, agriculture is also held hostage by the uncertainty of climate change, with differential effects on men's and women's lives (Yocogan-Diano and Kashiwazaki 2009).

The other major economic activity that in the past has shaped rural regions globally is resource extraction. Wood, fish and minerals found in specific places have generated communities dedicated to removing and sometimes processing them. There is a well established literature that has examined the ways in which single resource communities are driven by class (e.g., Lucas 1971, Williamson 1982, Williams 1981) in ways starkly demonstrated by the social relations of these communities. More recently attention to gender (Luxton 1980, Mayes and Pini 2010) has been prompted by the fact that most resource related jobs in these communities have been intended only for men. Fishing dependent communities in the global North have been devastated by declining fish stocks and bans on fishing, while in the global South fish farming expands (Neis et al. 2005). These related trends undermine the cultural significance of locally embedded ways of life, with classed and gendered consequences in particular communities.

International economic shifts have made these activities in rural communities more significant than ever. Global trade has established minerals as one of the more 'safe' commodities for investment, leading to expanded exploration in many parts of the world. The international crisis in oil production has intensified the stakes for energy extraction in resource rich regions. Environmentally dangerous practices such as tar sands development and pipeline routes through sensitive ecosystems and the search for alternative energy sources such as wind farms, all provide new contexts for reshaping the social dynamics of rural areas.

These two major sectors of activity driving rural economies have in some regions also generated manufacturing activity, as food products are processed and the implements needed, especially for agriculture, are made close by (Winson and Leach 2002). In other places, rural workers have been employed by urban manufacturers, working around agricultural cycles (Rayside 1991). Global shifts have affected rural manufacturing through the concentration of capital and consolidation of production in a more limited numbers of sites. As a result, it is in the service sector that most rural job growth is occurring (Green 2007, Goe, Noonan and Thurston 2003). In rural areas this has taken the form of an expanded tourist industry, but it is also associated with the service requirements of migrants to rural communities from cities (Woods 2007). These changes have buffeted rural economies, with particular implications for working-class women who had found work in these sectors when they were unable to do so in resources. The rise in service sector jobs in rural communities has been associated more with those at the lower end of the wage scale, largely in the retail sector than, for example, at the higher end in financial services. Exacerbating the slow growth of better paid service sector jobs has been the effects of government services restructuring, which has reduced the numbers of public sector jobs (teaching, nursing, government officials), jobs that had formerly been among the best jobs that women were able to hold in rural areas (Leach 1999). Related has been the dramatic reconfiguration of the welfare state in Western industrial nations which has had critical implications for already disadvantaged rural groups such as the poor, people with a disability, the unemployed and the aged (White et al. 2003, Milbourne 2004, 2010).

What emerges from this discussion is a picture of rural spaces as dynamic and varied, both of these affected by capital's particular interest in those spaces that are rich in resources or agricultural potential, and a parallel disinterest in those deemed to be of no value. All of these areas then struggle through distributing and redistributing resources and reframing cultural meanings where relations of gender, class and racializations intersect with the particularities of the rural. In all of these processes, power is a critical consideration, as it is invested in property, but also as relational and mobilized through institutional processes (Panelli 2006: 78).

In order to understand the ways in which rural spaces are being reshaped, the contributors to this volume engage with theoretical frameworks for analysing class and gender that have developed both within the field of rural studies and outside of it. It is to developments in the latter, that is, theoretical understandings of class, to which we now turn.

Theorizing Class

The very limited attention to class in contemporary rural studies reflects a wider retreat from class analyses across the social sciences in recent decades. This is in contrast to the fundamental place class had traditionally enjoyed in rural social studies and broader disciplinary fields. As a result those who have continued to argue for the importance of class have been counselled to 'get over it' (Hey 2006: 295) and/or positioned as intellectually archaic (Savage 2002). The scholarly recoiling from class analyses was afforded considerable currency in the latter part of the twentieth century, with commentaries from Giddens (1991), Beck (1992) and Bauman (2000) arguing that as a result of changes in fields such as employment relations and technology, class was no longer a relevant identity or political category. They promulgated instead notions of 'individualization', 'reflexive modernization' and 'liquid modernity'. Such claims have subsequently been subject to detailed critiques in the literature. Nominated conceptual weaknesses and ambivalences of the 'death of class' thesis have included that it lacks empirical grounding, relies upon narrow and contested definitions of class, and generalizes the experiences of the middle class to the world at large (e.g., Atkinson 2007). The latter issue has been extrapolated in feminist critiques which have pointed to the gendered assumptions upon which they are based as well as gendered disparities in the new economic orders of globalization, neo-liberalism and twenty-first century capitalism. Adkins (1998, 2001, 2002, 2004), for example, argues that due to continuing inequality in the domestic division of labour and ongoing gendered occupational segregation, including in new knowledge industries, men and women are not equally placed to take up the biography of the 'individualized' worker of postmodern times. Rather, she contends that it is men who are the 'reflexivity gainers' and women who are the 'reflexivity losers' in the current economic realm. McDowell (2006: 828) takes up this argument about the ongoing importance of structural inequalities but takes it further chiding feminists for continuing to privilege only gender when there is significant evidence to suggest that it is the intersections *between gender and class* which may be most critical to social disadvantage. In her response to those who claim we may be living today in an era of self-creation as social roles such as class and indeed gender are no longer significant or binding McRobbie (2004, 2009) notes the absence of any discussion of power. Like McDowell (2006) she observes not only the continuing existence of profound gender inequality, but views such inequalities as most deeply experienced when reflected through prisms such as class and race.

Adding weight and strength to the feminist critiques of authors such as Adkins (2004), McDowell (2006) and McRobbie (2004, 2009) have been conceptual developments in the field of class studies itself which has seen the field re-emerge newly invigorated from its embattled position of previous decades (Atkinson 2009). New class theorists have not just argued for the continued relevance of class, but sought to address some of the theoretical dissent and tension that has a long history in scholarship on the subject such as the relationship between structure and agency, the role of the non-economic in class formation and impact of class as it melds with other social locations such as race or gender.

Indicative of renewed energies and trajectories around class is work that has been labelled the 'culturalization of class' (Hebson 2009: 28) or 'new cultural analyses of social class' (Reay 2006: 289). The work in this area is, as Bottero (2004) opines, too diverse to be categorized as a 'school', but cultural writing on class does mobilize around some common themes. Four can be identified. First, and perhaps most obviously, a cultural framing defines class as a relational practice, embodied and dynamic. This is, of course, a view of class, strongly influenced by Bourdieu (1990) and his associated notions of habitus, capital and fields (Lawler 2005b). These tools, as Skeggs (2004: 20) has written, have been particularly engaged by gender theorists to 'put the issue of class back on the feminist agenda' as they have enabled ways around some of the stumbling blocks of classificatory schemas and the bifurcations between the public/private. Secondly and relatedly, the cultural class literature has, as Sayer (2005: 948) has counselled taken 'lay normativity, especially morality, much more seriously'. In doing so they have emphasized the 'psychic landscape of class', that is, the importance of emotions in producing class and class differences (Reay 2005: 911) whether it be disgust, shame, pride or pain (Lawler 2005a, Reay 2002). Finally, an interest in understanding class as lived and experienced has meant that many culturally informed studies of class have largely relied upon ethnographic methods including participant observation, interviews and document analysis (e.g., Edensor and Millington 2009). A particular focus of documentary analysis has been on class representations and indeed, what has been reported as increasingly prevalent and pernicious representations of the working class in popular culture (Ringrose and Walkerdine 2008, Skeggs 2005, Tyler 2008).

Also reflective of the greater 'plurality and difference' (Crompton 2008: 152) in class analyses has been the emergence of 'new working-class studies'. This development in class scholarship is associated with the United States and most particularly, the Center for Working-Class Studies (CWCS) at Youngstown State University (YSU) established in 1996. However, it has also been given impetus in the United Kingdom with the European Social Research Council (ESRC) sponsoring a seminar series (2003) and *Antipode* (2008) publishing a special edition on the subject. In their book *New Working Class Studies* United States authors Russo and Linkon (2005: 14–15) delineate the key features of the approach including that it is interdisciplinary as well as action oriented and inclusive of working-class people and politics. They claim it aims to foster collaborative connections between community and political actors and academics and, in the process, champion new methodologies such as film, photography and art. Beyond this, much of what is cited as 'new' in 'new working-class studies' echoes the key tenets of cultural approaches to class described above. Strangleman (2008: 17) for example, evokes the cultural turn to issues of identity and subjectivity in class studies writing that new working-class studies 'seeks to understand working-class experience in its lived complexity and totality, attempting to grasp the processes of class' (see also Roberts 2007). Attempts to define the field are further complicated by the fact that different commentators make divergent claims about its orientation and priorities with, for example, some declaring that it ignores gender (McDowell 2008) and others maintaining it is primarily concerned with class relations as they are shaped by gender and other social locations (Stenning 2008, Wills 2008).

The epistemic shifts and debates in class studies, including advances, reversals and contestations can, in part, be mapped on to the discipline of rural studies. There have been spirited discussions about the appropriate methodologies for studying rurality and class and critiques of the epistemic assumptions upon which different methodologies are based whether they be ethnographies or large-scale surveys (see Abram 1998, 1999, Hoggart 1997, 1998, Murdoch 1995). Differences in opinion about the definition of class, its conceptual efficacy as a descriptive or explanatory device and its relevance to rural people have all been integral to these mediations. Phillips (2007) provides a thorough overview of these mediations as they have played out in the rural literature as well as gestures to the new and broader developments in class theory, specifically in terms of new cultural critiques of class. Adding a gender lens to this scholarship is a more recent study by Bryant and Pini (2009) which reports on class relations amongst farming men and women in two Australian rural communities using feminist cultural class theory. While both these papers review the literature on rurality and class in the context of the wider field of class studies important qualifications need to be made. That is, class has never been a major concern in rural studies, and moreover, gendered studies of class in rural areas, have, like all areas of gender inquiry of the rural, been incredibly limited.

The partiality of rural scholarship of class and particularly gender and class is due to a range of intersecting factors including the discipline's applied historical legacy as well as the ongoing failure of rural social scientists to take feminist concerns and theory seriously. An associated causal factor may be that the majority of rural scholars, like academics more generally, come from middle-class backgrounds and therefore may not name and see (or want to name and see) class and its virulent legacies. Certainly, within feminist studies it has been women academics from working-class backgrounds, not their middle-class counterparts, who have agitated and advocated for documenting and challenging class based advantage and disadvantage (Walkerdine, Lucey and Melody 2001, Mahoney and Zmroczek 1997, Hey 2003).

Overview of Book

The book begins with a chapter by Martin Phillips who continues his contribution to the literature on class and rurality by questioning how contemporary theoretical insights into class may further the study of gender inequality in rural areas. Phillips draws on a range of leading class scholars such as Michele Lamont (1992) and particularly her book *Money, Morals and Manners: The Culture of the French and American Upper Middle Class*, Bennett et al (2009) and their monograph *Culture, Class, Distinction* and the writing of feminist academic Dianne Reay (2000; 2004). The notion of 'symbolic boundaries', derived from Lamont's (1992) interviews with 160 elite French and American men, Bennett et al's (2009) more recent investigation into the cultural consumption practices of the contemporary British and Reay's (2000; 2004) empirical study of schooling and working-class and middle-class mothers are all overviewed. However, it is what these studies have to offer rural gender studies which is of concern to the author and thus he highlights Lamont's (1992) insistence on the importance of morality in assignations of class, Bennett et al's (2009) contention that the concept of 'cultural capital' needs to be disaggregated along with Reay's (2000; 2004) insights into emotional capital to enunciate future directions for rural gender studies. In terms of the latter, for example, Phillips asserts that detailed explorations of the emotions and class have yet to be undertaken and suggests that the notion of 'emotional capital' has much to offer future studies of rural communities, not least because emotion is imbued with gender. While Phillips utilizes British research to enrich his arguments, his reflections, grounded in theoretical debates about class, are clearly relevant beyond this national context and thereby provide a solid platform from which remaining authors present empirically based studies of the intersections between rurality, class and gender.

In the third chapter Machum explores a subject that has been well traversed by rural studies academics, including scholars of rurality and gender. That is, farming. Indeed, the earliest literature on rurality and class used the farm as a site of analysis (Newby 1972, 1977), while the more recent trajectory of scholarship on rurality and masculinities has, despite its nascent status, given significant attention to agriculture (Pini 2008). In considering the intersections between rurality, class and gender in the context of farming, however, Machum brings a new dimension to knowledge about agriculture as she investigates the variegated class relations *between* farming women and how such class relations are enacted in everyday discourses. She begins her discussion by identifying the dominant discourses by which academics in rural social science have theorized and understood class and farming noting the dominance of Marxist and Liberal frameworks. She then turns to interviews with thirty potato and dairy farming women in rural New Brunswick, Canada, to delineate the way in which symbolic markers (for example, expensive machinery or new infrastructure) along with material practices (for example, the presence of off farm employees and the farm's legal arrangements) are engaged to mark one's own class status and the class status of others. Many of the indicators of class that are typically used by academics in analysing farming such as level of technological inputs, the size of the operation, and use of off farm labour, are subsumed in the women's discourse by reference to discussions about motivations to farm. Machum explains that the women farmers tend to congregate within two classed groups she labels 'the expanders' and 'the sustainers'. The 'expanders' are focused on profitability and growth and denigrate 'the sustainers' as being financially untenable. In their turn 'the sustainers' draw on an ethic of care and criticize 'the expanders' for their lack of ecological stewardship. In concluding her chapter Machum returns to the frameworks of Liberalism and Marxism identifying the tensions between them and the farm women's own class narratives.

In Chapters 4 and 5, Rae Dufty and Edgar Liu, and Kerry Preibisch and Evelyn Encalada Grez respectively continue a critique of gender and class in the context of farming, but like Machum, investigate new territory. For these authors this is achieved by focusing on what feminist theorist Joan Acker (2006: 441) refers to as 'inequality regimes' that is, the intersections between gender, class and race in the context of agricultural employment. Dufty and Liu use a case study of Punjabi Sikh women's employment in the transnational corporation Blueberry Farms Australia (BFA) as their basis for discussion. Such a contextual setting provides a stark reminder that as the capitalist relations of agriculture continue to shift dramatically so too will gender, race and class relations change. To demonstrate this Dufty and Liu utilize Massey's (1984, 1994) notion of the 'spatial division of labour' together with a poststructuralist approach pioneered in rural studies by Philo (2002). The banana industry has operated through family farms owned by members of the Punjabi Sikh community, who have been established in the area for several decades. In contrast, blueberry farming is a recently established enterprise. Owned by a multinational corporation that has purchased declining banana farms, this industry employs a significant number of women as low paid pickers and packers. Often these women are the wives of banana farmers. Dufty and Liu found that the new blueberry industry both feminized and racialized rural labour in this region, in the process bringing about a renegotiation of women's community and family work. This occurs because the banana industry's declining fortunes coincided with a lack of alternative employment options in the region. The multinational blueberry company was therefore able to negotiate labour agreements that favoured itself, despite women's often high levels of education. The organization also capitalized on two absences: firstly, a history of women as major household breadwinners, and secondly, a lack of a union tradition. Blueberry farm work thus complicated women's gendered class position in relation to other members of their households as well as the racialized nature of their broader rural class relations. Dufty and Liu conclude that despite offering much needed employment for women, new jobs in the blueberry industry did nothing to secure the future of the Punjabi Sikh community.

At the centre of Dufty and Liu's analysis is globalization and the changes it has wrought to rural spaces, including, as this book reveals, to gender and class relations. This is similarly echoed in Chapter 5 in which Kerry Preibisch and Evelyn Encalada Grez detail the experiences of Mexican migrant women working in Canadian agriculture. The very large literature exploring the nexus between globalization and agriculture has often been celebrated for its disciplinary and conceptual 'diversity' but has had little to say about gender and rarely engaged feminist theory (see Goodman and Watts 1997: 5, Pritchard and Burch 2003: 15). Meanwhile, the growing literature on migration and gender has considered the labour conditions of women migrant workers in North America, but largely focused on those in the domestic sphere. Preibisch and Grez thus bring visibility to a group that has been largely overlooked. They explain that the number of women employed on temporary visas to work in Canadian agriculture has traditionally been small due to a range of factors such as the demands of the application process and dominant gender ideologies. Thus, the identity 'good farm worker' of the temporary agricultural visa programme has not only been racialized and classed, but also gendered. The authors note, however, that this is potentially shifting. Mexican women are seen as useful to corporate agriculture for embodying a range of essentialized feminine traits such as dexterity, responsibility, productivity and patience. At the same time they are in an incredibly precarious position because employers can choose staff on the basis of sex and nationality. Further, work permits are also only valid with a single designated employer so employees' options and mobility are highly constrained. The vulnerability of the Mexican temporary women worker is aggravated by employer regulatory mechanisms which seek to discipline their bodies and sexuality by creating barriers to developing social networks (for example, separating male and female employees, separating employees of the same nationality) and social connections (for example, restricting visitors). Despite the enormous hardships the women endure, including, for example, ongoing threats of sexual violence and harassment, they take temporary work visas in the hope of providing a better life for their children. It is in such a claim that the prisms of gender, race and class are refracted most potently.

The 'globalized countryside' (Woods 2007) and the transformation of gender and class in this space are addressed further in Chapter 6 by Barbara Pini and Robyn Mayes. The chapter draws on a case study of a community in the south west of Western Australia that has traditionally relied upon farming and only recently seen the establishment of a large nickel mine operated by BHP Billiton. The authors situate their discussion within the well known literature on class and gender in resource affected communities, but differentiate it in two key respects. Firstly, previous scholarship has typically focused on single industry resource towns and so not observed how class is enacted between women involved in different industry sectors, such as mining and agriculture. Secondly, much of this literature pre-dates significant changes in the resource sector which have the capacity to influence class and gender relations. These changes include the decline in union membership (Ellem 2006), an increase in the use of temporary and contract labour and outsourcing (Bowden 2003), the consolidation of global corporate resource and energy interests through mergers and acquisitions (Russell 1999) and the increase in women's employment (Eveline and Booth 2005). With their different foci the authors utilize an understanding of class consistent with the new cultural studies of class described above which emphasizes 'the moral significance of class' (Sayer 2005). To begin, Pini and Mayes detail the reticence and discomfort expressed by women associated with BHP Billiton when they are asked about class. Interestingly, women often responded to questions about class by referring to community divisions they believe result because of racial differences between South Africans and Australians. As the authors suggest, this may indicate that racial discord is more acceptable than class based discord. More explicit naming of class, and the invoking of moral attributions around class, occur in relation to discussions about contractors, that is, those who worked at the mine but were not employees of BHP Billiton. Contract workers are seen to embody a range of negative traits. They were viewed as overpaid, rough, ruthless and lacking community and family ties. While the BHP Billiton women attribute this type of moral bankruptcy to contractors, the farming women, in turn, label the broader group 'mining women' (and their husbands) in the same pejorative manner. The messiness of class relations in contemporary rural spaces is highlighted by Pini and Mayes as they observe the considerable economic capital of the contractors and BHP Billiton employees and the financial vulnerability of the farmers they interview. Despite this, the moral authority of farming people and their claims to class status appears (at this juncture) to remain intact.

How global capital has changed rural spaces and the classed and gendered subjectivities of the men and women who live in these spaces is further examined in Chapter 8 by Belinda Leach. Leach reminds us that the tendency to conflate rurality with agriculture has meant that there has been little research on rural manufacturing, despite the movement of transnationals into rural arenas over recent decades (see Harvey 1993). In responding to this lacuna she examines the continued under-representation of women in automobile employment in rural Ontario. In the rural communities under investigation, those with a long industrial history, Leach argues that a particular form of rural industrial masculinity has been predominant, and this has worked to exclude women from the better working-class jobs available. The association of men and the male body with heavy machinery, the prevalence of sexual and sexist harassment, the use of rotating shifts which make childcare problematic (even if it is available) are different manifestations of the privileging of rural industrial masculinity which limit women's employment in manufacturing. To varying extents, these practices are supported by cross class alliances between shop floor men and the male managers of the factories. Against this Leach draws upon research with unionized women workers in rural Ontario to demonstrate the critical difference access to a job in the automobile sector can make to working-class women. Such a position enables women to raise children independently or leave a partner, buy labour saving devices and perhaps buy a car allowing them a mobility they would otherwise be denied. It is important Leach explains that many of the new automobile plants that have been established in rural areas in the past decade are non-unionized, because it has been in unionized environments that rural women have been successful in achieving better employment conditions and opportunities.

It has not just been in the Ontario automobile industry that working-class men have mobilized masculinities to marginalize and exclude women employees. It has, as Suzanne Tallichet reveals in Chapter 8, also been in the coal fields of Appalachia in the United States. Tallichet examines a critical moment in the gendered and classed history of Appalachia when, as a result of a successful class action suit over sex discrimination in the coal industry, women began working in large numbers in the underground mines in the area. This represented a significant rupture in the sexual division of labour in the mining communities, to strongly held gender norms and to the conflation of masculinity with mining work. Tallichet records that the women miners were subject to overt and persistent sexist and sexual harassment as part of their everyday work life. She then reports on the way the women miners attempted to circumvent and obliterate the negative behaviours and practices to which they were subjected by drawing upon two key discourses which positioned them as 'the breadwinner' and/or 'the good miner'. The former relied upon constructing women's involvement in mining as a necessity rather than a choice as a result of divorce or separation while the latter emphasized women's equivalent expertise and capabilities in terms of a masculinized definition of miner. In the final part of the chapter Tallichet looks back on this period from the vantage point of the first part of the twenty-first century. She notes that women's participation in mining work was curtailed by the closure of mines throughout Appalachia in the 1990s. However, she wonders what the legacy of the early pioneers may be on today's Appalachian woman, particularly in terms of research by Miewald and McCann (2004) which highlights the active economic, political and social role many such women play in the contemporary public sphere.

The subject of employment and its relationship to class in the rural is taken up in Chapter 9 by Annie Hughes in a study of lone parents in two British non-metropolitan locales. As the author explains, the chapter needs to be read in the context of the radical restructuring of state welfare in western industrialized nations and the proliferation of 'workfare programmes' (Peck 2001). Such programmes, defined by the fact that they are compulsory, tied to welfare access and emphasize 'any job' over quality employment, have particularly targeted lone parents, specifically single mothers (Breitkreuz 2005, Evans 2007). Hughes' brings a spatial dimension to the feminist critiques of 'workfare' arguing that material and discursive dimensions of rurality influence lone parents' engagement in employment. She asserts that in the rural the type of distinction Duncan et al (2003) have made between the 'middle-class' mother who gives primacy to paid work as separate from their identity as 'mother' and the 'working-class' mother who gives primacy to the benefits of physically caring for their children themselves become blurred. For example, she explains that outside the urban occupational opportunities for middle-class professionals may be restricted and so will access to childcare thus limiting the employment options of middle-class women. Dominant socio-cultural narratives about the identity of 'rural woman' may also influence involvement in paid work for middle-class women living outside of urban centres. Hughes' central argument, that lone parents' decisions about participation in paid employment in rural areas of England cannot simply be read off a class based typology, is furthered as she considers the additional dimensions of relational and human capital. It is the case that access to these capitals, and the capacity to translate these into economic capital, is often classed. This is obvious in terms of educational credentials and employment history. However, in examining levels of support given to lone parents by their ex-partners and extended families, Hughes found no definitive class differences amongst her participants. What emerges is a much more complicated picture of lone parents than homogenising representations such as 'underclass' would suggest.

In Chapter 10 Yvette Taylor complicates the preceding discussions in a range of important ways. First, she employs past detailed ethnographic work on the life experiences of working-class lesbian and gay men (Taylor 2007, 2009) to bring sexuality to the fore in debates about gender, rurality and class. In taking up this challenge she destabilizes any bifurcated assumptions about 'rurality' and 'urbanity' and thereby opens up debate about the messy, shifting and complex nature of 'the rural'. Taylor establishes her argument by first explaining that dominant constructions of 'the rural' position it as a place of exclusion and homophobic intolerance against which sits 'the urban' as the imagined opposite. It is a construction of rurality that is echoed in the views of some of Taylor's research participants. However, others disrupt the rural/urban dichotomy in a number of ways. That is, they point out that the hyper trendy and commercial clubs and bars of major city centres that are referred to as 'scene spaces' for contemporary gays and lesbians are the preserve of the middle-class. In addition, participants differentiate between types of urban spaces (for example, suburbia or the inner city) as places of inclusion, but these too also marked by class. In furthering her argument Taylor unravels different gay and lesbian experiences of rurality and how these are shaped by class. For example, while the gentrified Yorkshire town of Hebden Bridge in the United Kingdom is nominated by some participants as a place 'for lesbians', the expensive nature of real estate in the area means it is predominantly middle-class space (see Smith and Holt 2005). Quite different from Hebden Bridge is an alternative experience of rurality as surveillance and discrimination. Again, class matters. It informs access to the types of capitals (social, cultural and economic) which could enable rural gays and lesbians to venture outside of their rural communities either temporarily or permanently.

Taylor's chapter provides a welcome corrective in reminding us of the importance of sexuality in studying rurality, class and gender. Maureen Reed and Debra Davidson, Chapter 11, make an additional contribution in this regard, by drawing out attention to the mediating influence racial identity may have in terms of inclusion in rural spaces. The particular arena of interest to the authors is the Canadian forestry sector, and the new committees established to involve local people in forest management decision-making. The chapter thus speaks to the literature which has problematized the gendered structures and practices of new modes of rural governance (Little and Jones 2000, Pini 2006), yet, at the same time, extends this scholarship as gender is only the starting point for the analysis presented. The question posed by Reed and Davidson is: How does gender intersect with classed and racialized identities and with local forms of forestry culture to influence involvement and participation in forest management groups? In addressing this question these authors invoke results from several research projects over the past decade. This work reveals some of the taken for granted and hidden gendered, classed and racialized practices of exclusion in terms of community engagement in forest management. Reed and Davidson note that the dominant model for participation is 'stakeholder based' whereby committee members are selected according to a designated interest. This tends to define participation according to one's employment (for example, municipal councillor, logger or hunter), favour more formalized domains (for example, unions, industry groups) and privilege economic concerns. Through these supposedly gender neutral processes women are filtered out. Once 'at the table' a range of practices continues to marginalize particular voices. Dominant definitions of knowledge circulating around discourses of science and expertise may mean the knowledge of Aboriginal or working-class members is dismissed or undermined. Indeed, the authors report on a national survey of forestry committees which found that women named scientists and men named industry representatives as those with the greatest legitimacy in terms of industry knowledge. As Reed and Davidson point out such groups (scientists and industry representatives) are predominantly constituted by white, middle-class men. It is thus that women, working-class and Aboriginal people find themselves written out of participatory forest management forums.

In the final chapter Edward Morris turns to Richard Sennett and Jonathon Cobb's (1972) seminal book *The Hidden Injuries of Class*. While Sennett and Cobb (1972) famously undertook participant observation in a wide range of settings from clubs and bars to workplaces and engaged in 150 interviews with working-class adult males, schooling, and more particularly, the way in which educational institutions actively reproduce class relations were major themes in the book. For the Boston working-class men at the centre of the study strongly internalized feelings of inadequacy, shame, anger and self-blame marked their experience of schooling. Morris adds to this work by introducing gender and rurality to an analysis of the lived experience of class of two teenagers, Kevin and Kaycee, from a high school in non-metropolitan Ohio, United States. As such, he provides further evidence that the 'hidden injuries' of class are 'beneath your clothes, under your skin, in your psyche, at the very core of your being' (Kuhn 1995: 98). He also demonstrates that these injuries are differently negotiated according to dominant scripts of rural masculinity and rural femininity, and potentially produce very different educational outcomes. Kevin, for example, responds to his disadvantage by asserting the hegemonic mode of masculinity in this rural area which prescribes physicality, strength and toughness. Ultimately, however, this alienates him from the educational environment as he is aggressive in his dealings with staff and students. In contrast, Kaycee navigates the shame of her class status (as experienced even by her surname) by taking up the behaviours and values of conventionally defined femininity. Her deference, submissiveness and emotionality facilitate the provision of support and care from the school to assist her with her education. Morris' chapter demonstrates the centrality of schools as sites for the production and reproduction of class and gender. While this is a subject that has been widely explored in the literature on education, it has not been through the purview of rurality. In this respect, the chapter should be read as sign posting the critical need for further work on this important subject. It is this issue, that of future scholarship on gender, class and rurality which is discussed in the following section.

Future Directions

The contributions to this book engage with a number of the issues identified in the discussion above, but there are also many areas of scholarship that are not explored here, but that provide an important lens with which to investigate what is happening in rural places. In this section we point to some work that takes the analysis of gender, class and rurality in some new directions that we feel are worth pursuing.

Attention has been paid to some aspects of consumption in the rural. Flora, Flora and Fey (2003), for example, describe changing patterns of food and other consumer goods provisioning, as fast food outlets and large-scale chain stores such as Walmart invade the rural landscape, cutting out locally and sometimes family owned restaurants and stores which cannot compete with the low prices of large companies. What gendered and class effects changing consumption patterns have on the health of poorer rural people, for example, remains to be fully investigated. Perhaps more attention has been paid by rural social scientists to rural tourism, promoted as a viable development strategy for struggling communities through investments in 'countryside capital' (Garrod, Wornell and Youell 2006) that build on particular rural heritages and more recently on the flourishing local food movement and interests in local ecologies. These kinds of changing patterns of consumption in and of the rural raise important questions about who is doing the work that allows others to consume. Reports of the growing rural service sector rarely reveal the shifting dynamics of gender and class (and race) that are associated with it. Susan Webb (2003) has described how women in inland African American communities in South Carolina, where poverty and unemployment are rife, are bussed a hundred miles to the tourist resorts that line the coast to perform the invisible work that tourism development demands, especially the 'back of house' work in kitchens and laundries and the cleaning of private and public rooms when they are not in use.

Tourism promotion of rural areas requires marketing rurality, that is representing the rural in particular ways. Arguably most tourism advertising is aimed at middle-class consumers who have disposable income for such pursuits. Jo Little (Forthcoming) has recently analysed how rural health spas capitalize on taken for granted understandings of rurality and use these as the subtle underpinning for the promotion of particular products and services that are so expensive that they could only rarely be enjoyed by most rural residents, especially women. But there are examples of tourism strategies that more consciously address class and gender dynamics. Gibson and Davidson (2004) analyse the marketing of Australia's 'country music capital', which involves recognising the music's association with white, working-class males, generating some ambivalence among the town's residents towards its newly constructed identity.

The type of gendered and classed representations of the rural, common in tourism media, also manifest in broader discursive arenas. Television drama series set in rural locales draw upon and reproduce many dominant symbols of the countryside which are classed and gendered (Phillips 2002). As the rural changes these cultural representations are likely to change as Pini, McDonald and Mayes (2011) demonstrate in analysing popular media depictions of the identity of the 'cashed-up Bogan' the newly well off beneficiary of the Australian mining boom. The 'cashed-up Bogan' is associated with the Australian resource boom of recent years when the unprecedented demand for resources from Asia allowed a group of working-class people (largely white men) to earn high wages for their labour. The economic resources of the 'cashed-up Bogan' has allowed entry into middle-class space, but this has caused unease for middle-class media pundits and their audiences who ridicule and denigrate this classed figure. Attending to class representations of the rural is important for as Skeggs (2004: 117) explains representations condense 'fears and anxieties into one classed symbol', and accordingly, critiquing them is 'central to any analysis of class'. Lawler (2005a: 431) adds to this, reminding us that depictions of the working class also 'produce middle-class identities'. Thus, attending to representations of the working class in the rural opens up to scrutiny the ongoing efforts of the rural middle class to reinscribe boundaries and differences, and the way in which middle-class values, attitudes and tastes are normalized and naturalized.

As the rural is restructured middle-class concerns taken up in the literature have tended to overshadow gendered forms of working-class agency in the face of the same social and economic processes. Aside from the fairly extensive literature on men's union activities in mining (which is in fact not usually characterized as rural), little scholarly attention has been paid to other forms of organizing and collective action taking place in rural spaces. Reed's (2000, 2003) work on women's actions in support of threatened forestry jobs and Neis' (2000) on women's activities in relation to the crisis of the fishery are exceptions, but both address support for men's work in single resource contexts. We know little about how unions operate in rural areas and what their effects there are, partly because of the hegemonic idea that agrarian ideology diverts energy away from labour militancy (Winson 1997). Leach's research on unionized rural workers points to how in rural areas union resources (in the form of people, knowledge and training, and finances) support not only workers' immediate interests, but extend further into other collective community activities with a social justice agenda, such as women's resource centres and anti-violence organizations. These actions have consequences for how rural communities apprehend and understand global change (Leach forthcoming).

A final way in which knowledge about gender, rurality and class could be furthered is through the experiences and perceptions of academics themselves. Feminist contributions to rural studies have been useful in bringing a reflexive lens to rural studies and thereby gesturing to questions of power, politics and representation in the knowledge production process as well as providing insights into gender relations in the rural (Pini 2003). Much could be gained by extending this critique of positioning to class. Illustrative is Langan and Morton's (2009) exploration of how their classed, rural and gendered biographies have situated them as outsiders within the academy.

Conclusion

The chapters in this volume take rurality to be a central problematic in the global restructuring of capital. Far from being reduced to backwaters irrelevant to global fields of power, we argue that spaces that are constructed and experienced as rural remain a requirement for capital's operations, as they have historically. In such a context the ways in which class and gender (and indeed racialization processes) are manipulated and transformed through the use and abuse of contested ideologies and practices of gender and class are necessary subjects for scholarship and for politics. The chapters address critical global themes as those touch down in particular rural spaces. These include the restructuring of global agricultural capital that seeks out cheaper and more malleable workers, and international mining and manufacturing operations that rely on rigid gendered divisions of labour to produce preferred workers and to reinforce class distinctions. They incorporate manifestations of an international debt crisis that, rather than erupting unexpectedly in 2008, has been long in the making in, and in the experience of, rural communities. By taking up these themes, despite local settings that encompass a limited range of rural communities in English-speaking settler colonies and Britain itself, the chapters traverse important global circulation routes of capitals, migrant peoples and commodities. While Australia, Canada, the United States, and Britain (the national locations of the studies we present) hold privileged positions in the global political economy, the rural areas described and analysed here are frequently subject to neglect by their respective governments and policymakers.

That neglect has particularly gendered and classed consequences. Also addressed here are global themes played out in the intimate spaces of daily life, and intimate relations rehearsed over a more public canvas. The contemporary vagaries of global capital restructuring present challenges for rural gender relations that are often tied to rigidly held gender ideologies. As the contributors show, new work opportunities and the loss of old ones have profound class effects and are far from gender neutral processes. Other authors demonstrate that in rural spaces where the preservation of gendered difference is held dear, the incorporation of alternative family structures (same sex couples, single parents) tests the capacity and willingness of communities to embrace change. Moreover, class and gender subjectivities shaped in either rural or urban spaces may not easily make the journey into the other realm. This, along with other factors, renders problematic claims that boundaries between rural and urban space are increasingly blurred. We join other scholars who have contended that geography is central to contemporary class distinctions (Butler and Robson 2003, McDonald et al. 2005) as well as to how class processes are also gendered (McDowell 2006). While subjected to the same global processes and reliant on its interactions with the other, we insist that for understanding the social relations of class and gender, rurality matters.

References

Abram, S. 1998. Class, countryside and the "longitudinal study": A response to Hoggart. *Journal of Rural Studies*, 14(3), 369–79.

Abram, S. 1999. Up the anthropologist: power, subversion and progress (another reply to Hoggart). *Journal of Rural Studies*, 15(1), 119–20.

Acker, J. 2006. Inequality regimes: gender, class, and race in organizations. *Gender and Society*, 20(4), 441–64.

Adkins, L. 1998. Feminist theory and economic change, in *Contemporary Feminist Theories*, edited by S. Jackson and J. Jones. Edinburgh: University Press, 31–50.

Adkins, L. 2001. Cultural feminization: "money, sex and power" for women. *Signs*, 26(3), 669–95.

Adkins, L. 2002. *Revisions: Gender and Sexuality in Late Modernity*. London: Open University Press.

Adkins, L. 2004. Gender and the post-structural social, in *Engendering the Social*, edited by B. Marshall and A. Witz. Maidenhead: Open University Press, 139–54.

Atkinson, W. 2007. Anthony Giddens as adversary of class analysis. *Sociology*, 41(3), 533–49.

Atkinson, W. 2009. Rethinking the work class nexus: theoretical foundations for recent trends. *Sociology*, 43(5), 896–912.

Bauman, Z. 2000. *Liquid Modernity*. Cambridge: Polity Press.

Beck, U. 1992. *Risk Society: Towards a New Modernity*. Newbury Park: Sage.

Bottero, W. 2004. Class identities and the identity of class. *Sociology*, 38(5), 985–1003.

Bourdieu, P. 1990. *In Other Words: Essays Towards a Reflexive Sociology*. Stanford: Stanford University Press.

Bowden, B. 2003. Regulating outsourcing. *Labour and Industry*, 14(1), 41–56.

Breitkreuz, R. 2005. Engendering citizenship? A critical feminist analysis of Canadian welfare-to-work policies and the employment experiences of lone mothers. *Journal of Sociology and Social Welfare*, 32(2), 147–65.

Bryant, L. and Pini, B. 2009. Gender, class and rurality: Australian case studies. *Journal of Rural Studies*, 25(1), 48–57.

Bryant, L. and Pini, B. 2011. *Gender and Rurality*. London: Routledge.

Butler, T. and Robson, G. 2003. *London Calling: The Middle Classes and the Re-making of Inner London*. Oxford: Berg.

Crompton, R. 2008. *Class and Stratification*. 3rd Edition. Cambridge: Polity Press.

Duncan, S., Edwards, R., Reynolds, T. and Alldred, P. 2003. Motherhood, paid work and partnering: values and theories. *Work Employment Society*, 17(2), 309–330.

Edensor, T. and Millington, S. 2009. Illuminations, class identities and the contested landscapes of Christmas. *Sociology*, 43(1), 103–21.

Ellem, B. 2006. Scaling labour. *Work, Employment and Society*, 20(2), 369–87.

Evans, N.J. and Ilbery, B.W. 1993. The pluriactivity, part-time farming and farm diversification debate. *Environment and Planning A*, 25(7), 945–59.

Evans, P. 2007. (Not) Taking account of precarious employment: workfare polities and lone mothers in Ontario and the UK. *Social Policy and Administration*, 41(1), 29–49.

Eveline, J. and Booth, M. 2005. Gender and sexuality in discourses of managerial control: the case of women miners. *Gender and Organization*, 9(5), 556–78.

Flora, C., Flora, J. and Fey, S. 2003. *Rural Communities: Legacy and Change*. Boulder: Westview.

Fuller, A.M. 1990. From part time farming to pluriactivity: a decade of change in rural Europe. *Journal of Rural Studies*, 6(4), 361–73.

Garrod, B., Wornell, R. and Youell, R. 2006. Re-conceptualising rural resources as countryside capital: the case of rural tourism. *Journal of Rural Studies*, 22(1), 117–228.

Ghorayshi, P. 2008. Canadian agriculture: capitalist or petit bourgeois? *Canadian Review of Sociology/Revue Canadienne de Sociologie*, 24(3), 358–73.

Gibson, C. and Davidson, D. 2004. Tamworth, Australia's 'country music capital': place marketing, rurality, and resident reactions. *Journal of Rural Studies*, 20(4), 387–404.

Giddens, A. 1991. *Modernity and Self-identity*. Cambridge: Polity Press.

Goe, W.R., Noonan, S. and Thurston, S. 2003. From extraction to amenities: restructuring and (In)conspicuous consumption in Missoula, Montana, in *Communities of Work: Rural Restructuring in Local and Global Contexts*, edited by W.W. Falk, M.D. Schulman and A.R. Tickamyer. Athens: Ohio University Press, 104–27.

Goodman, D. and Watts, M. (eds). 1997. *Globalising Food: Agrarian Questions and Global Restructuring*. London and New York: Routledge.

Gray, I. and Lawrence, G. 2002. *A Future for Regional Australia: Escaping Global Misfortune*. Cambridge: Cambridge University Press.

Green, G.P. 2007. *Workforce Development Networks in Rural Areas: Building the High Road*. Cheltenham and Northampton: Edward Elgar Publishing.

Harvey, D. 1993. Class relations, social justice and the politics of difference, in *Place and the Politics of Identity*, edited by M. Keith and S. Pile. London and New York: Routledge, 41–66.

Hebson, G. 2009. Renewing class analysis in studies of the workplace: a comparison of working-class and middle-class women's aspirations and identities. *Sociology*, 43(1), 27–44.

Hey, V. 2003. Joining the club? Academic and working-class femininities. *Gender and Education*, 15(3), 319–36.

Hey, V. 2006. 'Getting over it?' Reflections on the melancholia of reclassified identities. *Gender and Education*, 18(3), 295–308.

Hoggart, K. 1997. The middle classes in rural England 1971–1991. *Journal of Rural Studies*, 13(3), 253–73.

Hoggart, K. 1998. Rural cannot equal middle class because class does not exist? *Journal of Rural Studies*, 14(3), 381–6.

Kuhn, A. 1995. *Family Secrets: Acts of Memory and Imagination*. London and New York: Verso.

Langan, D. and Morton, M. 2009. Through the eyes of farmers' daughters: academics working on marginal land. *Women's Studies International Forum*, 32(6), 395–405.

Lash, S. 1994. Reflexivity and its doubles: structure, aesthetics, community, in *Reflexive Modernisation: Politics, Tradition and Aesthetics in the Modern Social Order*, edited by U. Beck, A. Giddens and S. Lash. Cambridge: Polity Press, 110–73.

Lawler, S. 2005a. Disgusted subjects: the making of middle-class identities. *The Sociological Review*, 53(3), 429–46.

Lawler, S. 2005b. Introduction: Class, culture, identity. *Sociology*, 39(5), 797–806.

Leach, B. 1999. Transforming rural livelihoods: gender, culture and restructuring in three Ontario Communities, in *Restructuring Caring Labour*, edited by S. Neysmith. Toronto: Oxford University Press.

Leach, B. Forthcoming. Producing globalization: gender, agency and the transformation of rural communities of work, in *The Social Transformation of Rural Canada*, edited by M. Reed and J. Parkin. Vancouver: University of British Columbia Press.

Little, J. and Jones, O. 2000. Masculinity, gender and rural policy. *Rural Sociology*, 65(4), 621–39.

Little, J. Forthcoming. Healthy rural bodies? Embodied approaches to the study of rural women's health, in *Rural Women's Health: Gendered Connections*, edited by B. Leipert, B. Leach and W. Thurston.

Lobao, L.M. 1990. *Locality and Inequality: Farm and Industry Structure and Socioeconomic Conditions*. Albany: State University of New York Press.

Lucas, R.A. 1971. *Minetown, Milltown, Railtown: Life in Canadian Communities of Single Industry*. Toronto: University of Toronto Press.

Luxton, M. 1980. *More Than a Labour of Love*. Toronto: Women's Press.

Mahony, P. and Zmroczek, C. (eds) 1997. *Class Matters. "Working-class" Women's Perspectives on Social Class*. London: Taylor and Francis.

Massey, D.B. 1984. *Spatial Divisions of Labour: Social Structures and the Geography of Production*. London. Macmillan.

Massey, D.B. 1994. *Space, Place and Gender*. Cambridge: Polity.

Mayes, R. and Pini, B. 2010. The 'feminine revolution in mining': A critique. *Australian Geographer*, 41(2), 233–45.

McDonald, R., Shildrick T., Webster, C. and Simpson, D. 2005. Growing up in poor neighbourhoods: the significance of class and place in the extended transitions of 'socially excluded' young adults. *Sociology*, 39(5), 873–92.

McDowell, L. 2006. Reconfigurations of gender and class relations: class differences, class condescension and the changing place of class relations. *Antipode*, 38(4), 825–50.

McDowell, L. 2008. Thinking through class and gender in the context of working class studies. *Antipode*, 40(1), 20–4.

McRobbie, A. 2004. Post-feminisms and popular culture. *Feminist Media Studies*, 4(3), 254–64.

McRobbie, A. 2009. *The Aftermath of Feminism: Gender, Culture and Social Change*. London: Sage Publications.

Miewald, C.E. and McCann, E.J. 2004. Gender struggle, scale and the production of place in the Appalachian coalfields. *Environment and Planning*, 36(6), 1045–64.

Milbourne, P. 2004. *Rural Poverty: Marginalization and Exclusion in Britain and the United States*. London: Routledge.

Milbourne, P. 2010. The geographies of poverty and welfare. *Geography Compass*, 4(2), 158–71.

Murdoch, J. 1995. Middle class territory? Some remarks on the use of class analysis in rural studies. *Environment and Planning A*, 27(8), 1213–230.

Neis, B. 2000. In the eye of the storm: research, activism and teaching within the Newfoundland fishery crisis. *Women's Studies International Forum*, 23(3), 278–98.

Neis, B., Binkley M., Gerrard, S. and Maneschy, C. (eds). 2005. *Changing Tides: Gender, Fisheries and Globalization*. Halifax: Fernwood.

Newby, H. 1972. Agricultural workers in the class structure. *Sociological Review*, 20(3), 413–39.

Newby, H. 1977. *The Deferential Worker*. Middlesex: Penguin Books.

Panelli, R. 2006. Rural society, in *Handbook of Rural Studies*, edited by P. Cloke, T. Marsden, and P.H. Mooney. Thousand Oaks: Sage.

Peck, J. 2001. *Workfare States*. New York: Guilford Press.

Phillips, M. 2002. Distant bodies? Rural studies, political-economy and poststructuralism. *Sociologia Ruralis*, 42(2), 81–105.

Phillips, M. 2007. Changing class complexions on and in the British countryside. *Journal of Rural Studies*, 23(3), 283–304.

Philo, C. 2002. Neglected rural geographies: a review. *Journal of Rural Studies*, 8(2), 193–207.

Pini, B. 2003. Feminist methodology and rural research: reflections on a study of an Australian agricultural organization. *Sociologia Ruralis*, 43(3), 418–33.

Pini, B. 2006. A critique of 'new' rural local governance: the case of gender in a rural Australian setting. *Journal of Rural Studies*, 22(3), 396–408.

Pini, B. 2008. *Men, Masculinities and Management in Agricultural Organizations Worldwide*. Aldershot: Ashgate.

Pini, B., McDonald, P. and Mayes, R. 2011. Class contestations and Australia's resource boom. The emergence of the 'Cashed-up Bogan'. *Sociology: Of the British Sociological Association*, Forthcoming.

Pritchard, B. and Burch, D. 2003. *Agri-food Globalization in Perspective: International Restructuring in the Processing Tomato Industry*. Aldershot: Ashgate.

Rayside, D.M. 1991. *A Small Town in Modern Times*. Kingston and Montreal: McGill Queen's University Press.

Reay, D. 2002. Class, authenticity and the transition to higher education for mature students. *The Sociological Review*, 50(3), 398–418.

Reay, D. 2005. Beyond consciousness? The psychic landscape of social class. *Sociology*, 39(5), 911–28.

Reay, D. 2006. The zombie stalking English schools: social class and educational inequality. *British Journal of Educational Studies*, 54(3), 288–307.

Reed, M. 2000. Taking stands: a feminist perspective on 'other' women's activism in forestry communities of northern Vancouver island. *Gender, Place and Culture*, 7(4), 363–87.

Reed, M. 2003. *Taking Stands: Gender and the Sustainability of Rural Communities*. Vancouver: UBC Press.

Ringrose, J. and Walkerdine, V. 2008. Regulating the abject. *Feminist Media Studies*, 8(3), 227–46.

Roberts, I. 2007. Working-class studies: ongoing and new directions. *Sociology Compass*, 1(1), 191–207.

Russell, B. 1999. *More with Less*. University of Toronto Press: Toronto.

Russo, J. and Linkon, S.L. 2005. *New Working Class Studies*. Ithaca: Cornell University Press.

Salmi, P. 2005. Rural pluriactivity as a copying strategy in small-scale fisheries. *Sociologia Ruralis*, 45(1–2), 22–36.

Savage, A. 2002. What Are You Worth?: Why Class is an Embarrassing Subject. *Sociological Research Online*, 7(3).

Sayer, A. 2005. *The Moral Significance of Class*. Cambridge: Cambridge University Press.

Sennett, R. and Cobb, J. 1972. *The Hidden Injuries of Class*. New York: W.W. Norton.

Skeggs, B. 2004. *Class, Self, Culture*. London: Routledge

Skeggs, B. 2005. The making of class and gender through visualizing moral subject formation. *Sociology*, 39(5), 965–82.

Smith, D.P. and Holt, L. 2005. 'Lesbian migrants in the gentrified valley' and 'other' geographies of rural gentrification. *Journal of Rural Studies*, 21(3), 313–322.

Stenning, A. 2008. Geography and the new working class studies. *Antipode*, 40(1), 9–13.

Strangleman, T. 2008. Sociology, social class and new working class studies. *Antipode*, 40(1), 15–19.

Taylor, Y. 2007. *Working-class Lesbian Life: Classed Outsiders*. Basingstoke: Palgrave Macmillan.

Taylor, Y. 2009. *Lesbian and Gay Parenting: Securing Social and Educational Capital*. Basingstoke: Palgrave Macmillan.

Tyler, I. 2008. 'Chav Mum Chav Scum' class disgust in contemporary Britain. *Feminist Media Studies*, 8(1), 17–34.

Walkerdine, V., Lucey, H. and Melody, J. 2001. *Growing Up Girl: Psychosocial Explorations of Gender and Class*. Basingstoke: Palgrave Macmillan.

Webb, S.E. 2003. The bus from Hell Hole Swamp: black women in the hospitality industry, in *Communities of Work: Rural Restructuring in Local and Global Contexts*, edited by W.W. Falk, M.D. Schulman and A.R. Tickamyer. Athens: Ohio University Press, 267–90.

Whatmore, S. 1991. *Farming Women: Gender, Work and Family Enterprise*. Houndsmills: Macmillan.

White, J., Tickamyer, A.R., Henderson, D.A. and Tadlock, B. 2003. Does welfare to work work? Rural employers comment, in *Communities of Work: Rural Restructuring in Local and Global Contexts*, edited by W.W. Falk, M.D. Schulman and A.R. Tickamyer. Athens: Ohio University Press, 240–266.

Williams, C. 1981. *Open Cut: The Working Class in an Australia Mining Town*. Sydney: Allen and Unwin.

Williamson, B. 1982. *Class, Culture and Community: A Biographical Study of Social Change in Mining*. London: Routledge and Kegan Paul.

Wills, J. 2008. Mapping class and its political possibilities. *Antipode*, 40(1), 25–30.

Winson, A. 1997. Does class consciousness exist in rural communities? The impact of restructuring and plant shutdowns in rural Canada. *Rural Sociology*, 62(4), 429–53.

Winson, A. and Leach, B. 2002. *Contingent Work, Disrupted Lives: Labour and Community in the New Rural Economy*. Toronto: University of Toronto Press.

Woods, M. 2007. Engaging the global countryside: globalization, hybridity and the reconstitution of rural place. *Progress in Human Geography*, 31(4), 485–507.

Yocogan-Diano, V. and Kashiwazaki, T. 2009. *Rural Women and Climate Change: Challenges and Recommendations*. Paper to the Asia Pacific Climate Change Conference: Consolidating the People's Movement on Climate Change Towards COP15, Asia Pacific Research Network, Bangkok, Thailand, 23–4 March 2009.

Chapter 2

Material, Cultural, Moral and Emotional Inscriptions of Class and Gender: Impressions from Gentrified Rural Britain

Martin Phillips

Bottero (2004: 986) has asserted that there has been a renewed interest in class, fostered by work that gives much more attention to 'processes of culture, lifestyle and taste', such that class analysis might itself be described as cultural or culturalist (see Devine and Savage 2000, Savage 2000). Others have made similar arguments, with Le Roux et al. (2008: 1050), for example, writing that recent work on class had tended to focus on cultural – or as they termed them, subjective – issues, such as 'identity, attitudes and morals (e.g. shame, worth, respect)', with even work on long standing issues of debates, such as the character of class structure, coming to address cultural issues, albeit often using quantitative forms of analysis (e.g., Bennett et al. 2009, Chan and Goldthorpe 2004a, 2004b, 2007). Bottero (2004: 986) suggests that together these studies have produced a 'substantial broadening' of class analysis and a 'much needed redirection of class theory and research'. She also notes that this movement has occurred 'concurrently' with studies exploring 'how class is lived in gendered and raced ways' (Bottero 2004: 986), and had heavily involved writers influenced by feminist concerns (e.g., Reay 1997, 2004, Skeggs 1997, 2004).

Similar arguments can be observed in the context of rural studies, with Bryant and Pini (2009) arguing that whilst gender and class have long been examined in isolation, and have had rather differing fortunes in terms of their recognition (gender receiving less attention than class in the rise of rural critical/political economy perspectives but being central to postmodern and poststructuralist rural studies from the late 1990s onwards), there has recently been greater recognition of the intersection, and one might add co-construction, of class and gender, along with growing appreciation of the value of feminist theorizations to understandings of class. Having said this, it can also be argued that the intersection of gender with lines of social differentiation such as sexuality and ethnicity has garnered much more attention than has the relationships of class and gender, as indeed have connections between gender, sexuality and ethnicity with spatialized identities such as rurality and nationality (e.g., Bell 2000, Campbell 2000, Law 1997, Little 2003, Little and Panelli 2007, Valentine 1997). More generally, Walkerdine, Lucey and Melody (2001: 12) have suggested that feminist studies have 'been more able to cope with differences of race and ethnicity ... than class differences', with social class having 'all but disappeared from mainstream feminist analysis', save for a small set of studies carried out, they argue, 'almost entirely ... by academics who themselves come from working-class backgrounds' (Walkerdine, Lucey and Melody 2001: 30).

Not only may the renewal of class analysis have some way to go in terms of its relative recognition, but significant theoretical questions still persist. Bottero, for example, whilst welcoming the renewed interests in class interest ends up being unconvinced by aspects of its reformulation, arguing that 'the "class" nature of such approaches must be questioned' because they, amongst other things, 'inflate "class" to include social and cultural formations' (Bottero, 2004: 986). By contrast, however, many analysts have explicitly welcomed these changes. McDowell (2006: 836), for example, suggests that analysts who have under-taken moves paralleling, if not necessarily explicitly enacting, those of post-structuralist analyses have 'deepened understandings of new forms of class differences and inequalities by placing bodies, meanings, representations and the significance of daily lived practices at the centre of their work'. Examples of such work includes, she suggests, feminist theoretical and empirical studies examining the concepts of Pierre Bourdieu (e.g., Adkins and Skeggs 2004) and Sayer's (2005a, 2005b) work on morality and class.

The work of Bourdieu and issues of morality have both been central to the work of Lamont (1992), who, as I have previously discussed in relation to rural class analysis (Phillips 1998a, Phillips 1998b), makes four significant claims. First, and in a manner that bears close parallels with many of the more recent reformulations of class, she argues that issues of self-identity need to be incorporated into the analyses of social classes. She focuses particularly on 'symbolic boundaries', or 'the type of lines that people drawn when they categorize people' (Lamont 1992: 1) and 'high status signals', or markers people use in social evaluations, suggesting that these are connected into the political-economic formulation of social classes. Second, Lamont (1992) claims that whilst self-identity can be connected to the formation of class, it is not as some formative or necessary relation but rather is 'the frequent unintended effect of the process of defining self-identity'. She further argues that the identity or culture a person holds cannot simply be accounted for by 'interests, the volume and composition of their resources (or capital), or the structure of their groups' (Lamont 1992: 7). Third, Lamont (1992) explicitly distances herself from a 'post-structural approach' to symbolic boundaries, which, in her view, sees symbolic differences as being a manifestation of power relations. Lamont, (1992: 6) by contrast, argues that rather than assuming that symbolic boundaries lead to exclusion and domination one should view these boundaries as 'a necessary but insufficient condition for the creation of inequality and exclusion'. Fourthly, while she 'builds directly' on the work of Bourdieu (Lamont 1992: 181), she also comes to challenge many aspects of it, including what she identifies as its over-emphasis on socioeconomic status. She suggests that it is necessary to widen the focus to include cultural and moral boundaries and to consider these in their own right, broadening Bourdieu's ideas about socio-economic status boundaries into a 'boundary approach' that examines how particular symbolic forms come to create social boundaries.

Whilst the arguments of Lamont have been subject to some critical comments (e.g., Bennett et al. 2009), her accounts, and the four issues raised in association with them, can be seen to provide a clear illustration of many of the key issues, and tensions, relating to recent reformulations of class analysis. In the rest of this chapter I will further explore some of these issues and tensions, considering their relevance to the understanding of rural communities.

Dis-identification, Socio-economic Differentiation and Cultural Distinction

One important task within 'culturalist analysis' is to explore people's understandings of class,[1] a point clearly made by Skeggs (2004), Sayer (2005b) and Wright (2005: 180). It is furthermore important to recognize that class can be conceived quite differently, it is also evident that within many countries a high proportion people dis-identify with any concept, rejecting any application of the term to identify themselves or any other people (see Skeggs 2004). Even in Britain where there has been a long history of class-consciousness, studies have recorded a growing dis-identification with class (e.g., Bennett et al. 2009, Marshall et al. 1988). In a rural context, I found in questionnaire surveys in Norfolk and Berkshire (Phillips 2002b) that over twice as many people agreed as disagreed with the statement that the countryside was becoming a 'middle-class territory', a finding which, whilst showing that the notion of an end of class consciousness is clearly inappropriate, also revealed that significant number of people did not readily identify with the concept (see also Bryant and Pini 2009).

Bryant and Pini (2009) and Phillips (2002a) both go on to outline other identities to which people apparently did ascribe, with the former suggesting that familial relationships to farming were a key constituent of identity, while the latter delimited four rural lifestyles to which people appeared to identify. As illustrated in Table 2.1, these were seen to variously draw upon and sustain aspects of the rural social identities of localism, ruralism, countryism and communalism previously described by Bell (1986, 1994). Localism refers to identities such as 'local' and

---

1   There are clear connections between culturalist approaches to class and those described as 'interpretivist' (see Phillips 1998a, 2002a, 2002b, 2007, Savage 1994, Savage and Butler 1995). However, one could argue that whilst interpretivist approaches focus on epistemological aspects of class analysis, culturalist analyses tend to concentrate more on ontological questions. Whilst in many instances there is clear connection, such that studies might be seen to adopt a culturalist and interpretivist approach, it is clearly possible to give greater recognition to cultural dimensions of class formation without seeking to move away from legislative/modernistic epsietmologies (e.g., see work such as Chan and Goldthorpe's 2004, 2005, 2007a, 2007b).

Table 2.1   Rural lifestyles and cultural textures of rurality and class

Rural lifestyle	General Character	Cultural textures of rurality	Primary cultural texture of class
Village gentry	Stress and seek to participate in 'traditional' rural society, which is seen to have a long standing and harmonious social hierarchy	Localism and ruralism.	Individualistic ethos
Move in and join in	Stress and seek to participate in an active rural community.	Communalism	Achievement ethos
Move in for self and show	Rural viewed as a space of consumption, either for nurturance of the self or for social display.	Pastoralism and recreationalism	Consumption ethos
Village regulators	Stressed and sought to organize spatial order.	Modernist pastoral	Individualistic ethos, but also achievement and consumption.

Source: Derived from Cloke et al. 1995, 1998, Phillips 1998a, 1998b, 2001, 2002a.

'incomer' constructed on the basis of people's association with a particular locality; ruralism constructs identities such as country person or non-country-person on the basis of associations with a rural locality; countryism involves the building of similar identities through connection to particular activities taken to be undertaken by country people; while communalism involves the establishment of identities focused on 'being part of a community' or remaining apart from it, as in the case of 'dormitory commuters' or the 'ghosts' identified in Abram (1998).

As illustrated in Table 2.1, it was argued that these lifestyles not only contain 'cultural textures' of rurality but also often embodied Eder's (1993) ethoi, or cultural textures, of class, even if they do not explicitly reference class. So, for example, whilst clearly not reducible to an expression of class identity, notions of localism and ruralism can be quite central to the 'village gentry lifestyle' because it draws on notions of distinct rural ways of living and a localized social hierarchy, viewpoints that simultaneously often draw upon cultural textures falling within Eder's (1993) individualistic ethos of personal identity. This ethos constructs socio-economic inequality as natural, unchangeable and indeed beneficial, ideas that can be seen to provide legitimacy to the ideal of a hierarchically ordered rural society. Advocates of a 'move-in and join-in' lifestyle, by contrast, may well reject notions of an inherent hierarchy, often asserting quite egalitarian sentiments about rural communities whereby everyone is seen as important as everyone else, although also frequently making assessments of people which stress their differences, particularly in relation to community involvement. However, these differences tend to be viewed, in line with Eder's (1993) achievement ethos, as the outcome of the efforts, competences and abilities of people. Adherents to the 'move-in and joint-in' lifestyle hence tended to value those who do things, be that activity within or outside the village community.

Table 2.2   Attendance at cultural events by residents of 5 villages in Leicestershire and Warwickshire

Cultural activity and frequency of attendance	Percentage of residents by social class, as indicated by classification of Goldthorpe, Llewellyn and Payne (1980)							
	I	II	III	IV	V	VI	VII	Total
Cinema								
Monthly or more	19.4	11.7	15.8	7.1	0.0	0.0	4.3	12.2
Monthly to 6 monthly	9.7	3.3	2.6	0.0	0.0	0.0	0.0	3.3
Six monthly or less	32.3	26.7	23.7	7.1	10.0	33.3	17.4	24.3
Annually or less	19.4	31.7	21.1	50.0	40.0	16.7	17.4	25.4
Never	19.4	26.7	36.8	35.7	50.0	50.0	60.9	34.8
Theatre								
Monthly or more	9.7	16.7	17.1	21.4	10.0	0.0	4.8	13.2
Monthly to 6 monthly	9.7	1.7	4.9	0.0	0.0	0.0	0.0	3.3
Six monthly or less	38.7	30.0	19.5	14.3	10.0	50.0	23.8	28.0
Annually or less	32.3	36.7	24.4	35.7	40.0	0.0	4.8	26.4
Never	9.7	15.0	34.1	28.6	40.0	50.0	66.7	29.1
Opera								
Monthly or more	0.0	1.7	4.9	0.0	0.0	0.0	4.3	2.2
Monthly to 6 monthly	0.0	0.0	0.0	0.0	0.0	0.0	0.0	0.0
Six monthly or less	6.5	5.0	2.4	7.1	0.0	0.0	0.0	3.8
Annually or less	29.0	13.3	12.2	14.3	10.0	16.7	4.3	14.8
Never	64.5	80.0	80.5	78.6	90.0	83.3	91.3	79.2

Source: Data from project entitled 'Recent social change in the Leicestershire and Warwickshire Countryside' funded by Coventry University; for details of study see Agg (2000), Agg and Philips (1998), Phillips (1998b, 1999).

These rural lifestyles hence incorporated assessments of socio-economic differentiation, albeit often indirectly. It was, however, also evident that these rural lifestyles, and the assessments of rural residents more widely, often incorporated more than socio-economic assessments. They often included, for instance, boundaries and symbols which resembled some of those associated with Lamont's (1992) identification of 'cultural' boundary drawing in that they drew attention to issues such as what and how people talk, dress and consume. As outlined in Phillips (1998b), some people in gentrified villages in England and Wales made clear use of 'high cultural' markers such as the presence of a historical, religious or educational establishment or person, in a manner akin to descriptions of 'positional consumption'. Furthermore, Bennett et al.'s (2009) claim that members of what they describe as a professional-executive class, composed of professionals and employers in large establishments, are, as a group, more regular attendees at 'high culture' institutions such as opera, cinema, theatre, museums and art galleries is born out to some extent within the results of a study of villages in Leicestershire and Warwickshire (see Table 2.2).

Bennett et al. (2009) also claim that tastes in reading and music express some class differentiation, arguments that also find some striking parallels with Tables 2.3 and 2.4. There appears, for instance, as argued by Bennett et al. (2009), to be a higher preference levels for biographies and modern literatures amongst higher or lower grade professionals than for people classified as lower-grade technical or skilled, semi-skilled or unskilled workers, as well as greater relative appreciation of classical music. Again, consistent with the contentions of Bennett et al. (2009), differences are also apparent in relation to jazz music and the reading of science, philosophy, politics, and science fiction, although a preference for this literary form was clearly highest amongst people classified as higher-grade professionals. Conversely, members of this group seemed less likely than members of other classes to express a liking for country and western or folk music, a finding that resonates with Bennett et al.'s (2009) claim that work form of music has become a 'stigmatized taste', with public expressions of enjoyment being avoided by all but a small group of largely working-class country and western 'enthusiasts'.

At least four other parallels with the work of Bennett et al. (2009) are worth highlighting in relation to Tables 2.3 and 2.4. First, whilst there are some clear differences in patterns of readership between people classified as being members of different classes, it was also apparent, as Bennett et al. (2009) remark, that reading books was a far from widespread activity, with even the most popular genre, biographies, still engaging less than half the respondents. Such findings might suggest that cultural capital, at least in the forms relating to book reading, is not significant for many people. Expressions of engagement were generally far higher for music, where, interestingly given the comments of Bennett et al. (2009), classical music appeared to be the most popular form of music, with approaching eight out of every 10 respondents expressing a liking for it. Such popularity might be reflective of the social stratification of the sample, which, given its focus on gentrified villages, was unsurprisingly dominated by middle-class residents (over 51 per cent of respondents with a classified social class position fell into social classes I or II), and also perhaps the age structure of the sample (66 per cent of respondents were over 40, and over 44 per cent over 50). Here is a second parallel

Table 2.3   Preference for musical genres by residents of 5 villages in Leicestershire and Warwickshire

Social class	Percentage of residents stating liked musical genres										
	Classical	Jazz	Pop	Avant-garde	Easy listening	Rock	Light orchestral	Country and western	Folk	Opera
I Higher grade professionals	80.6	45.2	51.6	3.2	54.8	38.7	35.5	12.9	19.4	38.7
II Lower grade professionals	93.4	45.9	39.3	8.2	65.6	39.3	49.2	27.9	41.0	42.6
III Routine non-manual/ personal service workers	78.0	29.3	58.5	4.9	70.7	39.0	56.1	34.1	24.4	41.5
IV Small employers/ self-employed	100.0	37.5	50.0	0.0	75.0	25.0	50.0	62.5	28.6	87.5
V Lower grade technical workers	50.0	20.0	40.0	0.0	70.0	10.0	50.0	20.0	20.0	20.0
VI Skilled manual workers	66.7	33.3	33.3	16.7	33.3	33.3	33.3	50.0	33.3	50.0
VII Semi-unskilled and agricultural workers	52.2	17.4	34.8	4.3	65.2	21.7	17.4	65.2	30.4	17.4
All classified	78.5	35.5	45.7	5.4	63.4	34.4	43.5	33.3	30.3	38.2

Notes: Social class derived using classification of Goldthorpe, Llewellyn and Payne (1980).

Source: As Table 2.2.

Table 2.4   Preference for literary genres by residents of 5 villages in Leicestershire and Warwickshire

Social class and gender	Percentage of residents stating liked literary genres											
	Biographies	Travel/ exploration	Historical novels	Thrillers	Classics	Modern Lit.	Love stories	Science Fiction	Poetry	Science	Political	Philosophy
I	51.6	54.8	35.5	64.5	38.7	32.3	3.2	35.5	16.1	22.6	22.6	12.9
II	57.4	55.7	50.8	44.3	52.5	41.0	14.8	18.0	14.8	18.0	18.0	8.2
III	51.2	39.0	43.9	29.3	34.1	17.1	39.0	7.3	17.1	7.3	0.0	0.0
IV	28.6	28.6	50.0	28.6	28.6	14.3	28.6	0.0	0.0	0.0	14.3	0.0
V	30.0	40.0	40.0	50.0	10.0	0.0	0.0	10.0	10.0	10.0	10.0	0.0
VI	16.7	50.0	33.3	50.0	0.0	0.0	16.7	16.7	16.7	16.7	0.0	0.0
VII	30.4	26.1	39.1	34.8	4.3	13.0	17.4	4.3	4.3	0.0	8.7	0.0
All classified	47.5	45.8	43.9	43.0	34.6	25.7	18.4	15.6	13.4	12.8	12.3	5.0
Male	47.6	52.4	42.2	53.0	27.7	26.5	1.2	24.4	12.2	12.2	22.0	18.3
Female	47.1	39.2	46.6	33.3	42.2	26.5	31.4	7.8	14.7	14.7	4.9	7.8
All classified	47.3	45.1	44.6	42.2	35.7	26.5	17.9	15.2	13.6	13.6	12.5	12.5

Source: As Table 2.2.

to the work of Bennett et al. (2009: 82), who suggest that there may well be an 'age-related cultural divide' in relation to music, whereby popular music appeals to younger people, classical music to the older, while the middle-aged, 'first exposed to music in the 1950s and 1960s, when popular music first challenged classical music's cultural visibility', were the group most likely to express a liking for both. The relative popularities of different forms of music and literature might also, in part, be reflective of geographical variations in the social structure, an issue not really examined by Bennett et al. who, as Gibson (2010) remarks, rather neglect issues of geography. They do, however, highlight that classical music, despite its elitist/high cultural associations and evident dislike by many people, still constituted the most popular musical form within their sample (42 per cent viewing it positively (Bennett et al. 2009: 79)).

Table 2.4 also includes information relating reading preferences to gender, an issue widely been recognized within feminist studies, particularly since the work of Radway (1984) on women and romantic fiction. In line with this work, Bennett et al. (2009: 105) suggest that this genre has a clear gender bias in terms of viewing figures, with women being 'almost 15 times more likely than men to choose romances as a preferred genre'. In Figure 2.4 the gender differences are even more stark, with women being over 26 times more likely than men to express a liking for love stories than men. Women also appeared to have a relative preference for classical literature, where they were around 1.5 times as likely to express a liking for this genre than men, whilst men appeared significantly more likely to express a liking for political literatures, science fiction, philosophy, thrillers and travel/exploration. These differences in taste might lend support to Bennett et al.'s (2009) claim that reading, along with participation in media such as film and television, expresses a gender-related distinction between 'inward' and 'outward' facing expressions of taste. They suggest that women, in general, preferred cultural representations relating to the domestic and the subjective – to life internal to the household and people's sense of identity and personhood – while men, in general, favoured images and narratives relating to activities outside of the household and beyond inner senses of the self. Table 2.4 suggests that men in the rural sample, in general, expressed an interest in literatures relating to such external worlds as politics, science, travel/exploration and crime, while women's reading preferences tended to focus, in general, on genres such as romance and classical literature, both of which may be seen to focus on intra-household and intra personal relations and identities.

Bennett et al. (2009: 222) are keen to stress that differentiation of 'outward' and 'inward' cultural orientations does not map directly on to gender, in the sense that neither are 'all men outwardly orientate and all women ... inwardly looking', nor is the outward simply masculinized and the inward feminized. Having said this, they do identify a 'crispness of ... separation' between men and women in relation to inward and outward orientations which they viewed as both 'striking' and rather clearer than those associated with class (Bennett et al. 2009: 222). Whilst such issues are important to recognize, the implications of Bennett et al.'s

(2009) findings, and indeed of Tables 2.3 and 2.4, are arguably to suggest, as they themselves conclude, that formations of cultural capital are often highly gendered, and gendered in ways that serve to establish distinctions of greater significance than those associated with class relations.

A fourth argument of Bennett et al. (2009) is, however, that cultural hierarchies are of less significance than assumed by people such as Bourdieu, at least in a British context. They suggest, for example, that whilst members of the professional-executive class generally have more educational qualifications and engage to a greater extent than other classes with activities high up on cultural hierarchies, participation in 'high culture' activities is 'not acquired by all the members that class; not by a long chalk' (Bennett et al. 2009: 253). They further argue that whilst participation in high cultural activities may be linked into class formation for elite elements of this class, 'where it oils the wheels of social connections' (Bennett et al. 2009: 253) and/or assists in the development of technical knowledges, even within this class it is widely accorded little value. Such claims have clear resonances with Tables 2.3 and 2.4, in that only within the musical genres of classical and easy listening, and the literary genres of biographies, thrillers and travel/exploration, did over half of the respondents classified as higher or lower grade professionals profess a liking.

The decline in cultural hierarchies and markers, along with evidence that socio-economic distinctions may be not be universally valued, provides evidence to support the dis-identification thesis, although their continuing presence in a significant number of accounts, along with some clear differences in participation levels, also suggests that societies are far from classless. One might argue, as Bennett et al. (2009: 211) do, that the language of class 'is in retreat', but notions of class have not disappeared completely but rather have 'gone underground'. As noted in Phillips (2002a: 94), many proponents of the death of class thesis operate with a very modernist/non-poststructuralist conception of class identity centred on its presence or absence, it being argued that there is actually 'a need for a fuller recognition of the diverse ways in which discourses act'.

Such recognition can be seen emerging within some reformulations of class. So, for example, Lamont (1992: 80) argues that non-recognition of class does not necessarily entail the non-operation of class relations, but may actually be a consequence of their pervasive operation in that they become 'taken for granted', or naturalized, and thereby 'non-salient at the discursive level', which focuses on 'the finer categories of the classification system ignoring the outer edges'. Another explanation of class dis-identification is that class relations become enmeshed within other social relations to such as extent that they come to be described through other social identities.

Rural parallels to this argument can be identified. In Phillips (2002b), for example, attention is drawn to the way that suburban space figured prominently in interviews with residents in two gentrified villages in Berkshire, England, it being suggested that this space was, in part, seen to signify people who were different from, or other than, the middle-class respondents. While the term working-class was rarely used, the description of suburban space exhibited many of the features that Skeggs (2004) and Lawler (2005) suggest have become associated with the working-class, as least within the perceptions of many middle-class residents. Lawler (2005: 430), for example, argues that locations inhabited by the working-class are often described by the middle-class in ways suggestive of abhorrence, lack and a status of being 'foundationally "other" to a middle-class existence', features also evidenced in accounts of rural gentrifiers who associated suburban spaces with a range of social ills, including poor parenting, high crime and violence. Rural space, as Cloke, Milbourne and Widdowfield (2000: 727) comment, is often conceived as 'a purified space, where social problems ... are out-of-place', displaced to some other of the rural, which in the case of gentrified areas of the countryside, often appears to be suburban spaces (see also Phillips, 2004). Another study indicating conflation of spatial and social identities is Pini, Rice and McDonald's (2010), which suggests that 'the rural' and the 'working class' are often fused within discussions of education in rural Australia, with 'the biography created for them being one and the same, that is, devoid of tertiary education and a career trajectory'. Such an argument not only reinforces Gibson and Davidson's (2004: 389) claim that the rural idyll has 'limited explanatory power' in Australia, but also highlights the needs to put geographical qualifiers on the claim of Cloke, Phillips and Thrift (1995: 238) that 'the cultural textures associated with the rural have expanded to a point where "rural" signifies the middle class'.

The issue of geographical variations within identity relations is given high prominence within the work of Lamont (1992), who observes that there are significant national variations in processes of boundary formation, including those associated with class and that further differences are enunciated according to gender and race/ethnicity. Illustrative is that working-class men tend to place greater emphasis on moral categories than their middle-class counterparts, but also that middle-class women tended to draw stronger cultural boundaries than middle-class men, while white working-class men tended to adopt a more individualist ethic than did black working-class men, who often 'put stress on solidarity and generosity' (Lamont 2000: 200), thereby exhibiting what the author identifies as a 'caring-self'. White working-class men, on the other hand, tended to place moral value of individual performance in relation to effort, responsibility and other facets of what Lamont identifies as the 'disciplined self'.

Such arguments have considerable significance for the dis-identification thesis, highlighting both complexity and variability in evaluations of identity. As yet there have been too few studies to enable evaluation of the specifics of Lamont's (1992) arguments concerning symbolic boundary drawing, although as demonstrated here, there are some interesting parallels with the UK-wide study of Bennett et al., as well as with a few more localised rural studies. As Heley (2010: 4) has remarked in a recent study that seeks to explore arguments of Lamont in relation to rural studies, what is needed is a series of 'empirically-rich studies that would (almost literally) flesh out understanding of the middle classes in rural areas'. The analyses in this section may have contributed slightly to such an endeavour by drawing together some existing and new empirical information relating to socio-economic and cultural boundaries and differences in rural areas. Heley's (2010) study provides further contributions, revealing the continuing significance of socio-economic boundaries within what is identified as a 'new rural squirearchy' composed of affluent financial and service workers, senior managers, professionals and business owners (who might be described as members of Bennett et al.'s (2009) 'professional-executive class', or even perhaps as rural 'supergentrifers' (Butler and Lees 2006, Lees 2003, Perrenoud and Phillips forthcoming)), as well as a range of middle-class identities which include but also extend beyond rural inscribed ones, such as the 'country set' which is described in a manner akin to the rural gentry lifestyle previously discussed. Heley highlights how this rural lifestyle was routinely enacted in conjunction with a series of other middle-class identities, including the 'business man', the 'yuppie', the 'jet-set' and the 'ex-pat'. Heley (2010: 10) also argues, in line with Lamont, that there is a need to recognize that socio-economic, and indeed cultural, identities are often enacted in association with moral categories, and also frequently involve 'sentimental attachments' and 'emotions'. It is to such issues that attention now turns in the next section of this chapter.

Beyond Cultural Assets and Boundaries: Explorations of Class, Morality and Emotion

It is noticeable that whilst commentators on the renewal of class analysis such as Bottero (2004) have called for yet further reflection on the conceptual meaning of class, there is little or no discussion of the concept of culture. This is despite there being claims that some of the social theorists invoked in the renewal of class analysis have quite problematic conceptions of culture. Bourdieu, for example, arguably developed a highly reductionist account of culture, seeming downgrading 'cultural complexity by recoding culture as simply the pursuit of symbolic advantage' (Cloke, Phillips and Thrift 1995: 223). Further, it is evident that quite diverse formulations of class have been adopted in much of the new, reformulated approaches to class. Even within the scholarship drawing on Bourdieu's notion of cultural capital significant differences are evident. Bennett et al. (2009: 29), for example, argue that Bourdieu's conception of cultural capital needs to be 'disaggregated' so that a range of 'different assets and markers' associated with the construction of 'cultural privilege' can be identified and explored. They highlight the distinction Bourdieu (1986) draws between objective, institutionalized and embodied forms of cultural capital, although supplementing this with notions of technical, emotional, national and sub-cultural forms of cultural capital. They add that although the 'exact provenance and content' of these forms of capital is hard to establish, they might be characterized as follows:

> Institutionalized capital confers honour deriving primarily from holding
> educational qualifications, where credentials bestowed and the institutions
> awarding them generate differential for individuals and groups. Objective capital
> refers to possessions and by implication, to the judgements of taste associated
> with their acquisition or in related areas. Embodied capital is manifest in
> demeanour, dress and bodily comportment generally (Bennett et al. 2009: 29)

Whilst still quite distant from clear definitions, these descriptions highlight diversity in conceptions of culture linked to processes of class formation, and also connect the work of Bourdieu to a range of other cultural and class analysts. The concept of institutionalized cultural capital, for example, encompasses much of what Lamont analyses through her notions of cultural and socio-economic boundary drawing. Indeed, Lamont in one of her early discussions of the concept of cultural capital, explicitly endorses an institutional perspective: 'we propose to define cultural capital as *institutionalized i.e., widely shared, high status cultural signals (attitudes, preferences, formal knowledge, behaviours, goods and credentials) used for social and cultural exclusion*' (Lamont and Lareau 1988: 156, original emphasis)

Lamont and Lareau (1988) note that many North American studies making reference to Bourdieu's concept of cultural capital in the 1980s tended to emphasize its connections to qualification attainment, seeing these as credential forms of knowledge whose successful attainment reflected the prior acquisition of legitimated attitudes and behaviours. Many of the recent studies associated with the new, reformulated, class analysis have adopted similar foci. Scherger and Savage (2010), for example, have examined whether educational attainment can be attributed to cultural capital associated with parental support and socialization, issues which have also been addressed by the likes of Reay (2004), Reay and Lucey (2000; 2003), Walkerdine, Lucey and Melody (2001), all of whom have incorporated examination of gender as well as class.

As well as focusing on gender in addition to class, the latter set of analyses also illustrates Pini, Rice and McDonald's (2010: 19) claim that much of the work on education 'associated with the newly invigorated class analysis' has focused on 'urban domains'. They do, however, go on to highlight a series of rural studies with links to such analyses, including Atkin's (2000) study of lifelong learning in rural Lincolnshire (see also Atkin 2003); Funnell's (2008) and Alloway and Gilbert's (2004) studies of young men in rural Queenslan; and Keddie's (2007) and Keddie, Mills and Mills' (2008) examinations of schooling in a Tasmanian working-class rural town. There have also been more quantitative studies in the UK suggesting that there may be rural-urban differences in educational attainment (Commission for Rural Communities 2007, 2008), which may in part be reflective of their respective social class composition rather than any specifically locational influences. Hoggart (2007), for example, identified marked differences in educational qualifications between middle and working-class adults which surpassed differences between urban and rural place of residence, while the Commission for Rural Communities (2010) argues that attainment amongst primary school children, as measured by Level 4 achievement at Key Stage 2 National Curriculum assessments (SATs), is uniformly lower in rural areas than urban areas when ranked according to decile position on an income deprivation index even though, overall, children in rural areas have higher attainment levels than children in urban areas. The reason for this apparently contradictory result lies, they suggest, in rural children being less likely than urban ones to be living in areas of income deprivation, which in turn might be seen as reflective of class positions, although the relationships should not be seen as direct, particularly if one adopts a multiple asset formulation of class position.

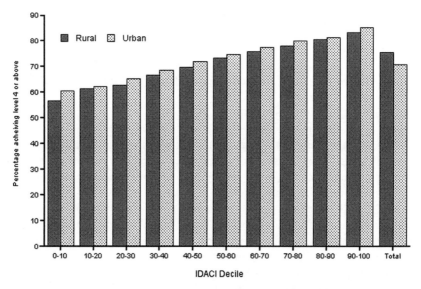

Figure 2.1   Key Stage 2 attainment by Income Deprivation Affecting Children Index (IDACI), 2008

Source: Based on Commission for Rural Communities (2010), using data available at http:// ruralcommunities.gov.uk/state-of-the-countryside-data, accessed 8/9/10.

Much work on educational attainment makes use of Bourdieu's concept of habitus, and in doing so can be seen to draw on aspects of what Bennett et al. (2009) characterize as embodied capital, and which might also be described as 'human' or 'social capital'. Bennett et al. suggest that embodied capital is often interpreted in two related, but rather different, ways. First, as referring to 'resources which others call human capital – skills and competences, cognitive and manual, which when deployed may be sold or gifted to others' (Bennett et al. 2009: 153). This sense of embodied capital might also be seen as closely related to notions of technical capital, and indeed to conceptions of skill that have long, if contentiously, been

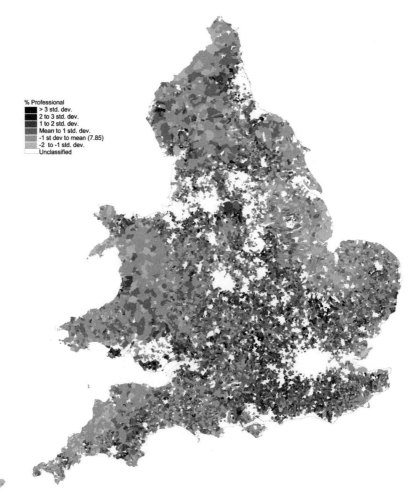

% Professional
- ■ > 3 std. dev.
- ■ 2 to 3 std. dev.
- ■ 1 to 2 std. dev.
- Mean to 1 std. dev.
- -1 st dev to mean (7.85)
- -2 to -1 std. dev.
- Unclassified

Figure 2.2   The relative significance of higher-grade professionals in rural areas in England and Wales, 2001 Census
Source: Phillips, M. 2007. Changing class complexions in and on the British countryside. *Journal of Rural Studies*, 23(3), 293.

employed in class analyses (e.g., see Dale, Gilbert and Arber 1985, Littler 1982, Marshall et al. 1988, Phillips 1991, Savage et al. 1992, Wright 1985, 2005). A second strand of interpretation identified by Bennett et al. (2009: 153) views embodied capital to referring to 'bodily hexis', that is, 'to accent, posture and demeanour' and 'to the appearance and presentation of the body to others'.

These two senses of embodied capital can be observed being employed explicitly or implicitly in a range of studies, including many rural studies. Some of the political-economy inspired studies of class and rural restructuring in the

1990s, for instance, suggested that skills and credentials had come to both be more prominent within capitalist divisions of labour and to exert a profound influence on the social geography of rural areas because members of a so-called service class, whose members were seen to have obtained the organizational and other skills required within emerging forms of post-industrial production, were attracted to living in the countryside (e.g., Cloke and Thrift 1987, 1990). Connected to this, it was also suggested that these groups would have a preference for residing in

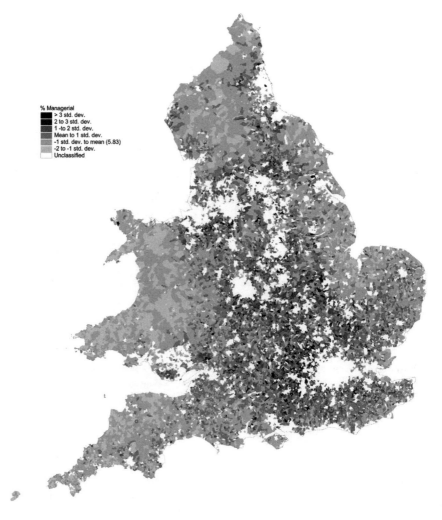

Figure 2.3   The relative significance of managers and industrialists in rural areas in England and Wales, 2001 Census

Source: Phillips, M. 2007. Changing class complexions in and on the British countryside. *Journal of Rural Studies*, 23(3), 292.

areas with good access to cultural facilities, or 'theatres of consumption' (Cloke and Thrift 1987: 327).

Some subsequent studies (Hoggart 1997, Phillips 2007, forthcoming, Phillips et al. 2009) have indeed identified highly differentiated geographies of rural residence amongst the middle-classes. Phillips (2007), for example, suggests that the 'service class' of industrialists/ managers and professionals was, within England and Wales, numerically most significant in rural areas in the South East and in a

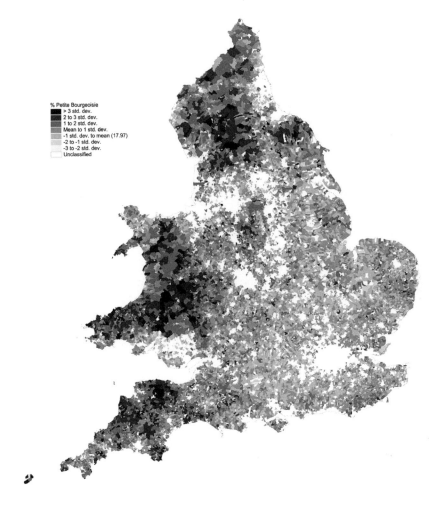

Figure 2.4   The relative significance of the petite bourgeoisie in rural areas in England and Wales, 2001 Census

Source: Phillips, M. 2007. Changing class complexions in and on the British countryside. *Journal of Rural Studies*, 23(3), 294.

corridor stretching from London, through the Midlands and into areas bordering the Merseyside, Greater Manchester and West Yorkshire conurbations, although the professionals exhibited a rather more dispersed pattern of concentration than did the industrialists and managers. However, the distribution of a further element of the middle-classes, the petite bourgeoisie of self-employed/own account workers and small-scale employers, was quite different, with rural areas in the north of England, Wales and the South West figuring as areas of relatively high presence.

It was further noted in Phillips (2007) that this group, although often over-looked in favour of examinations of a range of 'new middle-class' groups such as the service class, had long been viewed as a 'traditional' component of the middle-class, with this term being used not only to convey extensive temporality but also, in many instances, a particular set cultural values. Bourdieu advanced such a view in his counterpoising of a traditional and new petite bourgeoisie in *Distinction* (Bourdieu 1984). There would seem to be scope for exploring the degree to which such differentiated geographies might be reflective of, and indeed be at least in part constituted in association with, differential compositions of cultural and economic assets (Phillips, forthcoming). However, there is arguably also a need to consider their relationship to more embodied forms of capital, both because Bennett et al. (2009) suggest that there has been declining efficacy of institutional capital and because educational researchers have long suggested that attainment of institutional capital is predicated on more embodied forms of cultural capital.

Aspects of embodied capital can be seen to have figured quite prominently within rural studies, albeit described largely through what Lareau and Weininger (2003) have described as cultural capital's 'sister concept', namely social capital. They further suggest that social capital has been more extensively used than its sibling concept, which is indeed the case within rural studies, where the concept of social capital has been extensively used and debated (e.g., Shortall 2008, Shucksmith 2000). Whilst reference is made in many of these to Bourdieu's writings on social capital (e.g., Bourdieu 1980, 1983, 1986), rural studies also frequently draw on its elaboration by Coleman (1988) and Putnam (1995, 2000). Common across the work of all three social theorists is the notion that social capital relates to 'social networks and interpersonal relationships' (Schaefer-McDaniel 2004: 140). As such, the concept has clear connections to the notion of habitus, and to embodied capital, with all three concepts being emphasized and discussed within feminist influenced studies of Bourdieu and class (e.g., Hughes and Blaxter 2007, Reay 2000, 2004, 2005).

As Hughes and Blaxter (2007) have noted, there has been a tendency within such studies for the concept of social capital to be closely linked to notions of cultural capital, a feature which is not the case within policy related discussions of social capital, which have tended to view social capital as a distinct, and measurable, variable of social production. This latter view is very clearly evident within literatures on rural livelihoods and community development, where social capital has been viewed as one of a series of distinct assets or resources needed to foster successful, vibrant or sustainable communities (e.g., Carnegie Trust 2007,

2009, Ellis 2000, Emery and Flora 2006). There have, however, been calls within rural studies to develop more relational perspectives on social capital (e.g., Falk and Kilpatrick, 2000), although there is a potential danger that such perspectives end up dissolving the concept of social capital completely. As a way forward, Holt (2009: 233) suggests that embodied social capital can be conceptualized using Bourdieu's notion of the habitus, which she claims 'also resonates strongly with enduring concerns about the beyond consciousness, the reflexive and the affectual realm within human geography'. Mention has, however, already been made to criticisms relating to the singular and over-arching character of Bourdieu's concept of habitus, and there appears to be some danger that recourse to this concept serves to return class analysis to an overly undifferentiated concept of culture.

Sayer's 2005b critique is particularly instructive in this regard, in that he not only expresses concern over the instrumentalization/economism of culture implied by Bourdieu – suggesting that Bourdieu's use of terms such as capital and investment encourages people to view habits and cultural preferences as 'competitive reward-seeking behaviours' (Sayer 2005b: 39) but also highlights the importance of recognizing 'ethical dispositions' or 'moral sentiments', an argument which again has explicit connections to the work of Lamont, and suggests that Bourdieu's conception of habitus, rather surprisingly given its emphasis on tacit, semi-conscious orientations, neglects a key aspect of people's experience of social life, namely emotions. These two issues can be seen to have come to the fore in recent debates over class analysis, and indeed to have also figured, albeit arguably to a lesser extent, within rural studies of class.

I have, for example, explored the use of moral labels by residents of gentrified villages, suggesting the have similarities to some of those identified by Lamont (1992). Lamont, for example, suggests that the notion of the 'phoney' was a widely used moral category amongst middle-class American men, being used to 'describe people who are not sincere, who pretend to know more than they do, or to be something they are not' (Lamont 1992: 92). It is suggested in Phillips (1998b) that such a notion was very evident in the descriptions of life amongst rural residents, being used to both devalue social status symbols and in the enactment of rural identities. In relation to the former, for example, people displaying status commodities or known to engage in high cultural activities were described by some as 'not genuine', as well as 'selfish', 'arrogant' or 'types we don't like'. In relation to rural identities, the notions of localness, ruralism, countryism and communalism discussed previously were often conferred with connotations of authenticity, realism and/or naturalism, whilst opposing relational identities such as 'incomer' or 'townie' were described in ways that implied connections with in-authenticity, un-naturalness and/or being less than real. The last feature was of particular significance in descriptions of enactments of countryism and communalism in that these identities are more open to enactment by incoming residents (see Cloke, Phillips and Thrift 1998). However, performance of such identities required more than the input of money and time but also what Cloke, Goodwin and Milbourne (1998) characterize as cultural competence, and failure to competently enact such identities was often subject to moral criticism whereby people were viewed as adopting pseudo lifestyle which did not reflect who they 'really were'.

Heley (2010: 4) advances similar arguments, suggesting that terms such as 'plastic farmers' and 'wannabe-Hooray-Henries' were used by some rural residents to imply that others were seeking 'improper, inauthentic and undeserved' identities. He also highlights, in a manner which resonates with Sayer's (2005b) discussion concerning the complexity and ambiguities of lay normativities, how people at times refrained from expressing viewpoints so as to 'remain the "right" side of a ... moral boundary' (Heley 2010: 6), even if they did not necessarily ascribe to this morality.

Heley (2010) also argues that there is a need to integrate the study of boundary drawing with a growing strand of rural research investigating performance, embodiment, affect and emotion. The significance of such research within rural studies has been highlighted by the likes of Edensor (2006), Carolan (2008) and Woods (2010), although as Heley (2010: 3) notes, such studies, at best, 'make only fleeting references to ... class'. However, a number of authors associated with new culturalist approaches to class have highlighted these very same issues (e.g., Sayer 2005b: Walkerdine, Lucey and Melody 2001)

The significance of emotion is also evident in the work of Reay (2000, 2004), who, amongst other strategies, seeks to extend Bourdieu's 'conceptual framework' to encompass the notion of emotional capital. She notes how the term was used by Nowotny (1981) who viewed it as a variant form of social capital, although the author herself connects it more to the concept of cultural capital, and to ideas of habitus and embodied capital. Reay (2000) sees the family as an institution through which embodied and, in some cases, other forms of cultural capital are produced and conveyed, which in turn influences the accumulation of more institutional forms of cultural capital associated with school education. Feelings of anxiety, anger and embarrassment were, Reay (2000) contends, highly prominent in discussions of schooling by both working- and middle-class mothers, although the subjects and effects of these emotions were often quite different.

Reay's (2000, 2004) work suggests that there are complex relationships between emotional and other forms of capital, with emotional 'commitment', to use Sayer's (2005b) terminology, not necessarily translating into the accumulation of cultural capital in the form of educational qualifications but also being itself impacted by 'economic security and social status' (Reay 2000: 582). Whilst Reay's (2000) focus is very specific, her arguments about emotional capital can be seen to have wider significance. Studies of service sector occupations, for example, have long recognized that employees may require embodied skills related to 'looks, personalities and emotions' (Leidner 1991: 156) which are complexly related to cultural qualifications and constructions of identity: as Silva (2000: 3) notes, emotions are incorporated into classificatory systems, being widely contrasted and devalued against other facets of social life, such as thought and action, as well as differentiated and evaluated against one another, and associated and/

or disassociated with particular behaviours, types of people and situations or places. Emotion, for instance, is widely viewed as gendered: Nowotny (1981), for example, argued that women tend to have larger amounts of emotional capital than men, while Reay (2000) argued that men were often uninvolved in the emotional work surrounding children's schooling, and indeed may generally be involved in much less emotional work within households than women (Reay 2004).

Recognition of emotions has become an important strand of the new, culturalist, interpretations of class. They have, however, yet to become a subject of sustained investigation within rural class analysis, although there are some pointers that suggest scope for such studies. Abram's (1998: 373) claim that rural studies has an 'obsession with class', for example, could be interrogated from an emotional direction rather than in relation to discourses of class and classlessness, as has largely hitherto been the case (Hoggart 1998, Phillips 1998a, 1998b, 2002a, 2007). Cloke, Phillips and Thrift's (1998: 179) claim that people moving into rural areas are 'investing not only socially and economic but also culturally and psychologically' could also be explored, perhaps drawing on Sayer's (2005b) distinction between investment and commitment. It has also been argued that 'emotional and affective ties play a prominent, if rather unacknowledged role within conceptions of community vibrancy ... [and] community tensions', and that the concept of emotional capital might be employed to 'highlight the significance of the resources that people employ when interacting with the emotive dimensions of community' (Phillips 2010: 11).

Conclusion

This chapter has sought to demonstrate that class analysis has moved on from the debates over class identity and classlessness of the 1990s. Attention has been drawn to how the renewal of class analysis has been linked to notions of culture and the so-called dis-identification thesis. The role of feminist and gender analyses within this change has also been highlighted, as has the significance of the dis-identification concept to debates about class and the presence of some rural studies exploring socio-economic and cultural boundaries and their relationship to class. The chapter considered studies of social, economic and cultural boundary marking as outlined in studies such as Lamont (1992, 2000) and Bennett et al. (2009), before turning its attention to concepts of culture employed within class analyses. It has been argued that the renewed 'culturalist' approach to class needs to pay greater attention to the concepts of culture, not least because of the range of conceptions employed. This is clearly evidenced in the work of Bourdieu, which has been widely cited in relation to the formulation of more culturalist interpretations of class. Drawing on claims that Bourdieu's concept of culture needs to be disaggregated and moral as well as socio-economic and cultural forms of symbolic boundary drawing recognized, the chapter has advanced the notion that rural studies of class might usefully adopt an assets-based approach to class which recognizes institutional, objectified, embodied, social and emotional forms of capital, as well as economic forms of capital such as the forces of production long recognized in Marxist and other forms of class analysis.

The distinctions between these forms of capital are complex and not necessarily clear cut, particularly given that several of the analyses discussed here have stressed the inter-constitution as well as transferability of one form of capital with another. It does seem at least theoretically possible that notions of class as potentially contradictory positionings within multiply constituted social relations or social fields, as advanced by the likes of Wright (1985, 2005), Savage et al. (1992) and, less explicitly, Bennett et al. (2009), might be extended to encompass a wider range of assets or capitals. Less ambitiously, perhaps, the concepts might be used to, as Heley (2010) suggests, 'flesh out' accounts of class in rural areas by encouraging the production of 'thicker descriptions' of the operation of culture within class relations, which encompass moral, emotional, embodied and symbolic dimensions of recognition and distribution.

References

Abram, S. 1998. Class, countryside and the 'Longitudinal Study'. *Journal of Rural Studies*, 14(3), 369–79.

Adkins, L. and Skeggs, B. (eds.) 2004. *Feminism after Bourdieu*. Oxford: Blackwell.

Agg, J. 2000. Rural social change in Leicestershire and Warwickshire. Unpublished PhD thesis, Coventry: Coventry University.

Agg, J. and Phillips, M. 1998. Neglected gender dimensions of rural social restructuring, in *Migration into Rural Areas*, edited by P. Boyle and K. Halfacree. London: Wiley, 166–85.

Alloway, N. and Gilbert, P. 2004. Shifting discourses about gender in higher education enrolments. *International Journal of Qualitative Studies in Education*, 17(1), 103–18.

Atkin, C. 2000. Lifelong learning–attitudes to practice in the rural context. *International Journal of Lifelong Education*, 19(3), 253–65.

Atkin, C. 2003. Rural communities: human and symbolic capital development, fields apart. *Compare*, 33(4), 507–518.

Bell, D. 2000. Farm boys and wild men. *Rural Sociology*, 65(4), 547–61.

Bell, M. 1986. The fruit of difference. *Rural Sociology*, 51(1), 65–82.

Bell, M. 1994. *Childerley: Nature and Morality in a Country Village*. Chicago: Chicago University Press.

Bennett, T., Savage, M., Silva, E., Warde, A., Gayo-Cal, M. and Wright, D. 2009. *Culture, Class, Distinction*. London: Routledge.

Bourdieu, P. 1980. Le capital social. *Actes de la Recherche en Sciences Sociales* 31, 2–3.

Bourdieu, P. 1983. Economic capital, cultural capital, social capital. *Soziale-Welt*, Supplement 2, 183–98.

Bourdieu, P. 1984. *Distinction*. London: Routledge.

Bourdieu, P. 1986. The forms of capital, in *Handbook of Theory and Research for the Sociology of Education*, edited by J. Richardson. New York: Greenwood, 241–58.

Bourdieu, P. 2005. *The Social Structures of the Economy*. Cambridge: Polity.

Bottero, W. 2004. Class identities and the identity of class. *Sociology*, 38(5), 985–1003.

Bryant, L. and Pini, B. 2009. Gender, class and rurality. *Journal of Rural Studies*, 25(1), 48–57.

Butler, T. and Lees, L. 2006. Super-gentrification in Barnsbury, London. *Transactions of the Institute of British Geographers*, 31, 467–87.

Campbell, H. 2000. The glass phallus. *Rural Sociology*, 65(4), 562–81.

Carnegie Trust 2007. *A Charter for Rural Communities*. Dunfermline: Carnegie Trust.

Carnegie Trust 2009. *A Manifesto for Rural Communities*. Dunfermline: Carnegie Trust.

Carolan, M. 2008. More-than-representational knowledge/s of the countryside. *Sociologia ruralis*, 48(4), 408–22.

Chan, T. and Goldthorpe, J. 2004. Is there a status order in contemporary British society? *European Sociological Review*, 20(3), 383–401.

Chan, T. and Goldthorpe, J. 2007a. Social status and newspaper readership. *American Journal of Sociology*, 112(4), 1095–134.

Chan, T. and Goldthorpe, J. 2007b. Social stratification and cultural consumption: music in England European. *Sociological Review*, 23(1), 1–19.

Cloke, P. and Thrift, N. 1987. Intra-class conflict in rural areas. *Journal of Rural Studies*, 3(4), 321–33.

Cloke, P. and Thrift, N. 1990. Class change and conflict in rural areas, in *Rural Restructuring*, edited by T. Marsden, P. Lowe and S. Whatmore. London: David Fulton, 165–81.

Cloke, P., Goodwin, M., Milbourne, P. and Thomas, C. 1995. Deprivation, poverty and marginalization in rural lifestyles in England and Wales. *Journal of Rural Studies*, 11(4), 351–65.

Cloke, P., Goodwin, M. and Milbourne, P. 1998. Inside looking out, in *Migration to Rural Areas*, edited by P. Boyle and K. Halfacree. London: Wiley, 134–50.

Cloke, P., Milbourne, P. and Widdowfield, R. 2000. Homelessness and rurality. *Environment and Planning D*, 18(6), 715–35.

Cloke, P., Phillips, M. and Thrift, N. 1995. The new middle classes and the social constructs of rural living, in *Social Change and the Middle Classes*, edited by T. Butler and M. Savage. London: UCL Press, 220–38.

Cloke, P., Phillips, M. and Thrift, N. 1998. Class, colonisation and lifestyle strategies in Gower, in *Migration to Rural Areas*, edited by P. Boyle and K. Halfacree. London: Wiley, 166–85.

Coleman, J. 1988. Social capital in the creation of human capital. *American Journal of Sociology*, 94(Supplement), 95–120.

Commission for Rural Communities 2007. *The State of the Countryside 2007.* Wetherby: Countryside Agency Publications.

Commission for Rural Communities 2008. *The State of the Countryside 2008.* Wetherby: Countryside Agency Publications.

Commission for Rural Communities 2010. *The State of the Countryside 2010.* Wetherby: Countryside Agency Publications.

Dale, A., Gilbert, N. and Arber, S. 1985. Integrating women into class analysis. *Sociology*, 19, 384–408.

Devine, F. and Savage, M. 2000. Conclusion, in *Renewing Class Analysis*, edited by R. Crompton, F. Devine, M. Savage and J. Scott. Oxford: Blackwell, 184–99.

Edensor, T. 2006. Performing rurality, in *Handbook of Rural Studies*, edited by P. Cloke, T. Marsden, P. Mooney. London: Sage, 484–95.

Eder, K. 1993. *The New Politics of Class.* London: Sage.

Ellis, F. 2000. *Rural Livelihoods and Diversity in Developing Countries*. Oxford: Oxford University Press.

Emery, M. and Flora, C. 2006. Spiraling-up. *Community Development*, 37(1), 19–35.

Falk, I. and Kilpatrick, S. 2000. What is social capital? *Sociologia Ruralis,* 40(1), 87–110.

Funnell, R. 2008. Tracing variations within 'rural habitus' Queensland. *British Journal of Sociology of Education*, 29(1), 15–24.

Gibson, L. 2010. Culture, class, distinction. *Cultural Trends*, 19(3), 245–8.

Gibson, C. and Davidson, D. 2004. Tamworth, Australia's 'country music capital'. *Journal of Rural Studies*, 20(4), 387–404.

Goldthorpe, J., Llewellyn, C. and Payne, C. 1980. *Social Mobility and the Class Structure in Modern Britain.* Oxford: Oxford University Press.

Heley, J. 2010. The new squirearchy and emergent cultures of the new middle classes in rural areas. *Journal of Rural Studies*, published Articles in Press as doiI: 10.1016/j.jrurstud.2010.03.002. Available at: http://www.sciencedirect.com/science/ journal/07430167 [accessed: 5 November 2010].

Hoggart, K 1997. The middle classes in rural England, 1971–1991. *Journal of Rural Studies*, 13(3), 253–73.

Hoggart, K. 1998. Rural cannot equal middle class because class does not exist? *Journal of Rural Studies*, 14(3), 381–6.

Hoggart, K. 2007. The diluted working classes of rural England and Wales. *Journal of Rural Studies*, 23(3), 305–17.

Holt, L. 2008. Embodied social capital and geographic persepctives: performing the habitus. *Progress in Human Geography*, 32(2), 227–46.

Hughes, C. and Blaxter, L. 2007. Feminist appropriations of Bourdieu, in *(Mis) recognition, Social Inequality and Social Justice*, edited by in T. Lovell. Abingdon: Routledge, 103–25.

Keddie, A. 2007. Games of subversion and sabotage. *British Journal of Sociology of Education*, 28(2), 181–94.

Keddie, A., Mills, C. and Mills, M. 2008. Struggles to subvert the gendered field. *Pedagogy, Culture and Society*, 16(2), 193–205.

Lamont, M. 1992. *Money, Morals, and Manners.* Chicago: University of Chicago Press.

Lamont, M. 2000. *The Dignity of Working Men.* New York: Russell Sage Foundation.

Lamont, M. and Lareau, A. 1988. Cultural capital. *Sociological Theory*, 6(2), 153–68.

Lareau, A. and Weininger, E. 2003. Cultural capital in educational research. *Theory and Society*, 32(5/6), 567–606.

Law, R. 1997. Masculinity, place and beer advertising in New Zealand. *New Zealand Geographer*, 52(2), 22–8.

Lawler, S. 2005. Disgusted subjects. *Sociological Review*, 53(3), 429–46.

Le Roux, B., Rousnet, H., Savage, M. and Warde, A. 2008. Class and cultural division in the UK. *Sociology*, 42(6), 1049–1071.

Lees, L. 2003. Super-gentrification. *Urban Studies*, 40(12), 2487–509.

Leidner, R. 1991. Serving hamburgers and selling insurance. *Gender and Society*, 5(2), 154–77.

Little, J. 2003. Riding the rural love-train. *Sociologia Ruralis*, 43(4), 401–17.

Little, J. and Panelli, R. 2007. Outback romance? *Sociologia Ruralis*, 47(3), 173–88.

Littler, C. 1982. *The Development of the Labour Process in Capitalist Societies.* London: Heinemann.

Marshall, G., Rose, D., Newby, H. and Vogler, C. 1988. *Social Class in Modern Britain.* London: Unwin Hyman.

McDowell, L. 2006. Reconfigurations of gender and class relations. *Antipode*, 38(4), 825–50.

Nowotny, H. 1981. Women in public life in Austria, in *Access to Power*, edited by C. Epstein and R. Coser. London: George Allen and Unwin, 149–65.

Perrenoud, M. and Phillips, M. forthcoming. The craftsmen of 'rural gentrification', in *The Gentrified Countryside*, edited by M. Phillips. Aldershot: Ashgate.

Phillips, M. 1991. *Classifications of Class. ESRC Middle Class Project, Working Paper 5.* Lampeter: University of Wales, St. David's College.

Phillips, M. 1998a. Investigations of the British rural middle classes: part 1. *Journal of Rural Studies*, 14(4), 411–25.

Phillips, M. 1998b. Investigations of the British rural middle classes: part 2. *Journal of Rural Studies*, 14(4), 427–43.

Phillips, M. 1999. Gender relations and identities in the colonisation of rural 'Middle England', in *Gender and Migration in Britain*, edited by P. Boyle and K. Halfacree. London: Routledge, 238–60.

Phillips, M. 2001. Class, collective action and the countryside, in *Can Class Still Unite?* edited by G. Gyes, H. de Witte and P. Pasture. Aldershot: Ashgate, 247–74.

Phillips, M. 2002a. Distant bodies? *Sociologia Ruralis*, 42(2), 81–105.

Phillips, M. 2002b. The production, symbolisation and socialisation of gentrification. *Transactions, Institute of British Geographers*, 27(3), 282–308.

Phillips, M. 2004. Other geographies of gentrification. *Progress in Human Geography*, 28(1), 5–30.

Phillips, M. 2007. Changing class complexions in and on the British countryside. *Journal of Rural Studies*, 23(3), 283–304.

Phillips, M 2010. Rural gentrification and the built environment: exploring the connections, in *Built Environment: Design, Management and Applications*, edited by C.F. Hauppauge. New York: Nova Publishers.

Phillips, M. Forthcoming. Class analysis and sociologies of translation: an exploration of the paradoxes of the NS-SEC, submitted to *Sociology*.

Phillips, M., Page, S., Saratsi, E., Tansey, K. and Moore, K. 2008. Diversity, scale and green landscapes in the gentrification process. *Applied Geography*, 28(1), 54–76.

Pini, B., Rice, R. and McDonald, P. 2010. Teachers and the emotional dimension of class in resource affected rural Australia. *British Journal of Sociology of Education*, 31(1), 17–30.

Putnam, R. 1995. Bowling alone. *Journal of Democracy*, 6(1), 65–78.

Putnam, R. 2000. *Bowling Alone*. New York: Simon and Schuster.

Radway, J. 1984. *Reading the Romance*. Chapel Hill: University of North Carolina Press.

Reay, D. 1997. Feminist theory, habitus and social class. *Women's Studies International Forum*, 20(2), 225–33.

Reay, D. 2000. A useful extension of Bourdieu's conceptual framework? *Sociological Review*, 48(4), 568–85.

Reay, D. 2004. Gendering Bourdieu's concepts of capitals? *Sociological Review*, 52, 57–74.

Reay, D. 2005a. Beyond consciousness? *Sociology*, 39(5), 911–28.

Reay, D. 2005b. Thinking class, making class. *British Journal of Sociology of Education*, 26(1), 139–43.

Reay, D. and Lucey, H. 2000. 'I don't really like it here but I don't want to be anywhere else'. *Antipode*, 32(4), 410–28.

Reay, D. and Lucey, H. 2003. The limits of 'choice', *Sociology*, 37(1), 121–42.

Savage, M, 1994. Class analysis and its futures. *Sociological Review*, 42, 531–48.

Savage, M. 2000. *Class Analysis and Social Transformation*. Buckingham: Open University Press.

Savage, M. and Butler, T. 1995. Assets and the middle classes in contemporary Britain, in *Social Change and the Middle Classes*, edited by M. Savage and T. Butler. London: UCL Press, 345–57.

Savage, M., Barlow, J., Dickens, P. and Fielding, T. 1992. *Property, Bureaucracy and Culture*. London: Routledge.

Schaefer-McDaniel, N. 2004. Conceptualizing social capital among young people. *Children, Youth and Environments*, 14(1), 140–50.

Sayer, A. 2005a Class, moral worth and recognition. *Sociology*, 39(5), 947–63.

Sayer, A. 2005b. *The Moral Significance of Class*. Cambridge: Cambridge University Press.

Scherger, S. and Savage, M. 2010. Cultural transmission, educational attainment and social mobility. *Sociological Review*, 58(3), 406–28.

Shortall, S. 2008. Are rural development programmes socially inclusive? *Journal of Rural Studies*, 24(4), 450–57.

Shucksmith, M. 2000. Endogenous development, social capital and social inclusion. *Sociologia Ruralis*, 40(2), 208–18.

Silva, E. 2000. The politics of consumption at home. *Pavis Papers in Social and Cultural Research*. Milton Keynes: Open University Press

Skeggs, B. 1997. *Formations of Class and Gender*. London: Routledge.

Skeggs, B. 2004. *Class, Self and Culture*. London: Routledge.

Valentine, G. 1997. Making space, in *Contested Countryside Culture*, edited by P. Cloke and J. Little. London: Routledge, 109–22.

Walkerdine, V., Lucey, H. and Melody, J. 2001. *Growing Up Girl*. Basingstoke: Palgrave.

Woods, M. 2010. Performing rurality and practising rural geography. *Progress in Human Geography*, published OnlineFirst as doi: 10.1177/0309132509357356. Available at: http://phg.sagepub.com/content/early/recent [accessed: 5 November 2010].

Wright, E. 1985. *Classes*. London: Verso.

Wright, E. (ed.) 2005. *Approaches to Class Analysis*. Cambridge: Cambridge University Press.

Chapter 3

Articulating Social Class: Farm Women's Competing Visions of the Family Farm

Susan Machum

This chapter examines class relations between farming women. In doing so it adopts an understanding of class as a dynamic, lived and embodied concept. In this sense, social class is more than an abstract theoretical construct used to explain social phenomena. It is something we actively do: it is a performance, a way of acting and reacting that is observable in ongoing daily actions and interactions and in the outcomes those actions ultimately produce (Skeggs 2004). This notion of class is utilized by McMullin (2010) in recounting the life story of 'Anna'. McMullin (2010) demonstrates that Anna's options shift in life as her class status changes and as she ages. At the same time her classed position is always informed by her gender identity as a woman and her racialized identity as white. It is the constellation of the characteristics of class, age, gender and race that enable certain opportunities while disallowing others at any given time. To suggest one dimension can be disconnected and understood as the single 'causal' or driving force of the others is to lose sight of the way they are intertwined. McMullin (2010) argues that these different social locations need to be understood as the 'CAGEs' (Class, Age, Gender, Ethnicity) within which we regularly make choices and engage with the world.

Bryant and Pini's (2009) recent work adds the dimension of rurality to this mixture. They too argue that gender and class 'are constructed and reconstructed through daily interactions' (Bryant and Pini 2009: 55), but they found that rural farm women were contending with a different set of circumstances and issues than urban women. They conclude, 'There are some unique material and discursive aspects of rurality, which inform how class and gender come together in non-metropolitan spaces' (Bryant and Pini 2009: 55). From their work we can see that McMullin's (2010) CAGEs need to be considered in the context of rural space and place. In keeping with these arguments, an underlying principle of this chapter is that class, gender and rurality are interconnected and integral parts of farm women's lives.

This chapter furthers Bryant and Pini's (2009) analysis of class and gender in farming communities by exploring how farm women 'do' social class and how in the process of living and practising the expectations of specific class dynamics they create future rural farm communities. The analysis emerges from case study data collected in rural New Brunswick, Canada where family owned and operated farms are still the mainstay of agricultural production (Statistics Canada 2007a). Thirty semi-structured, open-ended, one on one interviews were conducted with women living and working on potato and dairy farms in the central and northwest parts of the province. With one exception interviews were conducted on the family farm; each interview was recorded and lasted between two and six hours. The interviews focused on how the women's family, farm and work had changed over their life course. The primary objective of the research was to assess how farm commodity production affected the work lives of farm women (Machum 2011), but quite apart from farm commodity type social class emerged as a major dimension of farm women's work lives. This chapter reports on how farm women articulate and accomplish social class in their agricultural settings.

The chapter uses Jones' (1995) notion of the presence and interconnectedness of multiple discourses to explore and locate farm women's social class discourse within larger agricultural debates. Jones (1995) endorses the work of Gregory (1994) by repeating his argument that discourse is much more than the words, symbols and texts we use to communicate with others, it is also 'the practices through which we make our world(s) meaningful to ourselves and others' (Jones 1995: 36). The vocal and written 'symbolic' representations of our actions have, in other words, a material basis. There is a dance between discourse and action, between abstract ideas and tangible deeds. In his study of 'rurality' Jones (1995: 38) argued that multiple discourses overlap and compete for legitimacy in any specific time or place. He contends there are four dominant discourses surrounding rurality. They are: the popular discourse present within mass media; academic discourses of researchers studying rural phenomena; the lay person or practitioner's discourse of their actions within rural contexts; and the professional discourses of rural policy makers, agricultural scientists and others who careers are directly and indirectly tied to rural places. Each discourse is spoken by a different group of actors, each has its own form and yet all are grappling with similar issues. The objective of this chapter is to explore how the academic and lay discourses articulate the dynamics of rural life and social class. In the process we gain insight into how the two discourses are interconnected and how social class is both communicated and practised by farm women in rural communities.

The chapter begins with an overview of the academic discourse on social class and farming. It demonstrates that social class is, and has been understood to be, an integral part of rural farm life, but at the same time, what exactly social class means and how it is applied remains contested within agricultural studies. The second section presents the farm women's – or to adopt Jones' (1995) language – the practitioners or lay, discourse surrounding social class and farming. Specifically it is the language and practices farm women and their families 'use and encounter in the processes of their everyday lives, through which meanings of ... [social class] ... are expressed and constructed' (Jones 1995: 38) that are developed in this chapter. Six key discursive practices are identified in the women's narratives as critical to the making of class. These are references to technology adoption, farm size, use of non-family labour, the farm's legal arrangements, visions of their farm's future and their motivations for farming. The concluding section argues that the competing social class discourses within the farm community are reflected in the academic rural studies literature, so practice and theory do meet. However, each group of actors has their own distinct discourse and within those discourses there is disagreement and debate.

Academic Discourse of Social Class in Farming

Academic discourse aims to capture, better understand and explain the observable outcomes of social phenomena. In the process it creates its own discourse and terminology which for credibility must reflect, but can often be quite distinct from, local practices, knowledge and communications (Jones 1995: 38). In terms of the academic literature on family farming two theoretical frameworks and associated discourses dominate; that is, the liberal and Marxist perspectives.

Liberal notions of class rank groups of people according to socio-economic criteria such as income, occupation and education. The group rankings are then stratified and compared. What emerges is an 'hierarchy of inequality' (Naiman 2008: 101–104). In the rural farm context, the 'elite' farms would be those with 'entrepreneurial' farmers and large farm cash receipts. Poor, 'lower status', farms would have little involvement in the market and provide low income. The middle strata would have modest cash receipts and middling success as farm businesses. In fact, a considerable portion of the work that ensues from this underlying theoretical model produces such rankings. The farm typology schemes developed by Agriculture and Agri-Food Canada (AAFC) and the United States Department of Agriculture (USDA) provide examples of this criterion in use. In the Canadian context the AAFC argue there are currently seven categories of family farms: pension, beginner, lifestyle, intermediate, large and very large (Niekamp and Zafiriou 2000). Likewise the USDA (2000) has seven categories for family farms: limited-resource, retirement, residential/lifestyle, farming occupation/lower sales, farming occupation/higher sales, large, and very large. Each set of typologies emphasizes the income, scale of operation and commitment of the farm operator to farming as a profitable occupation for delineating family farm types.

There are a number of challenges with these socio-economic based schemes. First of all, measurement of the farm family's commitment to farming is based on the level of farm versus off farm income, which ignores the family's motivations for farming and how they perceive the success of their operation. The more reliant farms are on external income sources, the more likely these typologies are to categorize them as non-serious 'lifestyle' or 'retirement' farms. Yet as Bessant (2006) demonstrates, all farms, regardless of size or rank, are increasingly dependent on non-farm income sources. Additionally, even though all farms are businesses providing self-employment and farmers' self identify as being 'their own boss', the entrepreneurial basis of farming as an occupation (Statistics Canada 2004, Pritchard, Burch and Lawrence 2007) is unevenly acknowledged.

It is the financially successful farms that are recognized as being governed by entrepreneurs, while the others are not.

The Marxist critique of liberal oriented farm typologies is that they 'layer' the farm community according to size and scale of operation without adequately taking into account the social relations of production or internal family farm dynamics (see Pritchard, Burch and Lawrence 2007: 77–8). The result is they do not produce a substantive picture of the various strategies family farms employ in order to keep their enterprises operating during difficult and challenging economic, social and political times. Rather their premise in the liberal schemes is that farm finances are the ultimate indicator of farm success instead of the capacity to survive and keep producing food in a highly competitive capitalist economic system. Much of the work of Marxist rural sociologists has been devoted to understanding the disappearance and resilience of subsistence farming, the rise of capitalist agriculture and the decline of traditional family farming (Buttel and Newby 1980, Friedland et al. 1991, Goss, Rodefeld and Buttel 1980, Sinclair 1984, Waters 2007, Winson 1985).

The Marxist political economy perspective focuses much more on the internal dynamics of the family farm enterprise. It examines labour relations, asking: Does the person earn their income from selling their labour power to an employer, from employing others to work for their enterprise, or from owning the enterprise and using their own (and family) labour to conduct it? These criteria provide the definitions of farm worker, capitalist farmer and petit bourgeois farmer. The farm typologies that emerge from this theoretical model emphasize the degree to which the family owned farm relies on family versus hired labour for day-to-day commodity production processes. Farms totally reliant on family labour are classified as petty, independent or simple commodity production farms. Farms totally reliant on hired farm workers are non-family corporate farms. Those combining family and hired labour are likely farms in transition from one set of social relations to another, but the point at which farms cease to operate as petit bourgeois production units and become capitalist enterprises is still debated (Ghorayshi 1986, Shaver 1990).

The actual labels adopted by rural researchers to capture these varying social relations of production are varied. For example Alston (1995) distinguishes between those farms that are capital intensive and those that are labour intensive. Whatmore's (1991) concern with what she calls the commoditization of farming, that is, the extent to which farms have become commercial operations reliant on wage labour, leads her to argue there are 'family labour farms' and 'family business farms'. Whatmore's (1991) position is reminiscent of Shaver's (1990) discussion of the extent to which farms have modernized and developed capitalist relations of production. In her research, Shaver (1990) concluded there were three kinds of family farms: 'family labour farms', 'semi-capitalist farms' and 'capitalist farms'. Gasson (1980) meanwhile, has tended to divide farms according to their physical size, though in her later work with Errington (Gasson and Errington 1993), she does concur with Shaver (1990) that 'the development of capitalist relations of production rather than size of business' (Gasson and Errington 1993: 164) is a more effective explanation for differences in farms. Gasson and Errington (1993) therefore, divide farms according to family worked farms and labour employing farms. All are observing the same phenomena, that is, different class positions among 'family farms'.

Each theoretical framework aims to understand how social class processes pervade agricultural production and family farm dynamics, but the initial criteria, and hence outcomes, differ. Academic discourses embedded in liberalism see variations among farms and the development of agriculture in terms of changing farm size, while academic discourses informed by Marxism view it in terms of changing labour relations. Both aim to understand and explain the presence of multiple farming practices, but they engage with a different discourse to do so. As the next section will illustrate, these competing academic discourses on farm typologies and social class are built upon and reflect the range of lived practices and discourses deeply embedded within the farm community itself.

The academic discourse on social class in rural social science focuses on the patterned outcomes of social processes. This is highly valuable, but what is needed is a better understanding of how those patterns come to be. As such, the following sections of the chapter concentrate on a number of the practices undertaken by farm women and their families that produce those outcomes. Its purpose is to illustrate how farm women 'do' social class as part of their everyday routines. This diverges from most academic literature on the topic: usually women are ignored and the rural social class trajectories described above are understood to be the result of male operators' decisions and actions. When the dynamics of farm women and social class are explored it is often in terms of gendered power relations within the family farm household (e.g., Delphy and Leonard 1986, 1992, 1994, Shortall 1999, Whatmore 1991), rather than as a power struggle amongst farm women themselves over competing class interests within the larger farm community. In contrast, the premise of the following analysis is that farm women actively engage in the production of social class differences and that they are just as responsible as their farming husbands for the formation of rural social class trajectories.

Farm Women's Discourse of Social Class and Farming's Future

The following sections explore how farm women, through everyday conversations and actions, articulate their social class locations within the farm community via: the adoption of farm technologies, farm size, their sourcing of farm labour, the farm's legal status, their visions of their farm's future, and their stated objectives and motivations for farming.

Farm Technologies as Signifiers of Social Class

Even though farm women are not inclined to self-referentially use academic social class categories, they do use general and farm specific status symbols to conceptualize, sort out and make sense of different farming practices. For instance, they talk about the 'state of the art' equipment they have, how much they have 'grown' their farms, and how the farm and their homestead have changed and evolved over their lifespan. What is evident from such comments is that: a) status symbols are used to indirectly signal and discuss relative status within the farm community; b) status markers are different in the rural farm community than in non-farm or urban contexts; and c) the relative status of individual family farms change over time as they continue to purchase new status markers. The use of status symbols to mark social class is no different for farm women than their non-farming rural or urban counterparts (see Schor 1998, Klien 2000). What is different is the status symbols meaningful to the farm community are not meaningful to outsiders.

In the urban context people make reference to their neighbourhoods, cars, jobs and recent vacations to mark their relative social position. In the farm context the status symbols are not the same. Here it is farm technology such as tractors and harvesting equipment, their acreage or herd size, expansion activities such as their ability to invest in the farm, in the house or to build a home office and so on that distinguishes one set of class relations from another. The farm women were cognizant of the social status conveyed via their own farm's purchases and investments. As well, they were very aware of and would make reference to purchases farming neighbours had made, especially highly visible ones such as a new barn or house addition, new vehicles and production equipment. During the interviews women used these kinds of social markers to describe their current situation and to elaborate on how their operations had changed over time. For example, Barbara[1] recounted how during her lifetime her farm had grown from producing 100 to 410 acres of potatoes and from milking 15 to milking 65 cows. It was commonplace for farm women to relate when and why they had purchased new technologies, improved their farm operations and, in some cases, built (or sometimes were in the process of building) a farm office separate but attached to the existing family farm household. In retrospect, as we will see below, the discourse surrounding these new offices and production technologies was meant to signal improvements in their social position. Danielle's comments support this position:

> In ten years we will be even more of a business and less a 'way of life' than
> we are today …We needed a farm office so all our records and bookkeeping

---

1   All the interviewees were given pseudonyms. Those who were on dairy farms have names beginning with the letter D and those on potato farms begin with P, those who farmed both commodities have names starting with B.

would be in one place. It was too hard to keep taking over the dining room table because we have more paper work than we used to. Now we have filing cabinets and a desk and we're going to set more things up on the computer. I can locate farm records and information a lot faster now.

The point to be made here is that farm families are not only continually purchasing new products, they understand those new purchases as reflective of new farming practices. Moreover, the farm women make reference to and are highly aware of how their own and neighbour's new purchases subtly and constantly shift their relative status and position within the farm community. In this way farm equipment and technologies operate both materially and symbolically as social class boundary markers.

In the case of potato production all farms have invested in machinery to prepare the soil, plant and harvest the crop. The newness and specific model details of such equipment vary considerably, but the newer and bigger the equipment model the more likely the women were to comment on it. This was especially true of the harvesting equipment and the potato storage facilities. In the past the biggest bottleneck for farm expansion was the autumn potato harvest which was historically handpicked, hence the emphasis women placed on the harvesting method. Plus as more is harvested, storage facilities gain importance. Within my case study only one farm continued to harvest by hand while three others had just recently converted to mechanical harvesters due to labour shortage issues. A potato harvester allows the operation to get larger sized crops in more efficiently. Bigger harvesters pick more rows in less time. Invisible in the list of equipment type is that the bigger the operation the more women reported a duplication of farm equipment. For example some women farmers explained they had two harvesters instead of one, to facilitate the planting and harvesting of large crop sizes in limited timeframes.

In the case of dairy farming multiple technologies were also in use. The emphasis here was on the milking system. Only farms with fewer than 25 cows reported using an automated milking pail system wherein the milking machine is individually attached to each cow. Many farms had started with this system but as their farms grew they shifted to pipeline systems and/or milk parlours. Farms using a pipeline system, characterized by milkers being attached to an overhead pipeline, milked between 30 and 55 cows. In this situation the greater the number of cows, the more milkers they attached to the overhead pipes. Once farms were milking 60 or more cows they had a milk parlour, again with varying numbers of milkers at any given time. Only two farms with fewer than 60 cows had milk parlours and these each milked around 40 cows. Both of these enterprises were situating themselves for expansion.

Each farm family selects the technologies they use in order to meet their production objectives. To expand without a proportionate increase in the amount of labour requires a path of more technological intensity. Introducing one new piece of equipment, such as a potato harvester or a double herringbone milk parlour, usually leads to the need for more or larger equipment purchases. The effect is an expanding production capacity, often accompanied by increased debt. Farm operations can, however, control the rate at which they participate in this expansion process. For some it is their *modus operandi*, in that they are continually in search of the latest technological advancements to integrate into their farm commodity production process. At this stage the technology acts as both a status marker and often as a precursor for changing social relations of production.

To reinforce how the technology was changing farm production processes, women would often refer to their 'new' purchases as being the best on the market, 'state of the art' or the 'only one of its kind' in the neighbourhood. They were establishing that their farm technology surpassed that of their farming neighbours. In fact, many women promoting expansion as the trajectory for farm success confided their bedtime reading was trade magazines, because it enabled them to keep abreast of new production implements and programs. However, for other farm operations technological change is much more gradual. Those pursuing more gradual change often purchased 'used' farm equipment, the cast-offs from those expanding. They argued this equipment was reliable and had proven itself. It was less expensive and therefore did not have the same debt consequences or require the same pressure to maximize production. Those discarding the technology see it as inefficient but the purchasers see it as more efficient than their current methods. They also frame their practice of utilizing older technology as being a 'greener' choice than purchasing new because, as they were quick to point out, the four R's are: reduce, *reuse*, recycle and reclaim. They were helping the planet by reusing perfectly good equipment.

Notably, all respondents had bought new equipment and made farm improvements throughout their tenure on the farm. It is both the meaning given to those purchases and how they change farm practices that explicates how social class is routinely enacted on family farms. But, as the following sections elaborate, technological innovation does not stand alone, farm size and labour needs are interconnected elements indicative of particular scales of production and class relations.

Farm Size as a Signifier of Social Class

Variances in technology adoption, farm size and labour needs can create divergence within a particular sector and yet promote alliances across sectors. This is because these farm characteristics elucidate how family farms growing the same commodity can have such different outcomes and experiences whereas those producing different commodities are engaged in fundamentally different jobs. Potatoes are a seasonal crop whereas dairy requires daily milking and animal care. The equipment needs are different and in New Brunswick marketing arrangements are vastly different: potatoes are sold in an open market and milk in closed market quota system. Despite differences between commodity sectors, similarities can emerge across sectors and differences can emerge within them due to the constellation of 'size related' variables noted above.

Among my case study participants, potato farms were growing between 25 and 30 acres on one end of the scale and 410 acres of potatoes on the other end. The active dairy farms ranged from milking 25 cows to milking 110 cows. The dairy farm with 25 cows was the only operation exclusively selling cream and therefore only milking seasonally. The other dairy farms in the sample were all milking twice a day for the fluid milk market. Size variations generally coincide with different technological inputs. Potato farms may or may not continue to hand harvest the crop, but the larger the operation the less likely they are to do so. Smaller dairy farms continue to use tie stall barns and pipeline milking systems while larger ones have open barns and use milk parlours equipped to accommodate varying numbers of milkers (more milkers mean milking is done faster each morning and evening).

The bigger the farm, in terms of acreage planted for potato farms and herd size for dairy farm, the more likely they are to be identified as a 'successful', serious farm operation by the liberal academic discourse. On the socio-economic scale these are the farms that have expanded and grown their operations often with the help of technological innovation. While relatively few in total numbers, the largest farms are generally supplying the food processing markets and account for the greatest proportion of total farm cash receipts (Statistics Canada 2007b). As a rule, their scale of production garners them more status and greater state support than their more numerous but 'smaller' counterparts (Machum 2009). Their capacity to dominate market share produces the social class discourse promoted by rural sociologists drawing upon a liberal framework. This discourse that 'bigger farms are more productive farms' is internalized and articulated by the farm women. As Paige explained:

> [The government] think[s] bigger is better. ... and they keep giving incentives for bigger farmers rather than small ones [like us].

In the academic and policy discourse, to be successful is to be big. As will be elaborated later, some farm women agree with the sentiment while others do not. However, as farm size increases so too does the labour needs of the operation as the following section will explain.

Labour Relations as a Signifier of Social Class

The bigger the farm, the more likely non-family labour is present. Frequently family farms manage to retain their status as family farms by combining a number of related nuclear families into the same farming operation (Sinclair 1984, Machum 2005). This was evidenced in the case studies where a number of sons, fathers, father-in-laws and brothers had expanded operations to accommodate several families in the 'family' operation. Usually farm expansion took place in order to accommodate and integrate multiple generations or brothers into the family farm unit. In the case of potatoes, full-time employment of non-family members was usually a result of farm diversification projects or the establishment of a non-related farm business.

For instance, several potato farms had trucking businesses. Other farms had garages where they repaired and maintained farm equipment, while two had elaborate, value added farm processing facilities. It was rare for a potato farm to have a non-family full-time employee devoted solely to potato production.

It was common practice for case study respondents to hire labourers on a part-time basis to assist with autumn harvest or summer haying. Given in the New Brunswick context all farms require some assistance during peak harvest periods less attention was given to the hiring of short-term seasonal labour.. Besides in many commodity sectors technology is also increasingly reducing the size of such seasonal work crews. The presence of seasonal labour is not, therefore, a strong differentiator of class relations. However, year round full-time and part-time employees are strong signifiers of social class relations.

Only on the smallest farm operations were family members the sole source of farm labour. For the most part, employing full-time or part-time labours on a year round basis, beyond the nuclear family, is more prevalent among the smaller and medium sized dairy operations than is true of the corresponding potato farms. This can be attributed to the intensity of daily milk production. In addition, being a supply managed system, milk production is a more lucrative and stable commodity sector than potatoes which are sold in an open market system. The relative financial stability and labour intensiveness of 365 days a year, twice daily milking are factors that help explain why small dairy operations can have full-time employees when their size category would suggest otherwise. Once there is one full-time herdsman on the dairy operation, the farm family is both freed from the daily responsibilities of milking, and integrated into a new set of social relations of production. Dairy farms with no employees are living on farms and producing milk under different working conditions than their full-time employee hiring neighbours.

In a similar respect, the more labour a potato farm needs to operate on a daily basis, the greater the degree of separation between them and those who are more reliant on family labour. For both commodity sectors the hiring of full-time, year round employees, signals a shift in the farm production process. In practice, the more labour you have the more time you need to spend managing that labour. What effectively happens is that farm families with regular staff see their own labour efforts shift from farm field to farm office. They spend less time in farm production and more time in farm management. There is likely to be a direct correlation between increased hiring and increased management work. As farm management work increases so too does the work of farm women because women tend to be the office managers responsible for payroll and farm bookkeeping.

Even though farm women readily shared information on the source and quantity of labour employed by the farm, they tended not to couch their employment of others in the class terms we might expect of small business owners. That is, while many saw themselves as running farm businesses, the majority did not identify or talk about themselves as employers or entrepreneurs. Perhaps this is a consequence of hiring a family member (often a son) who is no longer living in the family farm household to work for and with them. Those farms with larger numbers of hired labour did, on the other hand, use the discourse of 'employers' indicating the number of full-time employees they had regularly hired and when and why shifts occurred.

Expansion can, after all, only occur with more labour and/or more productive technology. Usually as the farm expands in size and technological inputs, so too do the labour needs. Once farms are highly dependent on non-family labour the farm is a capitalist production unit in Marxist academic discourse and a 'highly' successful farm in liberal terms. Among the farm women, family farms with only family labour (this included adult children being paid for their farm work) were more likely to describe family farming as 'a way of life' and less likely to identify themselves as being farm businesses. The inverse is also true. Those women who reported expanding their operations to accommodate full-time employees, especially non-family members, were more likely to identify their farms as 'businesses' seeking growth and profitability. The academic and lay discourses for the same farming production practices are thus most likely to converge around farm labour requirements.

Legal Status of Farm as a Signifier of Social Class

A characteristic frequently used to denote their class position and the distinction between farm types is their legal status. Many farms on an expansive trajectory seek to separate the legalities of the farm enterprise from the family household. According to Statistics Canada (2007b: Table 2.3), in 2006, the legal operating arrangements of farm establishments varied substantially. That is, only 17.6 per cent of New Brunswick census farms were incorporated, 13.5 per cent were partnerships with no written partnership agreement while 1.9 per cent were operations with written partnership agreements. The remaining 63.8 per cent were individual family operations with sole proprietorships. Amongst the case study participants nine were incorporated while 21 were not. Incorporation separates and protects family assets should the business fail. It also tends to bring with it different banking arrangements. The majority of incorporated farms had established a farm account separate from the family household account. Surprisingly two of the incorporated potato operations reported continuing to operate all household and farm income and expenditures through one bank account even after the farm had become a legal corporation. Generally the separation of farm and household income and expense streams is an indicator of the extent to which the farm is being operated as a business rather than as a farming 'lifestyle'. So while many farm operations were not legally incorporated, they did have clear and separate banking arrangements for the farm and the household. Lack of incorporation and still operating farm and household finances from one account coincided more often with the smaller operations. In these situations farm people self-identified as engaged in 'sustaining a way of life'.

Farm incorporation and creating separate family household and farm accounts are not the only strategies farm women employ to separate the family household from the farm business in a formal way. Farms creating these kinds of formal boundaries were also the ones most likely to be proudly displaying their up to date farm offices. Rather than the farm table, the farm office becomes the space and place to greet visitors, keep and analyse farm books, and engage in farm management activities. For many the home office came as a result of a room conversion, but for the most serious farm expanders it was the result of a household expansion. The dining room table is where the farm accounts and management decisions are made in the traditional family farm while the home offices are the site of such practices on family business farms. The degree to which farm women aim to demarcate family and farm life are indicators of the social class locations they are trying to establish and sustain as much as scales of production and farm labour sources. Overall the family household and the farm business activities are much more integrated in the 'farming lifestyle' than in the 'expansionist' farm households.

Visions of their Farm's Future as Signifiers of Social Class

To sustain the farming 'way of life', farm families must convince the next generation to farm (Small 2005: 491). Therefore, the discourse around whether or not farm women want their children to farm is highly indicative of their social class agenda. If they want to sustain their operation as a petit bourgeois, traditional family farm, they will want their children to farm. If their goal is to create a profitable business that they can divest when they want to retire, it is not necessary for their children to farm. Of course, lived experiences and discourses are never so clear cut, but the farm women's visions did generally cluster into these competing positions.

Among the case study respondents, passing on their farm to their children was impossible for three due to the sale of the farm, the poor health of a child and the occupational backgrounds and age of adult children. Of remaining participants just two, Perdita and Penny, did not want their children to farm. These women both came from non-farming backgrounds, had preschool age children and were living on potato farms growing roughly the same acreage (275 and 300 acres respectively). In each instance their husbands worked off-farm to make ends meet. They saw no future in farming and certainly did not want to encourage their children to take on this lifestyle.

In the cases where children were already farming alongside their parents, the women logically wanted their children to farm. For example, as one commented, 'Our son farms with us and he wants to stay in so we'll try to keep going. We probably wouldn't do it if our son wasn't in it'. In other cases participants described actively growing their business in order to have a sizable and viable investment to pass on to their children. One interviewee, Donna, who was in this position explained:

> People shouldn't be in business if they can't show a profit. The ones who are still here see farming as a business. ... Our ultimate goal is to set up all our [four] boys in farming if that is what they want. You can't force them, it must come from within. But our goal is for our children to farm.

Those who were undecided if their children should farm, saw farming as a difficult occupation with few certainties and/or they saw their farm in terms of sweat equity. In the later instance they reflected on the fact that they and past generations had invested their life savings and energy into the farm and observed that to lose the farm would be to lose the investment and activity of generations. Those who saw farming as a difficult occupation questioned how their children could make a living from farming.

Penny expanded on this position by indicating the growth in farm size, coupled with the increase in the non-farm population in her community, led to questions of whether future land for farming would even exist. She stated:

> We haven't encouraged our children to farm. There just isn't any farmland to be had, so I don't see how they could make a living from it.

For the most part, ambivalence around children working in farming was a position held by those family farm operations seeking to 'make a living' from farming. In contrast, women such as Donna argued farming was a family business, like any other business, and their children should only farm if they could make money by taking over the family business. This framing of *farming as a way to make a living* versus *farming as a profit oriented business*[2] endeavour affects present and future farm practices in that their visions embody particular class discourses. How farm women envision, discuss and articulate their children's future prospects within agriculture promotes a particular class agenda. One group is arguing for traditional family farming practices and the other group is promoting a farm business model. Each discourse reflects the women's own class location and experience.

Motivations for Farming as Signifiers of Social Class

Farm women made the most explicit comments about social class and class differences when they were asked to envision how they saw their farm and the rural community evolving over the next ten years. It was in this context that they first began to articulate how they were the same or different from others. They were no longer an isolated farming operation changing over time, but a farm operation that had pursued a different strategy than some of their farming neighbours.

What emerged was a twofold division where the women make distinctions on the basis of 'us' versus 'them'. Each group understands their own actions as being coherent and rational, but questions the rationality of the other group. They label themselves in positive terms but the 'other' in pejorative language. For those farm women who self-identified as being part of a family farm business operation promoting expansion

---

2 It must be acknowledged that both are 'ways of life'. One happens to have become the local discourse reflecting and capturing the activities of a particular group rather than the other. However, the premise that social class is communicated through both talk and practice is a powerful reminder that McMullin's (2010) CAGEs all represent a way of life for those practising them.

and growth, farms not following this model were 'backward' or 'cute' farms. Danielle summed up the 'expansionist' position best when she commented:

> Cute farms can't make a living. You must be a business first. It should be that way all along. We want a fair return for our product. You can still make money farming but you must be big and farming must be your main concern. Our goal is to have more hired people so we can enjoy life more.

This viewpoint stands in sharp contrast to those who see themselves as working to sustain farming as 'a way of life'. This second group is more concerned with the long-term sustainability of themselves as farmers and of the ecosystem upon which they depend. Delia exemplified this outlook when she confided, 'We are a small operation. We make a living from farming. ... We go with the flow'. Paige elaborated this perspective:

> It drives me crazy when people say it's farmers' mismanagement that drove them out of business. Farmers have good management skills. It's really the system ... The government is pushing farmers to get big. ... I don't know why they can't see the mistakes they're making. The government just doesn't realize how easily the ecosystem can be screwed up.

On one side we have farm women promoting their farm operations as profitable and expanding businesses and on the other we have farm women arguing that their farms are sized and operated to sustain the ecological base and their participation in farming across generations. The former can be labelled the 'expanders' and the latter the 'sustainers'. Each group self-identifies and places themselves in sharp contrast to the other. A summary of these positions is contained in Table 3.1.

Table 3.1　　Farm women's articulation of their farm's agenda

	The expanders	The sustainers
Sense of self	A 'family' *business* farm that must be focused on profitability and growth	Caring for themselves, their community and the planet
	Engaged in farm development and expansion	Engaged in ecological 'stewardship'
Sense of the 'other'	'Cute farms' which are not economically sustainable	Mega business farms with little ecological 'stewardship' (they're pushing the ecosystem too hard in order to meet short-term economic gains)

Each understands the other group as failing: one is failing to be a business while the other is failing to think beyond the short-term and to maintain the ecological and social basis for a viable farm community. The expanders have faith in the dictum 'get big or get out' as the key to farm survival. In contrast, the sustainers believe the expanders are following a trajectory that will inevitably bring financial and ecological bankruptcy. Each sees their own agenda as deeply meaningful and enduring, and the other as deeply misguided and delusional. Ironically neither group expects the other to be around much longer.

Rather than systematically make reference to the size of farm operation, the use of family versus non-family labour, the level of technological inputs and other variant characteristics of agricultural enterprises as academics do, farm women shorthandedly refer to differing class-related practices in terms of 'motivational' differences. They understand all these other farm practices as connected to and deeply embedded in their motivations for farming. While farm production practices represent the sets of physical activities and behaviours upon which farm women's class discourse is based, it is in their conversations surrounding their intentions and motives for farming, and their beliefs and dreams for their farm's future, where farm women most clearly express their class agendas and experiences. It is here that their everyday 'doing' of social class most readily moves into a more academically oriented social class discourse. Their 'social class' talk, thus, is not just a theoretical abstraction; it is a 'grounded theory' of their own behaviour. And they discuss their behaviour in motivational terms whereas academics discuss it in terms of their own social class categories.

Competing Visions and Discourses of Family Farms

This chapter began by identifying two dominant academic discourses around farming and social class. Within these discourses differences in scales of production and the concomitant range of technological innovations, farm incomes, labour needs and labour sources embedded in farm size have long been acknowledged. Liberal sociologists frame these variations in farming practices in socio-economic terms and thus rank farms from smallest to largest, whereas Marxist sociologists emphasize how the social relations of production change as farms expand beyond the capacity of the family labour supply. In liberal terms the bigger the operation, the more successful it is understood to be (Niekamp and Zafiriou 2000). In Marxist terms increasing farm size is a marker of the rise in capitalist agriculture to the detriment of traditional petit bourgeois family farms (Ghorayshi 1986).

The chapter then presented case study findings to illustrate how the class dynamics observed by academics are produced by farm women and their families through their daily practices. When farm families purchase new equipment, expand their operations, hire non-family labour to meet their growing responsibilities and make new financial and ownership arrangements to better manage their expansion efforts, they transform the class relations of farming. As the interviews illustrate, not everybody follows the growth trajectory with the same enthusiasm or at the same rate. Moreover, the trajectory each farm pursues, and hence their social class position, is no secret. Whoever passes by their farm (especially their farming neighbours, who may or may not engage in similar farming strategies), will regularly see the outwardly visible signs of their farming practices and attribute motivations to them.

Farm women thus understand themselves as not only producing milk and potatoes under different production processes, but also as producers with different underlying intentions and motivations. For them their motivations inform how they farm. The theoretically grounded groupings articulated by the farm women are, in effect, premised on their lived practices. That is to say, the farm community itself recognizes farming motivations as interconnected and linked to particular work processes and conditions. The aftermath is family owned and operated farms tend toward two types, what I have labelled the sustainers and the expanders. While there is more complexity than this duality would suggest, farm practices (such as the size of the operation, the technology it employs in the production processes, the form of legal ownership, the banking arrangements and the use or not of non-family labour) tend to *cluster* at the poles of sustainer or expander. These poles define the range of social class positions that are simultaneously embodied and performed within farm communities, and recognized and given meaning in academic discourse surrounding rurality and social class.

Jones (1995: 36) has argued that it is necessary for social scientists to recognize the terms in which social participants, the actual actors in the social activities being studied, understand themselves. This chapter has engaged with that agenda. To ignore the farm women's discourse on motivations and to insist on our own favoured frameworks of thought would be a mistake. The credibility of social science categories and theoretical understandings rests on their ability to account for both the behaviour and the thinking of the participants in the social phenomena under study. How then do the self-understood categories of difference held by these farm women compare to the liberal and Marxist conceptions of class discussed at the beginning of the chapter?

Let us begin with the liberal framework. As noted, the liberal understanding of class is a stratified 'hierarchy of inequality' (Naiman 2008: 101–104). In order to reduce the potentially infinite number of possible gradations to only three in the rural farm context: 'elite' farms are those with 'entrepreneurial' farmers and large farm cash receipts; poor 'lower status' farms have little involvement in the market and provide low income; and the middle strata has modest cash receipts and middling success as farm businesses. Given that the expanders in the case studies are the big farms with cutting edge technology and hired workers, or those seeking to attain this status, liberal sociologists could easily argue that successful and aspiring farmers are at the upper end of the inequality continuum. They would tend to identify the sustainers as belonging to the lower end of the spectrum along with the declining middle. What would upset liberals, for whom the goal of business expansion and increased profits is 'natural', is the idea that the sustainers appear to be rejecting 'economic rationality'. The sustainer position seriously challenges the liberal ideology as it represents a rejection of market logic and openly defies the business ethos of the market. One suspects they would be reluctant to take the category of 'sustainer' at face value, preferring instead to interpret the women's professed goals of ecological concern and a simple desire to make a living as a rationalization for failure to thrive as a business enterprise. To do otherwise would require explaining the origin of alternative goals to that of business in the marketplace, something that is akin to an act of social deviance in the liberal worldview.

The Marxist schema of class is more easily mapped onto the farm women's discourse, since different classes are understood to have different social goals and purposes for engaging in economic activity. While farm women's understandings of class are based on varying motivations for farming linked to, and grounded in, their own everyday farm practices, Marxists would understand the split between sustainers and expanders as a conflict between the petit-producers who aim to sustain and preserve traditional practices and their own livelihoods, and capitalist (and emerging capitalist) farmers pursuing expansion and profitability. Marxists argue the objective of capitalist enterprise is the open-ended accumulation of more and more capital for investment through one round after another of investment-production-profit-and-reinvestment in the enterprise. Petit bourgeois enterprises, by contrast, are not obsessed with this expansive dynamic, which can only be achieved through the hiring of workers whose wages are less than the value of their work. Petit bourgeois enterprises that do not, or cannot, move onto the path of wage labour employing enterprises are concerned with survival and the provision of living for the owners and their families. These differences correspond closely to the characteristics of the expanders and the sustainers, with the apparent exception of the latter's voiced concern for ecological sustainability. While the mainstream of Marxism has not traditionally associated ecological concerns with petit-producers, many of those participating in the emerging Green Marxism evident in *Capitalism, Nature, Socialism* and *Monthly Review* would be more open to accepting the sustainers' environmentalist aspirations at face value.

It is thus not simply valuable in itself to understand the thinking of farm women about the fundamental divisions within the farm community, but to see how their recognition both corresponds to, and challenges, thinking about class within the scholarly discourses on rurality. This chapter has created a fuller view of gender, class and rurality by mapping the social class dialogues occurring between and amongst academics and farm women. Further, it has illustrated how the two discourses are interconnected by relating the theories of social class to farm women's lived practices. In their everyday lives, farm women make choices, engage in particular work activities and not others because of how class, gender and rurality intersect and inform their experiences. Knowing how class is performed and how women participate in class formation in rural places advances an appreciation for both liberal and Marxist theories of social class. The case study findings indicate both are needed to better incorporate the layperson's discourse into the academic discourse.

Acknowledgments

The author wishes to thank the Social Sciences and Humanities Research Council of Canada, the Canadian government's Canada Research Chairs program and St. Thomas University for their financial support with this research.

References

Alston, M. 1995. *Women on the Land: The Hidden Heart of Rural Australia.* Kensington: University of New South Wales Press.

Bessant, K. 2006. A farm household conception of pluriactivity in Canadian agriculture: motivation, diversification and livelihood. *The Canadian Review of Sociology and Anthropology*, 43(1), 51–72.

Bryant, L. and Pini, B. 2009. Gender, class and rurality: Australian case studies. *Journal of Rural Studies*, 25(1), 48–57.

Buttel, F. and Newby, H. 1980. *The Rural Sociology of the Advanced Societies: Critical Perspectives.* Montclair: Allanheld, Osmun.

Delphy, C. and Leonard, D. 1986. Class analysis, gender analysis and the family, in *Gender and Stratification*, edited by R. Crompton and M. Mann. Cambridge: Polity Press, 57–73.

Delphy, C. and Leonard, D. 1992. *Familiar Exploitation: A New Analysis of Marriage in Contemporary Western Societies.* Cambridge: Polity Press.

Delphy, C. and Leonard, D. 1994. The variety of work done by wives, in *The Polity Reader in Gender Studies*, edited by A. Giddens et al. Cambridge: Polity Press, 159–65.

Friedland, W., Busch, L., Buttel, F. and Rudy, A. 1991. *Towards a New Political Economy of Agriculture.* Boulder: Westview Press.

Gasson, R. 1980. Roles of farm women in England. *Sociologia Ruralis*, 20(3), 165–80.

Gasson, R. and Errington, A. 1993. *The Farm Family Business.* Wallingford: CABI International.

Ghorayshi, P. 1986. The identification of capitalist farms: Theoretical and methodological considerations. *Sociologia Ruralis*, 26(2), 146–59.

Goss, K., Rodefeld, R. and Buttel, F. 1980. The political economy of class structure in US agriculture: a theoretical outline, in *The Rural Sociology of the Advanced Societies: Critical Perspectives*, edited by F. Buttel and H. Newby. Montclair: Allanheld, Osmun, 83–132.

Gregory, D. 1994. *Geographical Imaginations.* Oxford: Blackwell Publishers.

Jones, O. 1995. Lay discourses of the rural: developments and implications for rural studies. *Journal of Rural Studies*, 11(1), 35–49.

Klein, N. 2000. *No Logo: Taking Aim at the Brand Bullies*. Toronto: Vintage Canada Limited.

Machum, S. 2005. The persistence of family farming in the wake of agribusiness: A New Brunswick case study. *Journal of Comparative Family Studies*, 36(3), 377–90.

Machum, S. 2009. The farmers in the dell: recognizing the role of smaller diversified farms in the rural countryside, in *Connecting the Dots: Social and Scientific Perspectives on Agriculture and Rural Life in Atlantic Canada*, edited by E. Beaton. Sydney, Nova Scotia: Cape Breton University Press, 53–75.

Machum. S. 2011. *Farm Wives' Work: a Comparative Study of Dairy and Potato Farming in New Brunswick, Canada*. Lewiston: The Edwin Mellen Press.

McMullin, J. 2010. *Understanding Social Inequality: Intersections of Class, Age, Gender, Ethnicity, and Race in Canada*. 2nd Edition. Toronto: Oxford University Press.

Naiman, J. 2008. *How Societies Work: Class, Power, and Change in a Canadian Context*. 4th Edition. Halifax: Fernwood Publishing.

Niekamp, D. and Zafiriou, M. 2000. *Factors that Influence Farm Business Behaviour*. Ottawa: Statistics Canada, Catalogue No. 21–004–XIE.

Pritchard, B., Burch, D. and Lawrence, G. 2007. Neither 'family' nor 'corporate' farming: Australian tomato growers as farm family entrepreneurs. *Journal of Rural Studies*, 23(1), 75–87.

Schor, J.B. 1998. *The Overspent American: Why We Want What We Don't Need*. New York: HarperPerennial.

Shaver, F. 1990. Women, work and transformations in agricultural production. *Canadian Review of Sociology and Social Anthropology*, 27(3), 341–56.

Shortall, S. 1999. *Women and Farming: Property and Power*. Palgrave: New York.

Sinclair, P. 1984. From peasants to corporations: The development of capitalist agriculture in Canada's Maritime provinces, in *Contradictions in Canadian Society: Readings in Introductory Sociology*, edited by J. Fry. Toronto: John Wiley and Sons, 276–91.

Skeggs, B. 2004. *Class, Culture, Self.* London: Routledge.

Small, L. 2005. The influence of 'family' on agrarian structure: revisiting the family farm debate in Bulgaria and Southern Russia. *Journal of Comparative Family Studies*, 36(3), 489–503.

Statistics Canada. 2004. *The Canadian Labour Market at a Glance, 2003*. Ottawa: Statistics Canada Labour Statistics Division, Catalogue 71–222–XIE.

Statistics Canada. 2007a. 2006 Census of Agriculture: Farm operations and operators, in *The Daily*, May 16, 2007. [Online: Statistics Canada]. Available at: http://www.statcan.gc.ca/daily-quotidien/070516/dq070516a-eng.htm [accessed: 10 April 2010].

Statistics Canada. 2007b. *Agricultural Perspectives From Seven Censuses, Canada and Provinces: Census Years 1976 to 2006.* [Online: Statistics Canada]. Available at: http://www.statcan.gc.ca/bsolc/olc-cel/olc-cel?catno=95-632-X&lang=eng [accessed: 10 April 2010].

United States Department of Agriculture. 2000. *Agriculture Information Bulletin Number 759: ERS Farm Typology for a Diverse Agricultural Sector* [Online: United States Department of Agriculture Economic Research Service] Available at: http://www.ers.usda.gov/publications/aib759/aib759.pdf [accessed: 27 August 2010]

Waters, T. 2007. *The Persistence of Subsistence Agriculture: Life Beneath the Marketplace.* Lanham: Lexington Books.

Whatmore, S. 1991. *Farming Women: Gender, Work and Family Enterprise.* London: Macmillan Academic and Professional Ltd.

Winson, A. 1985. The uneven development of Canadian agriculture: farming in the Maritimes and Ontario. *The Canadian Journal of Sociology/Cahiers canadiens de sociologie,* 10(4), 411–38.

Chapter 4

'Picking Blueberries and Indian Women Go Hand in Hand': The Role of Gender and Ethnicity in the Division of Agricultural Labour in Woolgoolga, New South Wales, Australia

Rae Dufty and Edgar Liu

Travelling north along the Pacific Highway, approximately 25 kilometres from Coffs Harbour a coastal community in the Australian state of New South Wales (NSW), a large white temple appears on the right as you enter the township of Woolgoolga. The temple is a *gurdwara*, one of two in a town that has a population with fewer than 4,000 people. People of the Sikh faith, the majority of whom come from the Punjab region in northern India, use this Gurdwara for religious and community events. Members of the Woolgoolga Punjabi-Sikh community are also major participants in the local agricultural industries of bananas and blueberries. In the case of bananas there is a long history of family farming in the industry. The community's role in blueberries, however, has been a relatively more recent phenomenon, with participation predominantly taking the form of paid employment for the horticultural company, Blueberry Farms Australia (BFA).

In the last 20 years major changes to these agricultural industries in the region have impacted on family farms of the Punjabi-Sikh community and have produced new gendered and racialized labour relations. Using data collected through a series of interviews with various industry participants (for example, workers at BFA, union representatives, and members of the local community), this chapter builds on interventions made by Bryant and Pini (2009) and Panelli et al. (2009) through analysing how ethnicity intersects with and mediates the lived experiences of gender, class and rural economic restructuring processes. The chapter employs Massey's (1994) concept of the 'spatial division of labour' as a framework for this analysis, and finds that the labour relations that have emerged through the changes in the banana and blueberry industries in Australia are enabled, arbitrated and, therefore, inextricably linked to gender and ethnicity.

Class and the 'Neglected Other' in Rural Studies

Class analyses of rural societies emerged during the 1980s and gained traction during the 1990s, responding to critiques, such as that posed by Cloke and Thrift (1990: 165), of the fallacy of presenting 'the countryside as an essentially classless society'. Concurrently, the development of theory in rural studies has also been highly influential in how rural class analyses have evolved over the last three decades. For example, rural class research has been informed by classical Marxist approaches, such as Kautsky's 'agrarian question', to neo-Marxian understandings of rural restructuring and its class implications, to poststructuralist insights on rural class identities as being 'fluid' and 'multidimensional' (Phillips 1998, Bryant and Pini 2009). Accompanying the latter theoretical development in rural class research were concerns that the impact of a 'cultural turn' and the emergence of poststructuralist approaches have produced a 'dilemma' or 'hiatus' in the robustness of rural class analyses (Murdoch and Marsden 1994: 17). Phillips (2002: 99) argued that this created an unnecessary bifurcated dilemma for rural researchers between:

> a 'modernist class analysis' generally employing some variant of a political-economy perspective, and postmodernism/poststructuralism in which class has completely receded from view, to be replaced by a focus on the discursive construction of largely non-class identities.

This situation, Phillips (2002) contended, has effectively led to a neglect of class analyses in rural studies in more recent times. Yet if class has become neglected in contemporary rural research then the 'academic retreat' or even absence of any gendered or racialized critiques of class relations should be of equal, if not greater, concern to rural researchers (Bryant and Pini 2009: 55, Panelli et al. 2009). According to Bryant and Pini (2009: 55):

> it is notable that more specific work on gender in rural areas has often overlooked or obscured class ... [While] there has been a significant growth in rural gender studies in the last decades ... [it has] largely failed to address the way in which class may also connect with gender to render some women more invisible and disadvantaged.

Likewise the need to understand and directly engage with the construction of rural spaces as essentially 'white' landscapes is equally pressing when understanding rural class relations (Agyeman and Spooner 1997, Missingham, Dibden and Cocklin 2006, Panelli et al. 2009, Jordan, Krivokapic-Skoko and Collins 2009). In particular, the implications of how racialized constructions of rurality influence how rural class relations manifest and are negotiated is an important, yet hitherto vastly under researched, area demanding greater focus in rural studies. As Panelli et al. (2009: 356) point out the 'absence [of ethnic minorities in rural studies] serves to consolidate a stereotyped image of ethnicized Others as entirely urban'.

In seeking to understand the class implications of agricultural restructuring on the female members of a Punjabi-Sikh community in northern NSW, Australia, this research comes to a similar *impasse* as that expostulated by Phillips (2002). We are sympathetic to Phillips' (2002: 82) argument that there is scope for rural class analyses that are both 'Marxist and poststructuralist' for two reasons. First, it can be argued that rural class analyses, especially those relating to gender, may have passed too quickly over the political economic contributions to theory that were made during the 1980s and 1990s. In particular, we contend that returning to Doreen Massey's (1984, 1994) concept of the 'spatial division of labour' provides a useful framework from which to scaffold a feminist class analysis of a rural region experiencing the impacts of economic change. Massey's (1984, 1994) argument that regional inequality is exploited by capital to produce new ways of making profit, and that gender is central to the new spatial divisions of labour being sought by capital, has never been applied in the context of rural restructuring. This is despite Little (1994: 15) contending that 'we have yet to recognise the importance of gender relations on the nature of rural restructuring itself' (see also O'Neill 1989). As we will argue later in this chapter, the situation in Woolgoolga, an Australian agricultural context, has a number of correlations with Massey's (1994: 56–58) understanding of the impacts of global, national and regional economic changes on the spatial division of labour in an English industrial context. Specifically, Massey (1994) identified a number of regional, industrial and labour force features that informed structural change in this environment. For example, she observed that industries had shifted from seeking areas where a labour force was made up of 'male, highly paid, skilled craftsmen', to instead valuing regions 'where wages are low, and where there is little tradition amongst these workers of organization and militancy' (Massey 1994: 56–57). Massey's (1994: 57) investigation of such changes also led to the conclusion that 'these may be areas suffering from the collapse of a previously dominant industrial sector' and that in 'such cases, the labour drawn upon will not mainly be that previously employed in the former specialization, but more typically the women of the area'. A region was also found to be favoured if those employed 'do not become totally dependent upon (nor organized around) waged work', for example seasonal or part-time work (Massey 1994: 57). These regional, industrial and labour force characteristics are summarized in Table 4.1 and are used as a general framework for subsequent analysis in this chapter.

While this research takes Massey's (1994) model (used to examine industrial change in the United Kingdom in the late 1970s and early 1980s) and applies it to the analysis of agricultural changes in Australia in the late 1990s and early 2000s, we are also mindful of the important contributions poststructuralist approaches to rural studies have made towards examining 'neglected rural others' (Philo 1992). Indeed, as mentioned earlier, often it is the gendered and racialized dimensions of rural class relations that continue to be neglected in rural class based research. Like

Table 4.1   Features of new spatial divisions of labour emerging in declining regions

Regional features
Suffering the collapse of a previously dominant industry
Exposed to external economic changes
New industry features
Few local links
Low economic multiplier effect
Regional workforce features
Female
Low wages
No or minimal experience of waged work
Semi-skilled
Work is a secondary source of income
No or minimal tradition of unionism

Source: Massey (1984, 1994).

Phillips (2002), we do not see one theoretical approach as being inherently superior to the other; instead we view both as important and needing to be evaluated in terms of the quality of the analysis and new knowledges that each approach can produce. As the discussion that follows will show, a class analysis conducted at the macro scale of the rural region does not suffice when seeking to better understand how ethnicity arbitrates the lived experiences of class and gender. A poststructuralist perspective enables us to nuance Massey's (1994) approach and frame the analysis through an understanding of rural identities (be they class based, gendered and/ or racialized) as slippery and shifting (Phillips 1998, Pini 2003, Bryant and Pini 2009). In adopting a 'blended' approach, we are able to examine how class, gender and ethnicity intersect and inform the rural labour relations that emerge from wider regional economic change.

Research Context and Conduct: A Brief History of the Woolgoolga Punjabi-Sikh Community, the Banana Industry and our Approach to this Research

The migration of Sikh people from the Punjab region in British India began during the nineteenth century. According to Bhatti and Dusenbery (2001: 39) poverty was rarely the driving reason informing this early period of migration. Rather, it was the desire to improve the family's position, or *izzat*, at home that often motivated an individual's decision to move to Australia. The migration provided opportunities to remit the money earned in Australia back to the Punjab, using it to acquire land, build a brick home or to provide a sufficient dowry for a daughter to 'marry well'. This was particularly important as many of the Punjabi-Sikhs migrating to Australia at this time were *Jats*, a rural landowning caste (de Lepervanche 1984, Bhatti and Dusenbery 2001). This rural background meant that early Punjabi-Sikh migrants tended to look for and obtain work as seasonal labourers in agricultural industries, travelling between the Atherton Tablelands in Queensland and the Northern Rivers region in NSW. Early migrants regularly worked as cane cutters and farm hands on cane and banana farms in these areas. While the introduction of the White Australia Policy in 1901 made such migration more difficult for Punjabi-Sikhs, unlike many other non-Anglo-Celtic ethnic groups, this legislation did not make migration to Australia impossible. This was because of India's position as a colony of the British Empire which meant that its citizens could migrate if they could pass a dictation test or prove, through a certificate of domicile, that they had resided in Australia prior to the introduction of the White Australia Policy (Bhatti and Dusenbery 2001: 44). As a consequence, Punjabi-Sikh migration to Australia continued throughout the early decades of the twentieth century, although at a reduced rate.

Prior to World War II, Punjabi-Sikh migration to Australia was generally pursued as temporary 'sojourn', as an opportunity for men to accumulate savings through their work in Australia and, on their return to the Punjab, use those earnings to contribute to the family's *izzat* (Bhatti and Dusenbery 2001). A number of events during and after World War II, however, shifted this migration from being a temporary visit to becoming a permanent move. Central to this was the partitioning of India and Pakistan in 1947[1] and the political, economic and social instability that ensued. As Bhatti and Dusenbery (2001: 75) explained, 'migration overseas became a solution for many people whose lives were disrupted ... conditions were seen to be more favourable to progress in Australia than in India'. Work also became more readily available in Australia during this time. For Punjabi-Sikh migrants, now wishing to establish themselves in Australia permanently, Woolgoolga emerged as a preferred location.

According to Bhatti and Dusenbery (2001: 129), 'for the Punjabis, the banana industry has been solely responsible for their firm establishment in the Woolgoolga-Coffs Harbour area'. Bananas were first introduced into this region in 1891 (Yeates 1982: 94). The region has unique conditions for growing bananas. Geographically, it is where the Great Dividing Range meets the east coast of Australia, providing steep gradients to prevent frost, and relatively temperate climates all year round to enable the growing of an albeit smaller, but sweeter banana. Initially, bananas were grown on a relatively small scale in the region, mainly to supply local shops. It was not until the 1930s, when an outbreak of the 'bunchy top' virus in Queensland decimated the local banana industry, that NSW experienced an increased demand for its disease free fruit. Furthermore, the region's relative proximity to the southern consumer markets in Sydney and Melbourne meant that, prior to the extensive use of refrigerated transport, Woolgoolga-Coffs Harbour bananas arrived in these major consumer markets in a 'fresher' state compared to Queensland produce. As

---

1   The Radcliff line segmented the Punjab region, causing much dislocation as families were forced to move between the new countries of Pakistan and India depending on their religious affiliation.

a result, by the 1960s NSW supplied as much as 80 per cent of Australia's bananas (Banana Industry Restructure and Recovery Project 2000).

Seeking employment during the 1930s and 1940s, a number of Punjabi-Sikh men had moved south from the Northern Rivers region in NSW to work on banana plantations in the Woolgoolga-Coffs Harbour area. By the early 1940s, a number of men had decided to stay in the region, with the employment in bananas, along with some itinerant cane cutting work, sufficient to warrant establishment in the area. As they became able to support their families, these Punjabi-Sikh settlers brought their wives and children to join them. Eventually these families were able to buy their own banana plantations. Their success drew other Punjabi-Sikhs from India and northern Australia to migrate and establish themselves in Woolgoolga (Bhatti and Dusenbery 2001). Described as a 'poor man's [sic] industry' (de Lepervanche 1984: 90), banana farming provided a comparatively easier start than most other agricultural industries (for example, cane, wheat, dairying). This was due to the relatively low level of capital needed to establish a plantation. Bananas required little outlay for machinery and other equipment, with success mostly relying on a farmer's access to sufficient manual labour, something that was provided through family and community networks (Bhatti and Dusenbery 2001). Punjabi-Sikh settlers were also assisted by the NSW State Government's policy at the time to lease State Forest land to facilitate its development for agricultural purposes (de Lepervanche 1984). This enabled individuals to transition from labourers to sharecroppers to eventually becoming owners of banana plantations within a relatively short time frame. Banana farming also offered the advantage of being familiar work for those who had come from an agricultural background in India. Furthermore, the independence of being farmers, and therefore their own 'boss', meant that Punjabi-Sikh settlers were able to more easily capture the profits from their own labour. This independence also provided many members of the community with the flexibility of pursuing and maintaining important religious and cultural traditions (Bhatti and Dusenbery 2001). The success of this community in establishing themselves in the region's banana industry over the last 70 years can be marked by the fact that Punjabi-Sikh men and women are today the dominant growers in the region, accounting for more than 90 per cent of the industry around Woolgoolga and more than 50 per cent around Coffs Harbour (Bhatti and Dusenbery 2001: 129).

While bananas have been integral to the establishment and ongoing success of the Punjabi-Sikh community, the industry, which had begun to face difficulties in the 1970s, experienced serious decline during the 1990s. When we first visited Woolgoolga in 2001, the future viability of the banana industry and the future of banana growers in the region were under question. Given their dominance in the banana industry, this was of particular concern to the Woolgoolga Punjabi-Sikh community. Employing a qualitative approach to this research two field trips, one in 2001 and a second in 2002, were conducted. Both fieldwork visits involved undertaking a series of semi-structured, in-depth interviews with a variety of participants, including Punjabi-Sikh banana farming families, religious and community leaders, and union representatives. The first trip was designed to gain a better understanding of the impacts of the decline of the banana industry on the broader community. The second was then used to develop an insight into how female members of the Punjabi-Sikh community were being employed by a large agricultural enterprise, at that time owned by the Transnational Corporation Chiquita Brands South Pacific, Blueberry Farms Australia (BFA). In analysing qualitative responses from the second trip, we returned to Massey's (1994) model of the 'spatial division of labour' (see Table 4.1). In the next section, we examine the regional features of the new industry (BFA) in relation to this model before going on to examine how specific labour force characteristics also fit within this framework. In each section, however, we also deviate from this conceptual basis to examine some of the more complex aspects of the new spatial division of labour that has emerged as part of regional restructuring.

Regional and New Industry Features

For a new spatial division of labour to emerge from a period of economic restructuring in a region, Massey (1984, 1994) identified that the region would generally be suffering from the collapse of a previously dominant industry. In the case of Woolgoolga, the decline of the NSW banana industry had its origins in the 1970s when regular periodic gluts and declining profits in the industry began to emerge (Banana Industry Restructure and Recovery Project 2000). This situation worsened during the 1980s and 1990s and was exacerbated by the inability of the NSW industry to organize and manage these gluts effectively. Fragmented marketing, a lack of regional cohesion and the consequent inconsistent quality in the bananas produced in the Woolgoolga-Coffs Harbour area meant that when large-scale banana plantations were established in North Queensland in the late 1980s and early 1990s, the NSW industry found itself unable to respond to this heightened market competition. The Woolgoolga-Coffs Harbour banana industry was also disadvantaged by a number of physical characteristics of the region. For example, the steep coastal slopes that prevented frost damage to crops and on which many banana plantations had been established meant that bananas could not be harvested mechanically. A lack of mechanization meant that the economies of scale that could be achieved on the large flat North Queensland plantations could not be obtained in this NSW region. The steep gradients of Woolgoolga-Coffs Harbour banana plantations also meant that topsoil was more easily eroded. Plantations thus required increasing quantities of costly chemical inputs, such as fertilizer, to compensate for a decline in soil quality. The cooler climate meant that a banana crop would take three months longer to mature than the North Queensland equivalent and that the bananas grown in the Woolgoolga-Coffs Harbour region tended to be smaller and less 'yellow' and therefore less aesthetically appealing to the consumer (Banana Industry Restructure and Recovery Project 2000). The growing domination of Queensland banana production and concurrent decline in

NSW, especially since the early 1990s, is summarized in Table 4.2. By the early 2000s, the Woolgoolga-Coffs Harbour banana industry was unequivocally an industry in decline, with ongoing survival essentially relying on the occurrence of freak events such as disease or cyclones wiping out the North Queensland competition.

Table 4.2   Australian banana market throughputs as a percentage proportion of national total by NSW and Queensland

Year	New South Wales	Queensland
1993	25%	68%
2000	14%	81%
2007	5%	94%

Source: Australian Banana Growers Council (2010).

The fierce competition from large plantations of bananas in far North Queensland became more aggressive when Chiquita Brands South Pacific, a subsidiary of world banana giant Chiquita Brands International, entered the Australian market in the 1990s, pursuing the agenda of leading the 'rationalisation of Australia's $4 billion horticultural industry' (Featherstone 1999: 14). This included the purchase of large banana holdings in the Tully Valley in North Queensland and the acquisition of the recently incorporated horticultural venture BFA. Located approximately 15 km north of Woolgoolga, BFA represented a new approach to agriculture, with production conducted at a scale and in a way that was unheard of in a region that had previously been made up of many small farmers. The General Manager of BFA boasted that the enterprise was the 'biggest single [blueberry] farm in the southern hemisphere' and that '95 per cent of the fresh blueberries in the world' were 'being picked right at this farm'. Consistent with Massey's (1994) framework, the corporate structure of this agricultural enterprise had few local links in terms of actual shareholdings, and its economic multiplier effect was limited to the wages it injected into the local economy through the workers it employed. The emergence of BFA as a source of employment in the Woolgoolga region also enabled a new spatial division of labour to emerge in the region and inadvertently provided an opportunity for Punjabi-Sikh banana farming families to survive.

Regional Workforce Features

In addition to certain regional and industrial characteristics that produced new spatial divisions of labour in regions experiencing economic change, Massey (1984, 1994) noted a number of features specific to the region's labour force that were also influential in precipitating such change. In this section, we focus on the following features: firstly, feminized and low waged work; secondly, no or minimal experience of waged work and work is semi-skilled; and thirdly, work as a secondary source of income and no or minimal tradition of unionism.

Feminized and Low Waged Work

Massey (1984, 1994) found that women, especially married women, in regions experiencing economic change often formed a reserve army of labour from which capital could draw. Gender was thus found to be a key feature in determining how the new regional agricultural industry, in the form of BFA, selected its workers. According to a union representative 'they [BFA] pick women because they don't get motion sickness [from the motion of the conveyor belts in the packing sheds] … and men don't like those jobs and women can easily do them'. Indeed, one of the most striking features of the work at BFA was the high proportion of women in the low level positions of pickers and packers of blueberries, the most menial and lowest ranked positions within the BFA labour hierarchy. In the 2001–02 growing season, almost two thirds of the Punjabi-Sikh workers at BFA were women. This situation was confirmed by the General Manager of BFA who stated that, 'the women are *the stars* [interviewee's original emphasis] shall we say, because they do it … they always put their hands up for extra hours and work at the packing sheds or in processing'. However, it was not just gender that was a key characteristic of this new spatial division of labour, blueberry class relations in Woolgoolga were also racialized. The BFA General Manager commented:

> No we've been very lucky. I mean you'll find in nine out of ten horticulture ventures of this scale in Australia labour is their biggest problem. … The local Indian community are one of the backbones of the operation because they are very good at the work that they do here.

The extent to which this work had become both feminized and racialized can also be observed in the way that the blueberry harvest time affected wider cultural and community activities in which Punjabi-Sikh women are central. A local community worker, a member of Woolgoolga's Punjabi-Sikh community herself, noted:

> We plan all of our programs that involve ethnic groups for winter. The whole community is affected. From April to August [winter time] I have no Saturday free because there is always something have to go do at the temple … these things [community and cultural activities] are all planned around the blueberries. … And people say things like "Oh the women are not going to be available to do the cooking" … so people try to have all the stuff in the winter. And it's been like that for a number of years. So that's affecting the community.

This situation not only points to the gendered nature of various facets of rural work such as community work and domestic labour, but the way in which the multiple burdens placed on rural women have been renegotiated at the community level. Cultural activities shifted from being something that could occur any time of the year to predominantly taking place in the winter months when there was little work to be obtained at BFA.

The gendered and racialized nature of this work was enabled by the fact that in the Woolgoolga region there was a general lack of employment opportunities (cf. Alston 1995). This was identified as a reason for why many Punjabi-Sikh women chose to work at BFA. As one of these women who was an ex-worker at BFA explained, 'actually there was no other work around here … [T]here were not many jobs around here back then, even now there is very little'. In addition to the central role of gender and race in this new spatial division of labour, high regional unemployment rates also enabled BFA to obtain the right to pay below award wages. This specifically geographical factor contributing to Woolgoolga's spatial division of labour was acknowledged by a union delegate:

> When they [BFA] did their non-union agreements [with the Federal Government[2]], they were actually less than the award rates were, but as I said they filed those applications "In the Public Interest", and they used two and half thousand people employed in a high unemployment area to justify why they should pay less than what they were legally required to … Yeah well there isn't that much opportunity for people to get much work up here at the moment, there is no doubt about that.

BFA's General Manager was at pains to justify this highly unfavourable Enterprise Bargaining Agreement, arguing that it was a necessary measure that enabled the company to remain globally competitive, while also emphasising that it continued to be a win-win situation for workers and BFA,

> [W]e're competing against particularly the South American companies, countries where the labour resources, they are much, much cheaper than we can ever compete with here. Even allowing for the fact that we've got what is fairly regarded as a very flexible enterprise bargaining arrangement here on the farm, which is probably different to a lot of other places in Australia. But it's a win-win situation again, for us and for the staff … And without it we couldn't be, we wouldn't be in the business. We wouldn't be competitive. Our hourly rates of pay, that's based on is still about 25 per cent higher than our [overseas] competitors.

High levels of regional unemployment and the global pressures of comparatively low cost labour sourced in other nation states enabled BFA to construct the decline

---

2   BFA was able to successfully petition the Australia Federal Government to obtain an exemption from adhering to the industrial award that had been established for agricultural workers in Australia.

in wages and conditions for its employees to be a positive for the workers, the region and the company.

No or Minimal Experience of Waged Work and Work is Semi-Skilled

Massey (1984, 1994) also contended that the work undertaken by new sources of labour was generally semi-skilled and that the conditions of this work remained this way because many of those with jobs had limited experience of waged work previously. In Woolgoolga, this situation was also gendered and racialized. As Alcorso (1991: 20) points out, 'Non English Speaking Background (NESB) women have historically been a cheap, flexible and dispensable source of labour in Australia'. This was also the case for the blueberry workers in Woolgoolga. In this rural spatial division of labour, the majority of the Punjabi-Sikh women at BFA were employed as either pickers or packers. This work was unskilled and provided little, if any, opportunity to develop skills that could be effectively transferred to other employment situations. In addition to the blueberry work offered by BFA being unskilled, the relative lack of 'recognizable' work experience and skills that many Punjabi-Sikh women had meant that employment opportunities in the region were extremely limited. The previous work experience of many Punjabi-Sikh women was often restricted to their role within the family household and as helpmeets on the family banana farm. As Bhatti and Dusenbery (2001: 84) explained, in the early years Punjabi-Sikh women 'were wholly dependent on their husbands ... they were left in the house when the men went to work, with little to do except housework. They did not know the English language and this was perhaps the main source of their loneliness'. This was the case for a female BFA employee, whose daughter translated on her behalf that she worked at BFA because: '[S]he is not educated. [BFA] is the only place she could work. She had no other choice I suppose'.

In more recent years, Punjabi-Sikh women coming to live in Woolgoolga have arrived with a level of work experience and/or tertiary qualifications obtained in India. Such qualifications are, however, generally difficult to have recognized in Australia, with further limits to employment opportunities being placed on women because of their English-speaking skills. As a Punjabi-Sikh woman who had previously worked for BFA reflected:

> ... a lot of women [migrate to Australia from India] who had been living in a city
> and were working; you know some had been working in a factory and some had
> been working in offices, and these women, I think they think that they won't be
> able to get any other job except blueberries because their language is a barrier.

What 'work experience' many women did have was generally in the packing sheds of the banana plantations, yet this was work that assisted a patriarchal system of property ownership and remained essentially semi-skilled (cf. Shortall 1999). The gendered nature of banana farming in Woolgoolga was recognized by one of the Punjabi-Sikh woman BFA employees interviewed:

> Well there was nothing else we could do you know [but work at BFA]... Because it is usually the sons that carry [the banana farm] on, so we were just helping out.

As a consequence, many of the Punjabi-Sikh women from the area had limited formal and recognized skills. At the same time, the limited skills developed through the banana work on the family farm was identified as a reason why many Punjabi-Sikh women were successful pickers and packers for BFA. According to the BFA General Manager:

> Picking blueberries and Indian women seem to go hand in hand, for what reason I'm not too sure ... they are the best, well they are the quickest pickers ... Be that culture; be that the physical attributes of the work they are doing. They're probably used to being out in the banana plantations and all the rest of it, in the packing shed and all that.

Even so the work at BFA was understood by many women as a mixed blessing. For instance, some women found that the work at BFA enabled the process of settling in a new country to be easier. One observed, 'I found [living in Australia] a bit hard at first but then not any problem. This [the work at BFA] is really good'. In contrast, others experienced farming work as both physically and emotionally draining as was the case with the woman who told us, 'It was quite hard emotionally and it was very different work wise, I had never done any farming in India'. Similarly, while the idea of women working at BFA was generally supported locally, beyond Woolgoolga it was another matter. One woman, who had begun a university degree in India, explained that her decision to undertake the semi-skilled work offered by BFA rather than seek work relevant to her qualifications had elicited criticism from her parents in India. She stated:

> I felt it was not fair for me to find a job elsewhere and work there five days a week while the ladies were here packing bananas ... For my in-laws, because of their farming background, for them it [her work at BFA] was a plus, because you're getting an income... For my parents it was a bit of disappointment. They said that it was up to me and my in-laws, because you have to get along with them. But yeah...

The work at BFA thus produced a conflict for more educated women who wanted to respect the investment their parents had made in their education prior to their marriage, but also wished to establish and maintain good relations with their new families in Australia. This situation reflects a constant theme in the literature on rurality and gender; that is, that rural women must adhere to household and wider community expectations as to the 'correct' performances of 'rural women' or risk censure (Little 1994, Alston 1995, Bryant and Pini 2009).

Work is a Secondary Source of Income and No or Minimal Tradition of Unionism

According to Massey (1994) one of the key aspects of the new spatial divisions of labour likely to emerge in declining regions is that new work in the region often performs the role of a secondary source of income. Certainly the work at BFA was constructed as being secondary, principally as a consequence of its gendered nature. For example, a Punjabi-Sikh male farmer talked of female blueberry income as 'money to keep them happy'. The understanding that the income earned from the blueberry work performed a supplementary role was also readily commented upon by many of the female BFA employees interviewed. For instance an ex-BFA employee explained that she had 'started there for pocket money for myself. A lot of women, they actually worked for their pocket money'.

The multiple roles that many Punjabi-Sikh women continued to fulfil within their family and community also assisted in the construction of the BFA income as secondary. In particular, the flexible nature of the work (undertaken mainly under casual and/or seasonal arrangements) was often understood to be a positive feature of this form of employment. Such flexibility was seen to enable those women, employed as pickers and packers at BFA, to continue to perform their other household, farm, family, religious and social obligations. A female ex-employee of BFA readily identified that the 'flexibility' of the blueberry work was a positive aspect of this work, saying that she was 'really happy [with the BFA work] when my kids were young and I needed that flexibility'. The General Manager at BFA also recognized that many of the female employees had other responsibilities beyond their role at BFA asserting:

> [Punjabi-Sikh women] can fit it [the banana work] in because normally we only work six hours a day picking … [they can] get back into the packing shed and whatever else … the men look after the cutting of the bananas and all the rest of it.

The secondary role of the income and flexible conditions of employment have been noted elsewhere as producing specifically gendered outcomes in rural class relations. As Little (2002: 102) observed, with agricultural employment becoming increasingly casual, part-time and seasonal, this work has shifted from being understood as 'men's work to women's work'. The 'flexibility' used to describe the BFA work suggests that this aspect is designed to benefit the Punjabi-Sikh women employed by the corporation. This understanding, however, neglects to take into account the job insecurity and lack of conditions that are associated with flexible employment. It also fails to acknowledge that this flexibility also produces the classic situation of women taking on the multiple burdens of household, farm, waged work and community work. Furthermore, this research found that it was not always as easy for women to juggle their multiple roles as is suggested by the quotations above (cf. Singh 2001). A number of women explained that they missed the time they might otherwise spend with their family because of the blueberry work. One noted, 'It gets hard at times because you know that you're spending less time at home and more hours here'. Others told of how tired they were at the end of the day to the extent that it was reported, 'When I get home late and just go to sleep, I miss talking to my children'.

Some participants also reported that blueberry income was actually used and relied upon by banana farming families in a manner markedly different from the construction of this employment as secondary. Far from being 'pocket money', blueberry work during financial down periods had become the primary source of income for many families (Kelly and Shortall 2002). During such times, many of the Punjabi-Sikh women employed at BFA effectively became the 'breadwinner' for the family unit. For many Punjabi-Sikh families, their banana farms had only remained viable through the waged work undertaken by mostly female family members at BFA. As one interviewee explained:

> There were times when banana prices were really down for a few years and those were times when we managed with that money – blueberries money. I would spend it on the groceries and a few bills and all that. That was a great help for the boys in the partnership [the farm] … The years we had good years in bananas the boys said 'you can keep the money and do whatever you want to do' so we could buy something at home, things like that. But the years that were really hard, hard on bananas, we could help the boys, help our husbands.

A telling feature of the above quote was the way the family banana farm (a male workspace) was positioned as more important and hence more deserving of the resources produced from the work at BFA (a female workspace). Similarly, it is important to note the way in which the patriarchal relations of the household determined how such income was to be used. This hierarchy was, however, not resented; instead the situation was constructed as a positive opportunity to help the family, and more specifically to assist the male heads of the family.

While these circumstances were exploitative (Bhatti and Dusenbery 2001: 140), a further layer of complexity was introduced to these rural class relations by the fact that they were also understood to be empowering. As the local community worker explained:

> I think the women have become more empowered in themselves. The way they walk. It's self-esteem. They walk taller in the blueberry season … they're economically contributing to the family and some of their incomes are now crucial to the economic survival of the household. Whereas before they would work on their husband's banana farm … and they never saw any cash.

The money earned from BFA was not only used to support the family banana farm, but engaged to enable many women to maintain family and cultural linkages in India. The money paid for return trips to India as well as contributed to the obtaining of higher education qualifications by future generations of Punjabi-Sikh women. One woman explained: 'Well I used my money a couple of times to go to India for holidays [and] it has helped out with my daughter's uni [university costs]'.

The final key labour force characteristic identified by Massey (1994) was the limited tradition of unionism amongst those employed. This was found to be especially the case amongst the Punjabi-Sikh women for a variety of reasons. First, this situation reflected an historical legacy, that is, the active union antagonism towards earlier migrant groups in the late nineteenth and early twentieth century Australia. As Bhatti and Dusenbery (2001: 44, 49) noted, 'As early Punjabis tried to find agricultural work in Queensland and northern NSW, they also faced union hostility and resentment ... They were well aware that union restrictions had limited their opportunities'. Indeed, the union representative interviewed as part of this research was also aware of the consequence of this past treatment, stating that, 'It was one of those industries we sort of gave up on ... the Sikh community obviously do not have too many ties with the Union'. As small farmers, many Punjabi-Sikh banana growers viewed themselves as small business people, rather than employees. The fact that their class identities were more closely aligned with the owners of BFA only served to cement their long tradition of non-affiliation with unionism.

Conclusions

There is a general acknowledgement of the dearth of research examining the lived experiences of rural women from Non-English-Speaking Backgrounds (NESB) (Wilkinson 1998, Missingham, Dibden, Cocklin 2006, Pini 2003, Panelli et al. 2009; Bryant and Pini 2011). As Wilkinson (1998: 235) points out, NESB 'women occupy a hidden, but crucial space within the discourse about agriculture in this land [they are] ... frequently rendered invisible by virtue of the intersectionality of their rurality, ethnicity and gender'. This chapter addresses this absence through an examination of the rural class relations of Punjabi-Sikh women employed in the blueberry industry near Woolgoolga, NSW. This research adopted a blended theoretical approach, returning to earlier political economic explorations of class relations, specifically Massey's (1984, 1994) concept of the spatial division of labour, to provide a framework for this rural analysis. The gendered and racialized nature of the class relations of Woolgoolga's blueberry industry, however, also required this research to employ a poststructuralist perspective that enabled a micro scale examination of how multiple rural identities intersected and arbitrated this new spatial division of labour.

Despite the disparity between the contemporary Australian agricultural context and the English industrial environment at the centre of Massey's (1994) analyses, a number of parallels can be drawn. Having dominated the local banana industry for a number of years, Woolgoolga's Punjabi-Sikh community experienced the negative impacts of the decline of this industry during the 1990s. Employment at BFA enabled this economic change to be managed by providing an additional source of income. A significant feature of this new source of employment was the way in which it was predominantly undertaken by female members of the Punjabi-Sikh community, making this new rural spatial division of labour both gendered and racialized. Blueberry work is associated with poor conditions and low wages that offers employees limited opportunities to develop further transferable skills. Indeed, a historical distrust of unions, a lack of prior experience in waged work (or the non-recognition of overseas qualifications) and the treatment of the work as a secondary source of income were all features that made Punjabi-Sikh women from Woolgoolga ideal employees from the company's perspective.

The gendered and racialized nature of these rural class relations also added a number of layers of complexity to the experiences of Punjabi-Sikh women employed at BFA. At the outset was the way in which community responsibilities mostly undertaken by women had been rearranged so as not to conflict with the demands of the blueberry season. Similarly, while constructed as secondary, in reality the income earned by Punjabi-Sikh women had become central to the survival of the local banana plantations. When the household and banana farm could spare this income, it had also enabled women to pursue their own interests such as making return trips to India. Such positives, however, are tempered by the fact that this work remained casual, unskilled and had low wages and poor conditions. Despite domestic and community responsibilities being adjusted to accommodate the needs of BFA, Punjabi-Sikh women still juggled multiple roles and responsibilities between the home, the family farm, their work at BFA and the wider community. Furthermore, while the work was more than just a secondary or supplementary form of income, blueberry wages were often resumed to serve the patriarchal structures of the family farm. Such was the marginal nature of this new spatial division of labour that Bhatti and Dusenbery (2001: 163) concluded, that while 'blueberry picking has provided an economic lifeline for many Punjabi agricultural families, it is unlikely that the local Punjabi community as a whole can be sustained through this in the absence of other economic opportunities'. Far from securing the long-term prospects of the community, it is the gendered and racialized nature of this new rural spatial division of labour that makes the future viability of Woolgoolga's Punjabi-Sikh community uncertain.

References

Agyeman, J. and Spooner, R. 1997. Ethnicity and the rural environment, in *Contested Countryside Cultures: Otherness, Marginalisation and Rurality*, edited by P. Cloke and J. Little. London: Routledge, 197–217.

Alcorso, C. 1991. *Non-English Speaking Background Immigrant Women in the Workforce*. Wollongong: The Centre for Multicultural Studies, University of Wollongong.

Alston, M. 1995. *Women on the Land: The Hidden Heart of Rural Australia*. Kensington: University of New South Wales Press.

Australian Banana Growers Council 2010. *Industry Statistics*. [Online: Australian Banana Growers' Council Inc.]. Available at: http://www.abgc.org.au/?industry/banana-industry [accessed: 1 February 2010].

Banana Industry Restructure and Recovery Project 2000. *Australia's Holiday Coast Sub-Tropical Bananas: What's the Future?* Available at: http://coastcall.com.au/agribus/bananas/gonebananasfinal.htm [accessed: 18 September 2002].

Bhatti, R. and Dusenbery, V.A. (ed.) 2001. *A Punjabi-Sikh Community in Australia: from Indian Sojourners to Australian Citizens*. Woolgoolga: Woolgoolga Neighbourhood Centre Inc.

Bryant, L. and Pini, B. 2009. Gender, class and rurality: Australian case studies. *Journal of Rural Studies*, 25(1), 48–57.

Bryant, L. and Pini, B. 2011. *Gender and Rurality*. London and New York: Routledge.

Cloke, P. and Thrift, N. 1990. Class and change in rural Britain, in *Rural Restructuring: Global Processes and Their Responses*, edited by T. Marsden, P. Lowe and S. Whatmore. London: David Fulton Publishers, 165–81.

Featherstone, T. 1999. Ripe for the picking. *Shares*, 1 October, 14.

Jordan, K., Krivokapic-Skoko, B. and Collins, J. 2009. The ethnic landscape of rural Australia: Non-Anglo-Celtic immigrant communities and the built environment. *Journal of Rural Studies*, 25(4), 376–85.

Kelly, R. and Shortall, S. 2002. 'Farmer's wives': women who are off-farm breadwinners and the implications for on-farm gender relations. *Journal of Sociology*, 38(4), 327–43.

de Lepervanche, M.M. 1984. *Indians in a White Australia – An Account of Race, Class and Indian Immigration to Eastern Australia*. Sydney: Allen and Unwin.

Little, J. 1994. Gender relations and the rural labour process, in *Gender and Rurality*, edited by S. Whatmore, T. Marsden and P. Lowe. London: David Fulton Publishers, 11–30.

Little, J. 2002. *Gender and Rural Geography: Identity, Sexuality and Power in the Countryside*. Harlow: Pearson.

Massey, D.B. 1984. *Spatial Divisions of Labour: Social Structures and the Geography of Production*. London: Macmillan.

Massey, D.B. 1994. *Space: Place and Gender*. Cambridge: Polity Press.

Missingham, B., Dibden, J. and Cocklin, C. 2006. A multicultural countryside? Ethnic minorities in rural Australia. *Rural Society*, 16(2), 131–50.

Murdoch, J. and Marsden, T. 1994. *Reconstituting Rurality: The Changing Countryside in an Urban Context*. London: UCL Press.

O'Neill, P. 1989. National economic change and the locality. *Environment and Planning A*, Spatial Divisions of Labour in Practice special issue, 21(5), 666–70.

Panelli, R., Hubbard, P., Coombes, B.L. and Suchet-Pearson, S. 2009. De-centring White ruralities: ethnic diversity, racialisations and Indigenous countrysides. *Journal of Rural Studies*, 25(4), 355–64.

Phillips, M. 1998. Social Perspectives, in *The Geography of Rural* Change, edited by B. Ilbery. Harlow: Addison Wesley Longman, 31–54.

Phillips, M. 2002. Distant bodies? Rural studies: political-economy and poststructuralism. *Sociologia Ruralis*, 42(2), 81–105.

Philo, C. 1992. Neglected rural geographies: a review. *Journal of Rural Studies*, 8(2), 193–207.

Pini, B. 2003. The question of 'the Italians' and women's representation in leadership in the Australian sugar industry. *Australian Geographer*, 34(2), 211–22.

Shortall, S. 1999. *Women and Farming: Property and Power*. Houndmills: Macmillan Press.

Singh, R. 2001. Sikh community of Woolgoolga: a comparative view, in *A Punjabi-Sikh Community in Australia: from Indian Sojourners to Australian Citizens*, edited by R. Bhatti and V.A. Dusenbery. Woogoolga: Woolgoolga Neighbourhood Centre Inc. 230–41.

Wilkinson, J. 1998. Prejudices: reconceptions or progress in agriculture? Rural non English speaking background women and leadership. *Rural Society*, 8(3), 235–55.

Yeates, N. 1982. *Woolgoolga: Past and Present*. Coffs Harbour: Advocate-Opinion Press.

Chapter 5

Re-examining the Social Relations of the Canadian 'Family Farm': Migrant Women Farm Workers in Rural Canada[1]

Kerry Preibisch and Evelyn Encalada Grez

Throughout the global South, women are becoming the predominant waged labour force in commercial agriculture. In particular, the rise of high value agriculture has resulted in a marked preference for female labour. This contemporary rise in female employment has roots in women's long experience in agriculture; historically, women have played a central role as unpaid labour within subsistence and small-scale production and, in many countries, as the temporary workforce sustaining commercial enterprises. The incorporation of workers from the global South into commercial agriculture within high income countries, however, has had a decidedly masculine bias. In North America, for example, guest worker programs for agriculture have predominantly recruited men, while women are sought to fill jobs in the hospitality or caregiving sectors. These processes underscore how central the social construction of gender is to employment relations in agriculture's multiple sites of production.

While academics have made inroads in documenting and theorizing the gender relations that organize migration and farm work, important limitations remain. Research in high income countries tends, within the scholarship on gender and migration, to adopt gender analysis when processes appear to be feminized, as can be seen in the now ample literature on migrant domestic caregivers. Further, the literature on women in agriculture in the global North has focused on female producers and gendered access to productive resources, failing to acknowledge the deeply gendered, classed and racialized relations beyond the 'family farm'. Our chapter focuses on women employed in labour-intensive agriculture in the global North, specifically women from rural Mexico who take up waged work as migrant workers in Canadian agriculture.[2] By tracing the incorporation of women into a highly

1   This chapter has been adapted from the article Preibisch, K. and E. Encalada (2010). "The other side of 'El Otro Lado': Mexican Migrant Women and Labor Flexibility in Canadian Agriculture," Special Issue on Women in Agriculture. *Signs: Journal of Women in Culture and Society*, 35(2), 289-316. http://www.journals.uchicago.edu/doi/pdf/10.1086/605483 © 2010, The University of Chicago.

2   We use the term 'migrant worker' to refer to people employed in Canada under temporary visas who do not hold Canadian citizenship or permanent residency (landed

masculinized, guest worker program for agriculture, we highlight a less visible facet of women's migration and a highly gendered and racialized set of employment relations. Further, by exploring employment practices on commercial farms, we expose less visible aspects of the social relations of agriculture in high income countries.

We begin by weaving connections between the literature on women in agriculture and gender and migration studies. We then turn to our empirical study of the Mexican women who leave their rural communities to work as migrant farm workers in Canada. The main focus of our analysis is on the lived realities of these women and the gendered, racialized employment relations that characterize their workplaces, an exercise that necessitates analysing gender at the crossroads of citizenship, class, and race. We argue that temporary migration programs further entrench existing structures of labour segmentation in farm work. Further, they grant employers access to a highly vulnerable group of workers (people who embody the economic, social, and political marginalization within their home countries) who are then placed at a disadvantage within the Canadian labour market through a range of legal disentitlements that hinge on their immigration status. Our analysis provides insight into the gendered incorporation of migrant workers in agricultural production in the global North and, by focusing on southern women on northern farms, provides new understandings of gender, class and rurality.

The Gendered Relations of Global Agriculture

Global restructuring of agrifood markets has resulted in rising levels of female employment in high value agriculture in the global South. Women tend to form a smaller percentage of the permanent workforce employed in commercial agriculture, often constituting the majority of the temporary, seasonal, and casual workforce that provides the greater portion of labour, in addition to filling most positions in packinghouses and other value added processing activities (Barrientos et al. 2005, Dolan 2005, Barrientos and Dolan 2007). The rise of contract farming, another trend associated with global patterns of restructuring, has also heightened demand for women's labour (Dolan 2005, Smith and Dolan 2006). Scholars have attributed growing female employment in commercial agriculture to a global trend toward flexible labour strategies instituted by firms struggling to maintain a foothold in increasingly competitive markets. In this context, flexibility is created by employing a temporary and informal workforce that can be mobilized and disbanded according to varying labour needs, thus depressing labour costs and reducing the non-wage related costs of employment (Standing 1999). Maintaining women in casual, informal employment and paying them less (or through their

---

immigrant status). Although people from economically marginalized regions and socially marginalized groups in Canada migrate to work in agriculture, we prefer to delineate our particular use of migrant here rather than use 'foreign worker', a term that contributes to the discursive disentitlement of international migrants (see Sharma 2006: 53).

male partners) have often been justified by, and made possible through, their roles in social reproduction (Lara Flores 1998, Raynolds 2002, Dolan 2005). As Arizpe (1988) has noted, the comparative advantage of agrifood industries in global markets rests on the comparative disadvantage of rural women in national labour markets. Further, capitalist agriculture benefits from women's previous skills and experience in agriculture. Women are central to food systems throughout the world, producing food crops but also many of the high value crops on which commercial firms depend (Sachs 1991, Lara Flores 1998). Employer preference for women's labour in tasks requiring dexterity, precision, and care is also considered to result from abilities women have acquired through their reproductive responsibilities (Lara Flores 1995).

Feminist scholars have also made contributions to understanding gender relations in agricultural production in the global North (Sachs 1991, Whatmore 1991a, 1991b, Brandth 2002, Saugeres 2002). The bulk of these studies have focused on women living on farms as wives, daughters, farm operators, or off farm workers and have attempted to make visible women's labour contributions to farm households, to theorize the gender relations of farming, and, in general, to expose the meanings and practices of agrarian patriarchal culture. This literature has made important contributions to understanding the social relations of agriculture and rural life. First and foremost, it has exposed agriculture as a decidedly patriarchal arena in which work is highly stratified by gender while emphasizing the consequences for women's positions in rural households and communities. On the farm, work is assigned and ranked according to gender; male bodily qualities are valued for most, if not all, forms of agricultural tasks and have come to symbolize farm work (Leckie 1993, 1996, Saugeres 2002, Brandth 2006). Overall, 'the masculine is valued over what is considered feminine, and as a consequence farm women's bodies and abilities are inferiorized and devalued' (Brandth 2006: 20). Further, scholars have shown how gender differences in farm labour participation reflect and reinforce women's social and economic marginalization in the rural sphere (Whatmore 1991a, Leckie 1993). The literature on gender in agriculture in the global North, however, remains focused on the family farm (Sachs 1991, Brandth 2006). While some research has explored how the modernization of farms masculinized formerly female responsibilities and appropriated agricultural technology from women, examination of the gender relations of labour-intensive, corporate farming is conspicuously absent (Sachs 1991, Brandth 2002, Saugeres 2002).

This lacuna in the literature can be explained partly by the persistence of the family farm as the dominant unit of agricultural production in high income countries throughout the twentieth century, despite extensive restructuring (Whatmore 1991a, Winson 1993). The rise of corporate agriculture and growing labour demand for migrant workers in North America, however, has triggered some scholarly consideration of farm workers (e.g., Findeis 2002, Mines 2002, Martin 2003, Walker 2004, Barrón Pérez 2006, Griffith 2006). Very few studies explore the situation of women farm workers; those that do tend to focus on labour rights, health risks, and sexuality, engaging only weakly with gender analysis (e.g., Van Hightower, Gorton, and DeMoss 2000, Villarejo 2003, Griffith 2006,

Castañeda and Zavalla 2007). Although Canada has a much smaller labour-intensive agricultural industry than the United States, its growth in the last decade has inspired some research on women farm workers and the gender dynamics of agricultural labour (Preibisch 2005, Preibisch and Hermoso Santamaria 2006, Barndt 2007, Becerril 2007). These examples aside, the general lack of research on women farm workers in the academic literature on northern agriculture corroborates the marginalization of *rural* and *women* in the social sciences. It is no surprise that within this context, less visible women such as waged workers (often im/migrant members of racialized groups) have fallen off the radar and that gender analysis is rarely invoked when farm labour issues are examined.

One body of literature that has generated significant research and theorizing on the involvement of women of colour in northern labour markets is gender and migration studies. The field of migration studies has been gendered over the past 20 years, with feminist scholars giving visibility to migrating women who had been obscured by decades of research based predominantly on male subjects and, moreover, exposing gender as a relation of power shaping the movement of people (e.g., Kanaiaupuni 2000, Sassen 2000, Parreñas 2001, Erel, Morokvásic-Müller, and Shinozaki 2003, Pessar 2003, Oishi 2005). Among its contributions, this literature has encouraged integrative approaches to migration studies that consider the intersectionality of gender with a wide range of social relations of power. Nana Oishi (2005), for example, uses a multilevel analysis to explain the feminization of international labour migration, taking into account a range of factors from the social legitimacy of women's workforce participation abroad to gendered and racialized preferences that have shaped occupational demand. Much of the gender and migration literature, however, has focused on women working as domestic caregivers or nurses (e.g., Arat-Koç 1989, Macklin 1994, Stiell and England 1997, Pratt 1999, Chang 2000, Parreñas 2001, Stasiulis and Bakan 2003). Very little work has been done on migrant women entering male dominated occupations or on how masculinized migratory flows are also gendered. Our focus on migrant farm workers in Canada intends to fill this gap.

Methodology

Our study is part of Rural Women Making Change (a Community University Research Alliance www.rwmc.uoguelph.ca.) a program of research that seeks to make visible the challenges facing rural women in their everyday lives, to bring a rural and gendered analysis to bear on the local and global processes from which these challenges stem, and to propose effective strategies to get rural women's concerns into policy agendas. Our project within Rural Women Making Change sought to include the small but rapidly growing population of migrant women in rural Canada. Our fieldwork focused on Mexican and Caribbean women who migrate seasonally via a highly managed temporary migration program for agriculture and Low German-speaking Mennonites who engage in circular migration between Canada and Mexico via Canadian passports. Co-author Evelyn

Encalada Grez has considerable experience working with migrant farm workers and various migrant sending communities as the cofounder of Justicia for Migrant Workers, a migrant rights advocacy group.

This article concentrates on our Mexican guest worker participants, which included 16 in-depth interviews, one focus group, and innumerable hours of ethnographic observation.[3] All participants were employed under the Seasonal Agricultural Workers Program and had worked between one and 16 seasons. They ranged in age from 25 to 49 years old, and all but three had children. About half of the mothers had divorced or separated from their husbands; the other half had never married, nor had the three women without children. Most were from states in central Mexico with the exception of two from Oaxaca. Participants were recruited in three localities in the province of Ontario: Niagara, the region employing the majority of women migrants; Leamington, the second highest employer of women; and a remote, small locality (unidentified to preserve anonymity) employing very few migrants. Since social isolation characterizes the lived experience of transnational migration to rural Canada, our purposive sample sought to include women in areas of high and low migrant concentration. We conducted interviews in 2006, all of which were subsequently transcribed in the original Spanish.

As well as the data described above this chapter also relies upon ongoing research on migrant farm workers in Canada, including some 60 in-depth interviews with men and women migrants as well as their allies, employers, and government representatives (Preibisch 2004, 2007) and doctoral research in Mexico and Canada.[4] Since our research was not designed to be representative of the diverse range of agrifood operations hiring migrant workers, it should be interpreted within its limitations and, hopefully, kindle further research in this area.

Migrant Workers in Canadian Agriculture

Global restructuring of agrifood markets has initiated significant changes in the employment of migrant workers in Canadian agriculture. The number of workers employed under temporary visas is increasing rapidly, practically doubling within the last decade. The Seasonal Agricultural Workers Program (SAWP), Canada's principal guest worker program for agriculture, now grants over 27,000 temporary visas annually. In addition, a newly created temporary migration program known as the NOC C and D Pilot,[5] which is not sector specific, approved over 11,000 work

---

3   All quotations are our translations; some have been edited with care to remain true to respondents' accounts. Any names that appear are pseudonyms.

4   The dissertation, by Encalada Grez, is currently in progress and is titled *Mexican Women Organizing Life, Love and Work across Rural Ontario and Rural Mexico: A Practice of Transnational Storytelling and a Proposed Translation for Change.*

5   The full name of this initiative is the Pilot Project for Occupations Requiring Lower Levels of Formal Training (National Occupational Classification C and D).

permits for jobs in agriculture in 2008 (Human Resources and Skills Development Canada No date). The range of industries eligible to receive temporary migrants has also widened considerably, as has their geographical distribution. While the province of Ontario still employs some 65 per cent of migrant farm workers, they are now present in most provinces (Human Resources and Skills Development Canada 2010). Moreover, migrants' work seasons have lengthened both through extended visas and as a greater number of employers hire workers for the maximum period under the SAWP. Furthermore, in 2007 it became easier and faster for employers to hire migrant workers as a result of a concerted policy agenda of the Canadian government and policies within sending countries designed to improve the management of their worker abroad programs. Finally, there is evidence to suggest that migrant workers account for the greater share of total hours worked in some agricultural labour markets and that employers consider them to be their core labour force.

The increasing demand for migrant workers reflects the growth of labour-intensive agrifood industries in Canada that have shown success in global markets (Preibisch 2007). It also highlights a national labour market in which job shortages have been created in certain occupations that citizens with other employment opportunities reject (Bolaria 1992). Indeed, the working conditions in agriculture the world over are, to a large extent, socially created through low wages and poorly regulated labour environments (Castles 2006). Canada is no exception: farm work is at the bottom of the occupational ladder and among the most dangerous types of work. Although there is enormous variation in agricultural jobs, in general they are poorly rewarded in material and status terms, involve inconsistent hours, and often entail considerable physical exertion under variable climatic conditions. Agriculture is also less regulated than other sectors; farm workers have historically been excluded from the protections other workers enjoy, including the right to unionize.

The social construction of labour conditions in Canadian agriculture has a long history. Throughout the postwar period, growers met their seasonal labour needs through marginalized or less than free populations, including prisoners of war, conscientious objectors, and orphans (Parr 1985, Satzewich 1991, Bolaria 1992, Wall 1992, Basok 2002). In the 1960s, growers began incorporating non-citizen migrant labour into their operations, a practice that was institutionalized in 1966 with the SAWP. The program operates under bilateral frameworks of agreement between Canada and a set of migrant sending countries. Under the SAWP, growers are able to hire migrants from these countries for as little as six weeks to as long as eight months and, in subsequent seasons, to request workers by name. The creation of the NOC C and D Pilot in 2002 liberalized the international labour pool available to Canadian employers, allowing them to hire migrant farm workers from outside the SAWP bilateral partner countries. This policy change has opened the door to a range of new nationalities in agriculture, principally Guatemalans, Thais, and Filipinos, as employers seek out the country they perceive will offer the most hardworking, reliable, and flexible workforce.

Migrant workers constitute a desirable alternative to Canadian citizens or permanent residents for a number of reasons that have been amply documented (Bolaria 1992, Colby 1997, Smart 1997, Basok 2002, Binford 2002, 2004, Verma 2003, Preibisch 2004). To begin, migrants' labour mobility is highly constrained through work permits that are valid only with a single, designated employer. Migrants are unable to work legally for another employer without negotiating a government approved contract transfer. Labour sending countries and employers exert considerable pressure for migrants to return home upon completion of their contracts (or when they are injured or sick) in order to avoid visa overstays. This grants employers tremendous power to institute mechanisms of labour control, including the repatriation of workers when they are no longer required, if they demonstrate undesirable behaviour, or if they fall ill or are injured. Recruitment policies also play an important role in generating a premium pool of workers. To illustrate, Mexico recruits primarily married applicants with dependants in an attempt to reduce visa overstay, premised on the assumption that these candidates are more likely to return after their contracts end (Basok 2002). Together with visa restrictions that compel migrants to move without their families, these policies deliver workers with greater willingness to accede to employer requests to work longer hours and over weekends relative to Canadians (Basok 2002, Preibisch and Binford, 2007). Furthermore, migrant workers are recruited on the basis of need from countries with large populations in poverty, often from the rural working class, a strategy that helps constitute them as a much more willing and committed workforce than that available within Canada. Eligibility requirements in one Mexican state, for example, indicate that candidates must be rurally located agricultural workers with minimal education. Class is in fact the main eligibility criterion; until very recently, civil servants in Mexico City inspected not only potential applicants' paperwork that proved they were rurally located farm workers, but also the palms of their hands. Finally, in an apparent breach of human rights legislation in Canada, employers are able to select their migrant employees on the basis of nationality and sex. This is a crucial element of temporary migration programs, enabling employers to create competition among labour sending countries and workers themselves along a number of social hierarchies, in which gender, race and class figure prominently.

Gendered Demand, Gendered Supply

International labour migration to the Canadian agricultural sector has been highly masculinized. Women did not participate for almost a quarter century after the SAWP was founded and today represent only 2 per cent of the workforce. Tracing the masculinization of migrant labour to Canadian agriculture reveals a complex set of gender ideologies held by farm operators, civil servants on both sides of the border, migrants' households and communities, and migrants themselves. The supply side of this equation, involving the gender ideologies operating within migrant sending countries that constrain or facilitate men's and women's migration, has received considerable attention in the gender and migration studies literature (Hondagneu-Sotelo 1994, 2003, Kanaiaupuni 2000, Parreñas 2001, 2005, Pessar 2003, Oishi 2005). In the case presented here, women have faced a number of institutional barriers to their participation. The Mexican state did not allow women to participate in the SAWP until 1989, and only single mothers were eligible until 1998 (Preibisch and Hermoso Santamaria 2006). Although Mexican officials claim that sex and civil status are not bases for recruitment, propaganda used to recruit participants often specifies male applicants only. Moreover, our participants perceived the principal requirement for women's entry to be the status of single mother.

An additional factor that must be considered on the supply side is the social legitimacy of women's international migration (Oishi 2005). Despite women's rising participation in United States bound migration, women's mobility remains constrained by social norms and gender expectations (Hondagneu-Sotelo and Avila 2003, Curran et al. 2006). As Kanaiaupuni (2000) has argued, it is not the responsibility for children that explains Mexican women's lower participation in international migration but expectations of what it means to be a good wife or daughter. For all our respondents, the act of even initiating the application process required considerable fortitude, bravery, initiative, and perseverance. Two women spoke of their husbands deterring their eventual migration with ultimatums and how these men ended up leaving them, despite the fact that their inability to provide economically had motivated these women's wishes to enter the SAWP. A third woman's ex-husband threatened to gain custody of their children if she migrated abroad. Other women faced significant opposition from fathers and brothers.

Women also confront considerable challenges in completing the application process, particularly as this initially involved travelling to Mexico City several times. Although the costs of migration to Canada are relatively low compared with undocumented migration to the United States, they are still out of reach for most rural women. Angelina (born 1967), recounting her reaction when someone described the application process involved trips to the capital, said:

> To say "go to Mexico City" was like saying "go to end of the earth." Because of my economic situation I said: "where will I get so much money to go to that city? God knows that here I don't even have food to give to my children. Where will I get money from? Who is going to loan me money when I don't have anything?" I don't have land, I don't have livestock. "If you don't pay, we'll take away the house." But I didn't even have a house for them to take.

The journeys associated with the application process, while not as dangerous as those faced by undocumented, United States bound migrants, often place women in situations of risk. As Rosa (born 1950), among the SAWP's first women, related:

I would go to the Ministry [of Labour] and they would say "come back in eight days"; then, "come back in 15 days." And that is how it was for two years. Sometimes I'd have to borrow money to go to Mexico City, where I had to stay in the bus terminal. Sometimes I'd sleep in different places because I didn't have money to pay for a hotel or to eat properly. I'd have to wash up in public washrooms so I could look presentable among the administrators of the program and sometimes stay overnight outside of the offices of the ministry.

Stories like Rosa's must be read within the context of high rates of gender based violence in Mexico City (Comisión de Derechos Humanos del Distrito Federal 2008) and considering that at least one woman in the SAWP's history has been raped outside the Ministry of Labour. Despite these and various other obstacles, such as obstructionist government personnel or congested phone lines, our respondents persevered with their decisions to migrate.

Once in Canada, women have to contend with stigma from the migrant community and their home communities, who see them as questionable mothers and as sexually available women (Preibisch 2005, Preibisch and Hermoso Santamaria 2006). Gloria (born 1973) described the verbal abuse by male co-workers: 'Many of the men that pass you in the street call you a pile of stupid things. For the men, all of us women working here [in Canada] are prostitutes.' Migrant women are often criticized for leaving their children. In women's home communities, men are seen as fulfilling their primary gender role by engaging in transnational livelihoods, while women who do so are seen as deserting theirs, at least according to how motherhood has traditionally been defined. In addition, migrant women are seen as responsible for breaking up marriages. In particular, the wives of migrating men see their husbands' female co-workers as potential threats.

Of principal concern to our interviewees, however, is not how they are perceived by others but the outcomes of migration for their children. As Angelina related, 'I told my mother: "Look, I'm going to submit my paperwork, and if I manage to get in, you can be sure that my marriage is over, but I don't care. What I care about are my children"'. Our participants often emphasized that their migration was motivated by maternal love, even though it meant separating from their children for up to eight months every year. They frequently spoke of their migration as a sacrifice that could create alternative futures for their children, such as providing an education they never had. When women discussed the injustices they suffered in their destination experiences, these were often framed pragmatically, as inevitable burdens to carry as they focused squarely on their purpose for migrating: their children. While single women also participate in migrant farm worker programmes, often as the primary breadwinner in their households they confront stigma in different ways: they are not mothers leaving children behind, but they are engaging in two activities typed as male (international migration and farm work) without recourse to the justification that migration was imposed through male abandonment and/or parental responsibility.

The demand side of gendered migration flows is an equally compelling but less studied area in the literature, involving the highly ideological territory of immigration policy but also the gendered and racialized perceptions of employers offering work (Hondagneu Sotelo 1997, Oishi 2005, Griffith 2006). Indeed, the overwhelming preponderance of men as migrant farm workers (and conversely, the preponderance of women as caregivers under Canada's other flagship managed migration scheme, the Live-in Caregiver Program) illustrates how entrenched gender segmentation can become if the tools are made available to do so. Given the highly patriarchal agrarian culture operating within high income countries, it is not surprising that male migrants are the preferred candidates. Canadian employers and civil servants hold rigid gender ideologies that perceive women as less suitable for farm work (Preibisch and Hermoso Santamaria 2006).

Gender ideologies explain part, but not all, of the scarce presence of women as migrant farm workers in Canada. Historically the importation of racialized male labour was also aimed at maintaining images of migrant workers as temporary, asexual, and alien (Galabuzi 2006). Canadian rural communities remain racially homogeneous places within a nation that continues to hold strong political and cultural attachments to its history as a white settler society (Galabuzi 2006, Sharma 2006). Critical historical analysis of official discourse surrounding the SAWP has revealed racist, negative depictions of Caribbean and Mexican men that legitimized indenturing them to agricultural jobs and denying them the opportunity to apply for permanent settlement (Satzewich 1991, Sharma 2001). Indeed, migrants to Canada enter an ideological context that is by no means neutral, one in which difference based on race and social location within the global political economy plays a central role in organizing inequalities (Sharma 2006). Not surprisingly, growers' efforts to bring migrants into rural communities have been met with considerable resistance by local residents. In order to mitigate xenophobic opposition that could ignite political debate around guest worker programs, employers have tried to mute the visibility of their migrant employers, such as concealing their housing. They have also attempted to constitute the black and brown bodies of migrant men as less dangerous by limiting their sexuality by restricting their mobility or recruiting married applicants of a single sex.

Efforts to desexualize migrants have been complicated by a number of processes, including the rising recruitment of women throughout the 1990s as certain labour-intensive industries began achieving dynamic growth. Although today women constitute some 2 per cent of the migrant labour force, their numbers show modest increases. The incorporation of women into select commodities and particular stages of production reveals deeply gendered processes. In 2002, for example, close to half of all migrant women employed were involved in fruit production, with greenhouse horticulture and floriculture as the next main destinations. This contrasts to the SAWP overall, in which tobacco, tomato, and fruit production are the top employers (Weston and Scarpa de Masellis 2003). Our ethnographic research suggests that women are performing particular tasks within these commodity sectors, such as packing fruit, potting seedlings, and cutting flowers.

Ironically, the same gendered ideologies that pose obstacles to women's employment in agriculture have become the grounds for their recruitment (Preibisch and Hermoso Santamaria 2006). Employers and civil servants claim that women possess a finer, lighter touch and are more patient, responsible, and productive than men. Men's and women's suitability for farm work in Canada is also highly racialized (Preibisch and Binford 2007). This is expressed, for example, in employers' perceptions regarding the appropriateness of workers for tasks according to nationality and racialized perceptions regarding work ethic. The circulation of these gendered, racialized discourses has a number of functions. For one, they serve to characterize people from the global South as naturally suited to agricultural work and less deserving of the employment options, working conditions, and legal entitlements Canadian citizens enjoy. A second major function is their role in constituting the perceived ideal workers for production. As Salzinger (2003: 21) argues, 'femininity matters in global production not because it accurately describes a set of exploitable traits, but because it functions as a constitutive discourse which creates exploitable subjects'. When employers use racialized and gendered discourses to compare and contrast workers in terms of who is better at a particular task, harder working, or less problematic, they are communicating what they see as desirable traits for workers. As migrants are well aware, those who conform to this fantasy will be requested for the following season. The role of gender, race, and citizenship in organizing work is thus reflected not only in the lack of women's participation as migrant farm workers overall but in their specific insertion in production, the gender ideologies surrounding it, and shop-floor practices, an area to which we now turn.

Gendered, Racialized Employment Relations

Farm work is among the most gendered and racialized occupations in Canada, highly segregated by sex, race, age, and citizenship. Within the workplaces hiring a substantial amount of paid agricultural labour, the general contours of a social hierarchy can be discerned. At the apex are the best jobs, fewer in number and characterized as requiring lower physical exertion, monotony, or contact with dirt or the elements. Included here are positions involving control over machinery or personnel. At the base of the hierarchy are the famous '3-D jobs': dirty, difficult, and often dangerous. Jobs at the apex are often always assigned to white men and women, including members of the grower's family, even children. Local whites are near the top. Descending down the hierarchy, the next positions are filled by Canadian citizens or permanent residents who belong to racialized groups. Many of these workers can only take up flexible and seasonal work due to their reproductive responsibilities (mothers) or productive engagement elsewhere (students, part-time workers). Others include those who cannot find or retain employment in better paying, higher status jobs (elders or immigrants lacking English, for instance). Temporary visa migrants are located at the bottom rung of the social hierarchy, followed only by migrants without status, if present.

Temporary migration programs further entrench existing structures of labour segmentation by allowing employers to formally choose staff on the basis of sex and nationality (often a euphemism for race). They also enable and legitimize a range of employment practices that hinge on differentiating workers on the basis of gendered and racialized criteria. Most immediately, temporary migration programs enhance employers' ability to segment their production processes along linguistic and cultural lines. In those workplaces where employers have recruited women to work alongside men, for example, a trend has emerged to segment the sexes by country. In the fruit industry, for example, growers will hire Mexican women for the packinghouse of an orchard picked by Jamaican men, according to a litany of gendered and racialized essentialisms. Employers and civil servants frankly acknowledge that this hiring strategy is intended to create barriers within the workplace that will dampen the potential for greater socializing that is seen to accompany a mixed sex environment and reduce the formation of intimate relationships that could create new social commitments (Preibisch and Hermoso Santamaria 2006). The fact that migrants have fewer social obligations than local workers is precisely one of the reasons why they are valued by their employers (Basok 2002, Preibisch 2004). As mentioned earlier, employers also seek to reduce the extent to which rural communities perceive migrants in their full humanity as sexual beings, including as the potential partners of white women.

Temporary migration programs, moreover, allow employers to hire a range of workplace subjects that can be compared, contrasted, and ultimately placed in opposition to one another. The hiring of different groups of workers and their assignment to particular tasks, along with their accompanying discursive justifications (Jamaicans as stronger, Mexicans as more docile, women as patient, men as less complicated) send messages to workers that communicate 'specific understandings of who they are and what the work requires' (Salzinger 2003:20). One medium that communicates these discourses to workers is the numbers of workers hired (or not) year after year, a process that we describe in greater detail below. They are also communicated through praise or censure of performance and behaviour. Our respondents indicated that their employers commend them for their perceived greater compliance, attention to detail, and greater dexterity. The reinforcement of gendered subjectivities transcends the workplace and invades migrants' quarters, where women are praised for keeping tidier accommodations.

This register of positive feminine traits is also accompanied by negative ones. The most common negative stereotype of women that is communicated by employers and civil servants, and internalized by migrants, is that women are 'problematic', a broad label that encapsulates a range of behaviours considered uniquely feminine. Being problematic, for instance, often refers to a perceived female propensity to engage in dramatic infighting that affects the work environment or impinges on managers' time by forcing them to act as mediators. Being problematic also includes women's capacity to reproduce. Employers see women who arrive pregnant or become pregnant in Canada as a major inconvenience, and pregnancy is (unofficial) grounds for repatriation. When complications alerted one respondent's employer of her pregnancy, she was berated and deported immediately. Employers and migrant sending states attempt to avoid these scenarios through such measures as pre-departure pregnancy tests, but because the tests do not occur at the airport (as they do for Caribbean women), some women are pregnant during their work periods in Canada. Those who want to continue working, or at a minimum remain in the SAWP, go to great lengths to conceal their pregnancies, continuing to undertake arduous tasks and refraining from seeking medical care that could draw attention.

Being 'problematic' also refers to women who assert themselves by reaching out to advocacy organizations or Mexican authorities to solve their personal or workplace concerns, including the exercise of their legal rights and entitlements. In general, the migrants who do so, or who even raise complaints, risk immediate repatriation (Colby 1997, Basok 2002, Verma 2003, Binford 2004, Preibisch 2004). Employers' ability to select their workers on the basis of nationality and sex grants them immeasurable power to discipline the workforce by, for instance, firing a group of workers and hiring workers of another nationality when they are displeased with workers' behaviour or performance (Preibisch and Binford 2007). In one case, a farm only hired Mexicans until a wildcat strike by the men led to their immediate deportation and replacement with Jamaicans. As Gloria recounted:

> Imagine, the [Mexican] men were kicked out from one day to the next and that night the Jamaicans arrived. ... I think that owing to the strike the men held, the company wanted to do a test. Now that they've seen that, more or less, the Jamaicans have worked out well, there are more.

The practice of switching migrant sending countries, or threatening to do so, disciplines both workers and their states, whose economies rely heavily on remittance income (Preibisch and Binford 2007). Predictably, migrants mistrust the Mexican government agents in Canada charged with representing workers, given that their loyalty is compromised by their simultaneous duty to increase their country's share of job placements on farms and ensure the continued flow of remittances home.

The timbre of the disciplinary mechanisms that communicate to migrants their precarious hold on their jobs in Canada is amplified among women. The scarce number of female positions, a ratio of one position for women to 43 for men, serves as a constant reminder to women of their disposability. Rural women's subordination within their home countries and within the global economy means that they value these select positions greatly, most likely more than men do. Our interviewees repeatedly emphasized the challenges involved in acquiring their transnational livelihoods and stressed the importance of protecting their

Canadian jobs that maintain their families and allow them to access property, housing, and investment capital, endowments formerly far from their reach. Most interviewees had similar work trajectories prior to migrating internationally, including low paying industrial homework, seasonal farm work, domestic labour, petty commerce, or factory jobs. As women, particularly as rural women, their employment options were severely limited. For single mothers, their situation was further aggravated by the lone headship of their households. Indeed, a complex web of intersecting social relations based on race, class, gender and neocolonialism combine to position migrant single mothers among the most precarious workers within the Canadian labour market.

In protecting their jobs, migrant women constantly feel the need to prove themselves as able workers. This is reflected in Gloria's account of how Mexicans were replaced by Jamaicans at her workplace:

> Each year there were 60 [Mexican] women. Then they reduced the numbers by five less year by year. Now there are only 15 of us for picking, but we finish the work in the same amount of time as before. They even rated our work with scanners and punch cards which counted each row. For us it was terrible pressure. Even a supervisor inquired, "Why are you rushing like mad?" I think that we've fought hard among us to be the fastest, to produce more work. We've given so much of ourselves, and it is a form of protecting our work.

Likewise, Jessica (born 1980) claimed:

> We work harder than men; you can tell. Sometimes even our male co-workers tell us the same: "You women are harder workers than us." We see some of the men weeding and then they sit down and they start to talk, and we don't. We may talk but we do not stop working.

Women not only test their physical capacities to the limit in order to protect their jobs, but they also submit to substandard housing, poor working conditions, and a range of employer demands. Some will forego medical attention if they perceive it might jeopardize their jobs. It is likely that some women have had to tolerate workplace sexual harassment, as women have been repatriated for refusing to have sex with their employers. Women justify their compliance with workplace indignities first and foremost by citing their responsibilities to their children and families. For example, Jessica stated that: 'sometimes tiredness does not matter but rather money for the family so that they can be taken care of.' Indeed, it is likely that women's commitment to their gendered responsibilities constitutes them as highly valuable workers.

Disturbingly, women appeared to identify their precarious status as self-created. To illustrate, Lupe (born 1959) declared: 'We women are killing this source of employment due to the problems that there are in all the houses.' Another respondent claimed: 'We did damage to ourselves on our own, creating little problems and everything.' Further, Shadira (born 1974) explained: 'If we do not protect our place, they will divide half Mexicans and half Jamaicans in some of the farms.' Women's observations of continual labour replacement along gendered and racial lines make employers' verbal threats to enact such replacements almost superfluous.

As we have argued, the operation of temporary migration programs in Canada serves to create deeply divisive workforces in which employees compete with one another to hold on to their jobs. It is within this context that employer allegations that women are more problematic must be read. Whether or not women's perceived tendency to compete with one another is carried from Mexico as part of their psychological baggage allowance, it is certainly cultivated within Canada. More often than not, women are forced to live in tight quarters, sharing rooms with strangers owing to the heavy rotation of women from year to year on any given farm. Since the quality of migrant housing is very weakly regulated, it ranges from very good to very poor, with most somewhere in the middle. Overcrowded, underserviced accommodations exacerbate tensions. Racial divisions are aggravated by some employers who physically separate workers from different countries, as is the case on one farm where bathrooms, bedrooms, and kitchens were divided with signs labelled 'Mexicans' and 'Jamaicans'. Competition between women is also heightened in the male dominated migrant community in which women are highly sexualized. This further filters into the workplace when employers and supervisors enter into sexual relationships with migrant women. At times, women in these situations use their power over others; at the minimum, these arrangements intensify the existing tensions between women.

Women also face greater restrictions on their mobility. Women's movements and sexuality are highly constrained by practices restricting women to the farm property, prohibiting or curtailing visitors of the opposite sex, and establishing curfews (Preibisch and Hermoso Santamaria 2006, Becerril 2007). On some farms, women are under heavy surveillance, either by the employer and his or her kin on smaller farms or by supervisors and even security guards on larger operations. In one case, a sign dictated the times when visitors were allowed and ominously warned that a private security company was reporting violations. Another farm posted a notice warning that men were not allowed on the property. Control exercised through restrictive farm rules exacerbates tensions among migrant women housed in enclosed quarters on isolated farms without breaks from the monotony of their daily routines.

Migrant sending governments have been willing participants in the policing of women's movements and their sexuality. At one time, Mexico's pre-departure orientation for women involved warnings not to become involved with men and even required women to sign waivers signalling their agreement. The division fostered between women has resulted in some migrant women actively participating in these practices of labour control, including enforcing employer imposed curfews, passing information to the boss, or reporting women who form sexual relationships with men or, conversely, those who transgress heterosexual norms. As this discussion highlights, migrant women's position at the bottom of the social hierarchy within their Canadian workplaces and the subordination they face within their home countries as a result of their subject positions as rurally located, poor women constitute them as particularly vulnerable recipients of this peculiar panoply of labour control, with considerable consequences for their lives.

Conclusion

The global restructuring of agriculture is dramatically disrupting and realigning how women and men around the world relate to agriculture. Those seeking to understand the new social relations of agriculture within high income countries must look beyond the family farm if they are to comprehend fully the range and scale of changes underway. Increasingly, this involves turning our attention to rising international migration from the global South, an exercise that demands further interrogation of the factors that link agriculture's multiple sites of production, including models of economic growth that promote the redundancy of small-scale agriculture, favour export led strategies, and create highly competitive agrifood markets. In the case of Canada, temporary migration programs have played an essential role in allowing labour-intensive agricultural operations to withstand and even thrive under the pressures of recent global restructuring. While these programs are lauded for their role in meeting employers' labour demands, they do much more than that. They grant employers access to a highly vulnerable group of workers who, once in Canada, are positioned disadvantageously within the labour market through a range of social and political disentitlements. Furthermore, they allow employers to further entrench existing structures of labour segmentation and facilitate the implementation of a particular set of employment practices that would not be possible with only a domestic workforce.

As we have shown, the systems of labour control and forms of work organization made possible through these programs rely on multiple, reinforcing and contextual systems of oppression, particularly the power relations based on gender, race, and class, among others. These strategies have yielded a degree of success, infusing greater flexibility into the agricultural labour market. While the focus of this chapter was to document and analyse these processes, it would be disingenuous to ignore how these do not proceed smoothly, that is, how points of resistance emerge. Indeed, migrant women find ways to assert their agency in multiple ways in order to contest their terms of employment and social location within Canadian society. Despite attempts to prevent women from forming social relationships with one another or the broader community, for instance, they overcome linguistic, cultural, and racial barriers to become friends, lovers, and in some cases, parents. Despite efforts to divide women, they demonstrate remarkable solidarity with one another by, for example, helping hide a co-worker's pregnancy. Despite legal impediments to their permanent immigration, they seek ways to negotiate Canadian citizenship or to bring their children to visit them in Canada. Despite controls on their bodies and their sexuality, they actively contest efforts to dehumanize them by leaving farms on weekends to attend dances, by forming intimate relationships, or by breaking curfew. Finally, despite attempts to keep these rural women from making change, they speak to researchers and activists so their stories of struggle are not silenced. These forms of contestation, a topic for a future paper, are indeed the most remarkable facets of international labour migration to Canadian agriculture.

Acknowledgments

We are grateful to the Social Sciences and Humanities Research Council of Canada for funding through Rural Women Making Change and a Standard Research Grant. We thank Dr. Belinda Leach, Dr. Barbara Pini and two anonymous reviewers for their insightful comments on earlier drafts. Finally, we thank the Mexican women who so generously gave of their time to bravely share their experiences and insights with us.

References

Arat-Koç, S. 1989. In the privacy of our own home: foreign domestic workers as a solution to the crisis in the domestic sphere in Canada. *Studies in Political Economy*, 28(Spring), 33–58.

Arizpe, L. 1988. La participación de la mujer en el empleo y el desarrollo rural en América Latina y el Caribe: trabajo de síntesis [The participation of women in employment and rural development in Latin America and the Caribbean: a synthesis], in *Las Mujeres en el Campo: Memoria de la Primera Reunión Nacional de Investigación Sobre Mujeres Campesinas en México* [Women in the countryside: proceedings of the first national research meeting on peasant women in Mexico], edited by J. Aranda Bezaury. Oaxaca City: Instituto de Investigaciones Sociológicas de la Universidad Autónoma Benito Juárez de Oaxaca, 25–62.

Barndt, D. 2007. *Tangled Routes: Women, Work, and Globalization on the Tomato Trail*. 2nd Edition. Oxford: Rowman and Littlefield.

Barrientos, S. and Dolan, C. 2007. Transformation of global food: opportunities and challenges for fair and ethical trade, in *Ethical Sourcing in the Global Food System*, edited by S. Barrientos and C. Dolan. London: Earthscan, 1–34.

Barrientos, S. Kritzinger, A. Opondo, M. and Smith, S. 2005. Gender, work and vulnerability in African horticulture. *IDS Bulletin*, 36(2), 74–79.

Barrón Pérez, M.A. 2006. Jornada de trabajo, ahorro, y remesas de los jornaleros agrícolas migrantes en las diversas regiones hortícolas de México, Canadá y España [Workday, savings, and remittances of migrant farmworkers in diverse horticultural regions of Mexico, Canada, and Spain]. *Análisis Económico* [Economic analysis], 21(46), 95–116.

Basok, T. 2002. *Tortillas and Tomatoes: Transmigrant Mexican Harvesters in Canada.* Montreal: McGill-Queens University Press.

Becerril, O. 2007. Transnational work and the gendered politics of labour: a study of male and female mexican migrant farm workers in Canada, in *Organizing the Transnational: Labour, Politics, and Social Change,* edited by L. Goldring and S. Krishnamurti. Vancouver: University of British Columbia Press, 157–71.

Binford, A. 2002. Social and economic contradictions of rural migrant contract labor between Tlaxcala, Mexico and Canada. *Culture and Agriculture,* 24(2), 1–19.

Binford, A. 2004. Contract labour in Canada and the United States: a critical appreciation of Tanya Basok's Tortillas and Tomatoes: Transmigrant Mexican Harvesters in Canada. *Canadian Journal of Latin American and Caribbean Studies/Revue canadienne des études latino-américaines et caraïbes,* 29(57–58), 289–308.

Bolaria, B.S. 1992. Farm labour, work conditions, and health risks, in *Rural Sociology in Canada,* edited by D.A. Hay and G.S. Basran. Toronto: Oxford University Press, 228–45.

Brandth, B. 2002. Gender identity in European family farming: a literature review. *Sociologia Ruralis,* 42(3), 181–200.

Brandth, B. 2006. Agricultural body-building: incorporations of gender, body and work. *Journal of Rural Studies,* 22(1), 17–27.

Castañeda, X. and Zavella, P. 2007. Changing constructions of sexuality and risk: migrant Mexican women farmworkers in California, in *Women and Migration in the US-Mexico Borderlands: A Reader,* edited by D.A. Segura and P. Zavella. Durham: Duke University Press, 249–68.

Castles, S. 2006. Guestworkers in Europe: a resurrection? *International Migration Review,* 40(4), 741–66.

Chang, G. 2000. *Disposable Domestics: Immigrant Women Workers in the Global Economy.* Cambridge, Massachusetts: South End.

Colby, C. 1997. *From Oaxaca to Ontario: Mexican Contract Labor in Canada and the Impact at Home.* Davis: California Institute for Rural Studies.

Comisión de Derechos Humanos del Distrito Federal. 2008. Informe Anual 2007 Volumen II: Situación de los Derechos Humanos de las Mujeres en el Distrito Federal. Report. Mexico City: Comisión de Derechos Humanos del Distrito Federal.

Curran, S.R. Shafer, S. Donato, K.M. and Garip, F. 2006. Mapping gender and migration in sociological scholarship: is it segregation or integration? *International Migration Review,* 40(1), 199–223.

Dolan, C. 2005. Benevolent intent? The development encounter in Kenya's horticulture industry. *Journal of Asian and African Studies,* 40(6), 411–37.

Erel, U. Morokvasic-Müller, M. and Shinozaki, K. 2003. Introduction. Bringing gender into migration, in *Crossing Borders and Shifting Boundaries, Volume*

1: Gender on the Move, edited by M. Morokvasic-Müller, U. Erel and K. Shinozaki. Opladen, Germany: Leske and Budrich, 9–22.

Findeis, J. 2002. Hired farm labour adjustments and constraints, in *The Dynamics of Hired Farm Labour: Constraints and Community Responses*, edited by J. Findeis et al. Wallingford: CABI, 3–14.

Galabuzi, G. 2006. *Canada's Economic Apartheid: The Social Exclusion of Racialized Groups in the New Century.* Toronto: Canadian Scholars' Press.

Griffith, D. 2006. *American Guestworkers: Jamaicans and Mexicans in the US Labor Market.* University Park: Pennsylvania State University Press.

Hondagneu-Sotelo, P. 1994. *Gendered Transitions: Mexican Experiences of Immigration.* Berkeley: University of California Press.

Hondagneu-Sotelo, P. 1997. Affluent players in the informal economy: employers of paid domestic workers. *International Journal of Sociology and Social Policy*, 17(3–4), 131–59.

Hondagneu-Sotelo, P. 2003. Gender and immigration: a retrospective and introduction, in *Gender and US Immigration: Contemporary Trends*, edited by P. Hondagneu-Sotelo. Berkeley: University of California Press, 3–19.

Hondagneu-Sotelo, P. and Avila, E. 2003. 'I'm here, but I'm there': the meanings of Latina transnational motherhood, in *Gender and US Immigration: Contemporary Trends*, edited by P. Hondagneu-Sotelo. Berkeley: University of California Press, 317–40.

Human Resources and Skills Development Canada. 2008. *The Temporary Foreign Worker Program: Recent Figures and Policy Development.* Paper to the Tenth National Metropolis Conference: Expanding the Debate: Multiple Perspectives on Immigration to Canada, Halifax, 5 April 2008.

Human Resources and Skills Development Canada. 2010. *Temporary Foreign Worker Program Labour Market Opinion (LMO) Statistics: Annual Statistics 2006–2009.* [Online: Human Resources and Skills Development Canada]. Available at: http://www.rhdcc-hrsdc.gc.ca/eng/workplaceskills/foreign_workers/stats/annual/table10a.shtml. [accessed: 6 September 2010]

Human Resources and Skills Development Canada. No date. *Unpublished Data Request for Number of Confirmed Temporary Foreign Worker (TFW) Positions Under the Seasonal Agricultural Workers Program (SAWP) and NOC C and D, by Specific Employer Industry Sectors and Province / Territory.* Integrity and Horizontal Coordination Division, Temporary Foreign Worker Program. Gatineau: Human Resources and Social Development Canada [Received 26 March 2009].

Kanaiaupuni, S.M. 2000. Reframing the migration question: an analysis of men, women, and gender in Mexico. *Social Forces*, 78(4), 1311–348.

Lara Flores, S. 1995. *Jornaleras, Temporeras y Bóias-frias: El Rostro Femenino del Mercado de Trabajo Rural en América Latina.* [Farmworkers, Temporary Workers, and Day Laborers: The Feminine Face of Rural Labor Markets in Latin America]. Caracas: Editorial Nueva Sociedad.

Lara Flores, S. 1998. *Nuevas Experiencias Productivas y Nuevas Formas de Organización Flexible del Trabajo en la Agricultura Mexicana.* [New Productive Experiences and Forms of Flexible Work Organization in Mexican Agriculture]. Mexico City: Juan Pablos Editor.

Leckie, G. 1993. Female farmers in Canada and the gender relations of a restructuring agricultural system. *The Canadian Geographer/Le géographe canadien*, 37(3), 212–30.

Leckie, G. 1996. 'They never trusted me to drive': farm girls and the gender relations of agricultural information transfer. *Gender, Place and Culture*, 3(3), 309–25.

Macklin, A. 1994. On the inside looking in: foreign domestic workers in Canada, in *Maid in the Market: Women's Paid Domestic Labour*, edited by W. Giles and S. Arat-Koç. Halifax: Fernwood, 13–39.

Martin, P. 2003. *Promise Unfulfilled: Unions, Immigration, and the Farm Workers*. Ithaca: Cornell University Press.

Mines, R. 2002. Family settlement and technological change in labor-intensive US Agriculture, in *The Dynamics of Hired Farm Labour: Constraints and Community Responses*, edited by J. Findeis et al. Wallingford: CABI, 41–53.

Oishi, N. 2005. *Women in Motion: Globalization, State Policies, and Labor Migration in Asia.* Stanford: Stanford University Press.

Parr, J. 1985. Hired men: Ontario agricultural wage labour in historical perspective. *Labour/Le Travail*, 15(Spring), 91–103.

Parreñas, R. 2001. *Servants of Globalization: Women, Migration, and Domestic Work.* Stanford: Stanford University Press.

Parreñas, R. 2005. *Children of Global Migration: Transnational Families and Gendered Woes.* Stanford: Stanford University Press.

Pessar, P. 2003. Engendering migration studies: the case of new immigrants in the United States, in *Gender and US Immigration: Contemporary Trends*, edited by P. Hondagneu-Sotelo. Berkeley: University of California Press, 20–42.

Pratt, G. 1999. Is this Canada? Domestic workers' experiences in Vancouver, BC, in *Gender, Migration and Domestic Service*, edited by J. Momsen. London: Routledge, 23–42.

Preibisch, K. 2004. Migrant agricultural workers and processes of social inclusion in rural Canada: encuentros and desencuentros. *Canadian Journal of Latin American and Caribbean Studies/Revue canadienne des études latino-américaines et caraïbes*, 29(57–8), 203–39.

Preibisch, K. 2005. Gender transformative odysseys: tracing the experiences of transnational migrant women in rural Canada. *Canadian Woman Studies/Les cahiers de la femme*, 24(4), 91–7.

Preibisch, K. 2007. Local produce, foreign labor: labor mobility programs and global trade competitiveness in Canada. *Rural Sociology*, 72(3), 418–49.

Preibisch, K. and Binford, L. 2007. Interrogating racialized global labour supply: an exploration of the racial/national replacement of foreign agricultural workers in Canada. *Canadian Review of Sociology and Anthropology/Revue Canadienne de Sociologie et d'Anthropologie*, 44(1), 5–36.

Preibisch, K. and Hermoso Santamaría, L. 2006. Engendering labour migration: the case of foreign workers in Canadian agriculture, in *Women, Migration and Citizenship: Making Local, National and Transnational Connections*, edited by E. Tastsoglou and A. Dobrowolsky. Aldershot: Ashgate, 107–30.

Preibisch, K. and Encalada Grez, E. 2010. The other side of *el Otro Lado*: Mexican migrant women and labor flexibility in Canadian agriculture. Special Issue on Women in Agriculture, *Signs: Journal of Women in Culture and Society*, 35(2), 289–316.

Raynolds, L. 2002. Wages for wives: renegotiating gender and production relations in contract farming in the Dominican Republic. *World Development*, 30(5), 783–98.

Sachs, C. 1991. Women's work and food: a comparative perspective. *Journal of Rural Studies*, 7(1–2), 49–55.

Salzinger, L. 2003. *Genders in Production: Making Workers in Mexico's Global Factories*. Berkeley: University of California Press.

Sassen, S. 2000. Women's burden: counter-geographies of globalization and the feminization of survival. *Journal of International Affairs*, 53(2), 503–24.

Satzewich, V. 1991. *Racism and the Incorporation of Foreign Labour: Farm Labour Migration to Canada since 1945*. London: Routledge.

Saugeres, L. 2002. 'She's not really a woman, she's half a man': gendered discourses of embodiment in a French farming community. *Women's Studies International Forum*, 25(6), 641–50.

Sharma, N. 2001. On being *not* Canadian: the social organization of 'migrant workers' in Canada. *The Canadian Review of Sociology and Anthropology/ Revue Canadienne de Sociologie et d'Anthropologie*, 38(4), 415–39.

Sharma, N. 2006. *Home Economics: Nationalism and the Making of 'Migrant Workers' in Canada*. Toronto: University of Toronto Press.

Smart, J. 1997. Borrowed men on borrowed time: globalization, labour migration and local economies in Alberta. *Canadian Journal of Regional Science/Revue canadienne des sciences régionales*, 20(12), 141–60.

Smith, S. and Dolan, C. 2006. Transformation of global food: opportunities and challenges for fair and ethical trade, in *Ethical Sourcing in the Global Food System*, edited by S. Barrientos and C. Dolan. London: Earthscan, 79–96.

Standing, G. 1999. Global feminization through flexible labor: a theme revisited. *World Development*, 27(3), 583–602.

Stasiulis, D. and Bakan, A. 2003. *Negotiating Citizenship: Migrant Women in Canada and the Global System*. New York: Palgrave Macmillan.

Stiell, B. and England, K. 1997. Domestic distinctions: constructing difference among paid domestic workers in Toronto. *Gender, Place and Culture*, 4(3), 339–59.

Van Hightower, N., Gorton, J. and DeMoss, C. 2000. Predictive models of domestic violence and fear of intimate partners among migrant and seasonal farm worker women. *Journal of Family Violence*, 15(2), 137–54.

Verma, V. 2003. *Canadian Seasonal Agricultural Workers Program Regulatory and Policy Framework, Farm Industry-Level Employment Practices and the Potential Role of Unions*. Ottawa: The North-South Institute/L'Institut Nord-Sud.

Villarejo, D. 2003. The health of US hired farm workers. *Annual Review of Public Health*, 24, 175–93.

Walker, R. 2004. *The Conquest of Bread: 150 Years of Agribusiness in California*. New York: New Press.

Wall, E. 1992. Personal labour relations and ethnicity in Ontario Agriculture, in *Deconstructing a Nation: Immigration, Multiculturalism and Racism in '90s Canada*, edited by V. Satzewich. Halifax: Fernwood, 261–75.

Weston, A. and Scarpa de Masellis, L. 2003. *Hemispheric Integration and Trade Relations: Implications for Canada's Seasonal Agricultural Workers Program*. Ottawa: The North-South Institute/L'Institut Nord-Sud.

Whatmore, S. 1991a. *Farming Women: Gender, Work and Family Enterprise*. London: Macmillan.

Whatmore, S. 1991b. Life cycle or patriarchy? Gender divisions in family farming. *Journal of Rural Studies*, 7(1–2), 71–6.

Winson, A. 1993. *The Intimate Commodity: Food and the Development of the Agro-Industrial Complex in Canada*. Toronto: Garamond.

Chapter 6

Configurations of Gender, Class and Rurality in Resource Affected Rural Australia

Barbara Pini and Robyn Mayes

Historically, class has been a key concern in studies of resource affected communities (e.g., Williamson 1982, Warwick and Littlejohn 1992). While work continues, particularly in Britain, today it reflects the rationalization of the British mining sector, and thus focuses largely on mining heritage (e.g., Strangleman et al. 1999, Dicks 2008). In contrast, this chapter examines class relations as manifest in a contemporary setting in rural Australia. This site, the Ravensthorpe Shire in the south west of Western Australia, relied largely on agriculture until 2004 when BHP Billiton commenced construction of a nickel mine in the area. This affected the entire Shire as well as the two rural communities of Ravensthorpe and Hopetoun. The mine, which was officially opened in June 2008, is one of a large number of new mineral and energy developments being established in non-metropolitan areas of the country as high international demand for resources fuels significant growth in the sector. In a single six month period in 2009, for example, 15 major minerals and energy projects were completed across the nation and a further 74 projects were at advanced stages (Australian Bureau of Agricultural Economics 2009). A number of these were, as was the case in Ravensthorpe, in what had been traditionally agricultural communities.

Drawing on interviews with 18 women associated either with farming or mining we explore how the contours of class are given expression in a shifting and reconfigured rural landscape. As such the chapter engages with the body of literature that has considered rural restructuring and class. This is a rich literature which dates back to Pahl's (1965a, 1965b) classic work on the movement of middle-class commuters into the rural urban fringes of northern London. However, it is also a literature which has been subject to criticisms which are of key relevance to our analysis. The first of these is that it has been gender blind. This is an issue addressed explicitly by Agg and Phillips (1998) who assert that much scholarship on the subject of rural change and class has focused at the level of the (male) individual and ignored the domestic economy. They demonstrate the importance of a gender analysis in drawing on studies of changing British rural communities which reveal that, compared with rural men, rural women are disadvantaged in the labour market in terms of promotion possibilities, work conditions and remuneration and also undertake the majority of unpaid household labour. The movement of middle-class people into rural areas may thus be experienced very differently according to one's gender. A second concern raised about research on rurality, change and class and enumerated by Cloke and Thrift (1987, 1990), is that there has been a tendency to frame work in terms of an essentialized, singular external middle class imposing itself onto a similarly configured native working class. This has meant that attention to conflict within class fractions and the dynamism of class has been obscured. A related and final concern with the literature is that often class has been understood in fixed and predetermined ways. Phillips (1998a: 412) labels this a 'modernist legislative approach' and contrasts it with an 'interpretive' focus which he uses to interrogate data from studies of social change in rural communities in the United Kingdom. Phillips' (1998b) attention to affect and morality in ascriptions of class situate his work within the corpus of literature referred to as the 'culturalization of class' (Hebson 2009: 28), 'culturalist class analysis' (Bottero 2004: 988), or 'new cultural analyses of social class' (Reay 2006a: 289) which, by attending to the symbolic and affective in class production and reproduction, provides a rich addendum to a discussion of class focused solely on occupation.

This chapter attends to the criticisms that have been levelled at the literature on rurality, change and class by examining the influence of gender in changing class compositions and identities in the rural and exploring differences within class groups and indeed shifts across class categories. In addition, we engage with the literature on the cultural dimensions of class thus moving beyond an understanding of class as a 'system into which we are slotted' and instead as something that is 'done' (Lawler 2005: 804). We draw on the vibrant and growing body of work which has adopted this theoretical lens to examine class as lived and embodied and related to everyday practices and discourses (e.g., Lawler 1999, Reay 2003, 2005, 2006a, 2006b, Savage, Bagnall and Longhurst 2001, Savage 2000; Skeggs 1997, 2004). In exploring the 'psychic landscape of social class' (Reay 2005: 911) we give particular attention to 'lay normativity, especially morality' (Sayer 2005: 948) as it is embedded in the descriptions, assumptions and beliefs of interview participants.

The chapter begins with an overview of the literature on gender and class in resource affected communities as well as an outline of the methodology informing the study. The data are then presented in three sections. The first section traverses territory that has dominated previous explorations of class in mining environments, that is, the associations between management and employees working for BHP Billiton. Following this we examine the emergence of a relatively new category of employee on mine sites in Australia, that is, 'the contractor', and delineate the classed hierarchies which inform how they are represented in the community. In the final section we describe how the groups 'mining women' and 'farming women' are characterized by each other highlighting the way in which these are mediated by beliefs, norms and practices about gender and rurality.

Gender, Class and Resource Affected Rural Communities

The limited contemporary attention that has been afforded to class is a theme taken up by Panelli (2006: 76) in reviewing the literature on studies of rural communities, and particularly gendered studies of rural communities. At the same time she notes important exceptions including the classic Australian works by Poiner (1990) and Dempsey (1992) which explored the ways in which gender relations are manifest in the labour market, voluntary work, community and leisure activities of rural men and women. What is particularly critical about these early studies is that they drew attention to the heterogeneity of the categories 'rural man' and 'rural woman'.

Informing the studies of both Poiner (1990) and Dempsey (1992) was earlier seminal sociological research by Claire Williams (1981). Drawing on data from case studies of two open cut coal mines in central Queensland between 1974 and 1975 Williams (1981) explored gender and class inequities. She claimed that while men struggled with class inequality as manifest, for example, in a lack of control over their jobs, women were equally struggling with gender inequities in their marital relationship as they typically undertake all domestic labour and have limited opportunities for paid work. Following Williams' (1981) work was another study of central Queensland coal communities by Gibson-Graham (1991, 1994, 1996) which focused on the union movement, industrial strategy and gender. The research centres on predominantly working-class spouses variously termed 'mining wife', 'mining town women' and 'miner's wife' and whom Gibson-Graham (1992) describe as living a 'feudal' existence at the intersections between patriarchy and capitalism. Also focusing on 'mining wives', but those from a middle-class background is Rhodes' (2005) *Two for the Price of One: the Lives of Mining Wives* which documents the experiences of Australian mining women across three generations: pre-1960, 1960–1985 and 1985–2000. In moving across these generations she tracks the relationships between broader societal and industry changes and the expectations for and of these middle-class mining wives. For example, she describes the ways in which generations one and two were more accepting of the dominant 'good wife' discourse that shaped and validated their contributions, whereas generation three emerges as seeking to variously renegotiate this discourse. Collectively, the three studies demonstrate both the difference that class makes for women in resource affected communities, as well as the salience of gender in such communities, in terms of access to employment (and by association, housing), and responsibility for domestic labour.

The noteworthy Australian studies by the above writers are part of a larger international literature on women and mining in industrialized economies (e.g., Shaw and Mundy 2005, Hall 2004, Gier-Viskovatoff and Porter 1998). As with the Australian work this broader literature has tended to focus on class as lived and experienced by those who inhabit the broad identity 'mining women' and thus not attended to how interactions with women not involved in the resource sector may also be shaped by class. In contrast, this chapter explores not only the classed relationships between women associated with the mine, but also between mining and farming women. Before undertaking this task we provide a brief outline of the study's methodology.

Methodology

Ravensthorpe Shire in the south west of Western Australia has undergone rapid and profound social upheaval resulting from the arrival of a BHP Billiton nickel mine which commenced construction in 2004 and was officially opened in June 2008.[1] Though the Shire has a long history of mining this project was the first modern, large-scale mine in the area. In May 2008, upwards of 300 employees and their families were residing in the region making Ravensthorpe Shire one of Australia's fastest developing local government areas (Mayes 2007). Consisting of an open cut mine and hydrometallurgical process plant and requiring an operational work force of 650 staff the venture had an expected ore reserve lifespan of 25 years (Mayes 2007).

Data for this chapter were derived from 18 interviews with women in the town undertaken in 2008. No Indigenous people were in the sample which is reflective of the very small Indigenous mine related population residing in the area.[2] The mine boasted a large South African population, who typically congregated in management positions. The General Manager was South African as were five of the eight managerial men in the deputy positions. Two women who had emigrated from South Africa as a result of the Ravensthorpe mine were included in the sample. The remainder were all Australian born.

Of the 18 women four were involved in farming and were long term residents of the district. Ten women were associated with the mine. Of these ten, six were employed at the mine and two of the six in positions of management. Four of the women associated with BHP Billiton had husbands in managerial positions. The four remaining women in the sample had relationships with both mining and farming. In two cases husbands had sought employment at the mine to supplement their agricultural income while their wives took responsibility for the majority of farm labour. The final two cases were women who had been involved in agriculture but then took jobs at the mine. One was separated from her farming husband while the other remained on the farm where her husband continued to work. Two women from the sample were associated with contract labour at the mine through their own employment and/or the employment of their husbands.

Interviews covered a range of questions about community, inclusion, friendship, work and leisure as well as the more specific issue of class. In many respects class

---

1   The mine subsequently closed unexpectedly in January 2009 and reopened again in 2010.

2   According to Australian Bureau of Statistics 2006 Census Data (Australian Bureau of Statistics 2007), the Indigenous population in the region at 1.7 per cent of the total population is lower than the Australian average.

was, a 'slippery' concept in interview narratives with participants demonstrating ambivalence and reticence in relation to the use of the term (Skeggs 1997, 2004). This was most pronounced in discussions about class relationships between BHP Billiton women as the following section explains.

Class Relations Amongst Women Associated with BHP Billiton

There were clear differences in the naming of class between participants. In the main, women associated with BHP Billiton, either through marriage or employment, were the most uncomfortable and ambivalent about class as manifest in relations between general staff and management. For the majority of women in the town connection to the mine was through their husband's own employment. There were few employment opportunities outside of the mine and it, like the majority of others in Australia, was disproportionately staffed by men (Mayes and Pini 2010).

While reluctant to name class relations as important to the contemporary BHP Billiton worksite and the surrounding town, a number of participants shared anecdotes of class based interactions from past experiences in mining communities. The geographic and emotional distance from these past communities and the immediacy and potential longevity of their lives in the current community no doubt mediated these responses. There was also a sense that class may have been more important in the past than it is in contemporary times. One woman recounted the story of being given a t-shirt by a family member which was in support of striking miners and her husband expressed embarrassment when she wore it saying, 'We're past all that now'. This type of conflation of the notion of class with industrial/union action was common in interviews with participants responding to questions about class with claims such as, 'The mine is deunionized'. It may be a further reason why there was such hesitancy in naming class as unions have been strongly maligned in the public sphere in recent years due to the veracity of campaigns against them by large corporations and the former federal conservative Coalition government led by John Howard (Oliver 2008).

Some participants who did refer to there being different 'groups' amongst the BHP Billiton women in the town sought to rationalize and legitimate this referring, for example, to the fact that people tend to mix with whom they have the most in common or with whom they shared shifts. It was also common for Australian born women associated with the mine to respond to a question about class by stating that it was not class which was problematic but racial identity. They labelled the South African women (and men) in a range of negative ways. That is, as spoilt, outspoken, uptight, rude and authoritarian and suggested that this was a result of having lived in a country which has a history of institutionalized and hierarchical racial inequality.

Linda: I know it's horrible. But I think mainly that is … I mean I know a couple of the ladies because my girls go to school with their girls you know … because they are South African, they have a very high-class difference in that way.

Julie: They [South African women] stay in their own little cliques. I mean the girls get invited to all the parties and stuff but the men … their men won't talk to your men sort of thing if you went to a party so much.

Susan: I know for a friend of mine, she related a story to me when they were all out … everyone was out having a breast cancer awareness morning tea or something. And it was this lady and only a couple of others that helped to clean up and she was quite frustrated because she felt that all the South African women were out and not helping and basically treating the women in the kitchen like servants.

The types of characterizations of South Africans asserted in the above quotations relies upon positioning Australians as having an essential core set of traits common to imaginings about the Australian nation. That is, as egalitarian, welcoming, open and antiauthoritarian. Clearly, it also relies upon a fiction of racialized equality in both contemporary and past constructions of the Australian nation. In the women's narratives it provided a widely engaged rationale for explaining any conflict or tension between BHP Billiton managers and employees indicating that it may be more acceptable to claim racial difference than class difference.

Those participants who did ruminate about class in terms of race or friendship groups punctuated their comments with repeated assertions that even if class did exist in the community they were indifferent to it. The following quotations from a senior female manager at the mine and a female mine employee are indicative of this positioning.

Kirsten: You're probably asking the wrong person because it doesn't bother me, I don't pick up on it … But it's again probably, it's not to say it's not happening but in terms of my own personal frame of mind, it's not important who you belong to or you know what your husband would be doing. It's who you are, and it doesn't even matter what you do.

Tammy: I know that certain people will go and have barbeques at people's houses and other ones won't. And certain people will have tea with other people and other ones won't. But again, like I don't care [laughter].

In a further demonstration of the need to distance oneself from class a woman married to a mine employee noted that a good friend who had recently left the community had often remarked on the way class shaped relations between the BHP Billiton women. However, like others, she was less certain about the importance of class as a social category and named class as simply friendships and shared histories. She stated:

> Robina: I don't know. There may be something. Maybe they all [the wives of the managers] go to each other's houses, but maybe because they've got that common bond their husbands are managers. I don't know. I really don't know what it is. I don't know. Sometimes I think there is and then other days ... It depends on my mood. I think, "Oh yeah, they're all sticking together." Then, "No. It's just they've got that thing in common." But yeah there are a few managers wives that hang out together. You know their husbands' positions so you know. But yeah I don't seem to have a real problem with it. I don't know. I always say to my husband, "Don't you ever apply for a manager's job because I'm not management wife material type thing."

> Interviewer: What would management wife material be?

> Robina: I don't know. Like to me they're all educated whereas I never finished Year 12. I didn't even finish Year 11. You know, I only went to Year 10 and I'm not educated at all.

Robina's repeated, 'I don't know' highlights her struggle to name and explain class. She moves back and forth as she seeks to understand class relations in the community. Her response also highlights the way in which women's classed position in the community is closely tied to their husbands. We were told that women married to managerial staff are often introduced through reference to their husbands so their status is clearly signalled. Robina's quotation also resonates with urban based studies of working-class women for whom class is difficult, if not impossible, to leave behind. Many of these studies have been undertaken by feminist scholars and focus on the movement of women from working class to middle class either through marriage and/or education. Collectively, they have demonstrated the way in which class is deeply inscribed on our very beings and often embedded in painful emotions such as shame, relief, anxiety and sadness (e.g., Lawler 1999, Walkerdine, Lucey and Melody 2001, Maguire 2005). Robina's husband had recently returned from an extended and successful stint at an international site for BHP Billiton and had been promoted to take up his position in Ravensthorpe. She was clearly proud of his success (and also clearly contributed to his success through her emotional and domestic labour), but she was anxious about a possible shift to a management position highlighting the powerful but often overlooked 'subjective and positional aspects of economic relations' (Hey 2003: 332).

A similar discomfort about class was enunciated by two BHP Billiton women as they spoke about housing. This was a stark material indicator of one's classed status in the town despite protestations about the lack of importance of one's position, or the position of one's husband, at the mine. While there was not a clearly delineated segregation between employees and managers that characterized mining communities of the past, some areas of the community housed more managers than others. This spatial segregation was noted by participants who employed classed and racialized descriptors such as 'Snob Hill' and 'Captetoun' (a pun on Hopetoun) to describe the preponderance of managers/South Africans in particular areas of the community. Further, while it was the case, as one woman married to a superintendent argued that, 'people were all mixed up', the size of houses and blocks differed between employees and managerial staff. Earlier arrivals to the community had been afforded greater choice in housing and therefore some employees did live in larger houses and on larger blocks, but these were the exceptions to the norm. For two of the women interviewed the location of their houses generated a sense of unease. One commented, 'I wish my house could be picked up and taken to another part of town'. These women explained that their own class backgrounds meant they were uncomfortable in the surrounds of 'the corporates', and living in a space seen by the broader community for the more privileged and elite.

Class Relations and Women Associated with Mine Contract Work

Historical studies of class in mining communities examined class as manifest largely, or solely, in terms of the relationship between employees and management. However, our data reveal that in the contemporary mining sector there are new variegations in the category 'employee' that render such a singular analysis obsolete. In particular, there has been a dramatic increase in the use of temporary and contract labour and outsourcing as part of a broader agenda of deregulating and liberalizing labour relations in the sector (Bowden 2003). When asked about class women associated with mining were most vocal about distinctions and categorizations made about those who were employed by BHP Billiton and those who were contractors. Again, the nomenclature of class was not used; instead participants referred to there being 'divisions' or 'big differences' between BHP Billiton workers and non-BHP Billiton workers. Contract workers, like the managers and employers of BHP Billiton are easily identified by their housing. They are not entitled to the BHP Billiton company housing, and as a result of significant shortages in accommodation as well as exorbitant rental costs, many lived in temporary lodgings such as caravans and demountables in 'camps' surrounding the town. One female mine worker we interviewed who, along with her husband, contracted to BHP Billiton explained:

> Libby: If you work for BHP then they give you housing and they give you this and they give you that. When we arrived housing was quite tight and contractors were living in really crappy houses and the rents were like $400 to $600 a week. And now they're probably double that you know. We knew some drillers … it was a six man crew and they were living in a caravan for two weeks on.

This woman considered herself 'extremely lucky' as she had been able to obtain a rental property to house herself, husband and two children, but it was of a much poorer quality and condition than those allocated to BHP Billiton staff at a subsidized cost. Along with a second woman we interviewed whose husband was a contractor, there were other ways in which her contract status inflected daily life. Work related functions and communication and information channels for example, are typically reserved for BHP Billiton staff. Most pointedly, when the company hosted a weekend of festivities to celebrate at the opening of the mine only BHP Billiton staff were invited. Contractors who had been involved in the establishment of the mine and employed for periods of up to four years were excluded. This type of segregation, the women noted, spilt into their non-working lives and the lives of their children, even determining who would attend a child's birthday party:

> Libby: With the kids we have birthday parties. There was a few that didn't come but there's a few that didn't stay and there's a few that just sort of came in and got their kids and left.

The women associated with contract work at the mine, either as employees or as partners of contractors, were highly conversant with negative stereotypes about contactors circulating in the town. Even the farming women who were much less cognizant of the nuances within the category 'mining women', had a sense of the contractors as undesirable residents. Women connected to BHP Billiton clearly articulated a typology of 'the contractor' as overpaid, alcohol and drug dependent, lacking familial and community ties and potentially violent. When asked about class in the town, for example, one woman whose husband worked for BHP Billiton stated:

> Anna: During construction we had a lot of trouble because of the people that were employed as contractors; because they were just here to make big bucks. The workforce now is a lot more stable and they don't have that ruthless mentality. It's like we're part of the community. We want to be involved which is really good but, before, it was just shocking.

The BHP Billiton women we interviewed argued that any tensions in the shire between mining and farming people had resulted from the behaviour and actions of contractors, and that unable to distinguish between the two groups, the agricultural community had simply labelled everyone with a tie to the mine as abject.

Class Relations between BHP Billiton Women and Farming Women

The difficulties and potential limitations of reading class simply from occupation or income was highlighted in focusing on the relationships between the farming and mining women. The comparatively small size of the holdings of the Ravensthorpe farms and the relatively recent acquisition of their farming land, in the 1960s, has the potential to negate claims to the higher class status that might traditionally be afforded to farmers. Further, the farming land in the shire of Ravensthorpe is not particularly rich, and has, in recent years, been badly affected by drought. Farming women talked of financial struggles and strains they were under, the need for off farm income to sustain the farm and large debts they retained. Many of the homes and farms we visited to undertake the interviews reflected this situation. In contrast, the mining women's homes were all modern, newly built and surrounded by landscaped native gardens. Interior furnishings and modern appliances all indicated wealth. Along with their homes, mining people in the town enjoyed very high incomes as a result of a severe skill shortage in the industry and the high demand for minerals for export. The disparity between mining and farming incomes was acknowledged by one interviewee who referred to the fact that the town's progress association required $A700 for a new roof for a park toilet block. It was thought this was a small amount given the financial capacity of mining people in the community. One community member noted that for those involved in mining, 'You could put some more zeros on that and it's nothing'.

Despite their self acknowledged inferior financial status, it was the farming women who tended to judge the mining women negatively and, importantly, as morally deficient. In part, this relied upon familiar classed tropes about the superiority of individual ownership of property and self employment. A constant refrain in this regard was the assertion that farming people have a greater level of responsibility while mining people are cosseted and pampered. The farming women positioned themselves and their husbands as tough, industrious and self-directed and caricatured the mining women (and men) as indulged and lazy. Mining people were seen to be in receipt of significant amounts of money as a result of their relationship to the mine as well as afforded considerable largesse in terms of housing and other inducements, and yet lacking graciousness or industry. One farming woman summarized the thinking:

> Norelle: I can hear people in my community saying, "They have absolutely nothing to do all day and they still have to hire a cleaner to come in and clean the house and they still have to have a day care centre to take care of their children after school, what the hell are they doing all day?"

The financial rewards of being involved in mining were viewed by the farming women as largely undeserved. They dismissed the work undertaken on a mine site as straightforward and undemanding, particularly in contrast to agricultural labour. Mining people were also seen to be extravagant and excessive in their consumption practices buying leisure-orientated vehicles such as jet skis, boats and trail bikes. In contrast, farming people were said to be careful with their money as well as more likely to direct it towards more morally appropriate purposes such as to benefit the farm enterprise. The caricature of the mining woman as pampered and cosseted was extended by the farming women to include mining men. Similarly, their representation of themselves as tough, industrious and self directed also encompassed their designations of their farmer husbands. Indicative of the softness and fragility of the mining man compared to the farming man, was, according to two agricultural women, the high priority BHP Billiton gave to workplace health and safety. These women parodied the compulsory fluorescent reflective vests, the aerials on vehicles and the noises vehicles made on reversing as ridiculous and trivial. There were class dimensions to these discussions of occupational safety as mining men's position as employees was contrasted with that of the farming men's as self employed. The latter, it was asserted, are business owners and must therefore take responsibility for their own selves. As one woman commented, 'You know, on farming, we're the managers, we manage it, but we also own it. We don't report to anyone else'.

Tensions between the farming women and mining women erupted when the local council suggested that the community hall could be used by BHP Billiton as a temporary childcare centre. There was considerable consternation amongst farming women as numerous pre-mine community groups utilized the hall for meetings and activities. For those who had nursed concerns about the changes wrought by the presence of the mine and, in particular, the sense of a loss of community, the prospect of handing over the hall to the company was also highly symbolic and infused with emotion. On the other hand, for women who already worked at the mine and those who sought employment at the mine a childcare centre was a key priority. For these women feelings were strengthened by the fact that they had expected that a company childcare centre would be in operation when they arrived.

At a public meeting to discuss the issue discourses of gender, rurality and class were engaged by both the mining women and the farming women to legitimate their particular position about the use of the community hall. BHP Billiton women at the meeting, particularly those few who were in managerial positions, drew on notions of 'choice' and 'rights' as well as called upon their occupational identities, for example, as a lawyer or an accountant and educational status in arguing their case. In contrast, farming women characterized the childcare centre as unwarranted given that they themselves had never required such an amenity. One expressed the view that children required their mothers and that good mothers should be at home caring for children. More generally, however, the reconstitution of the community hall as a childcare centre was characterized by the farming women as indicative of mining women's lack of understanding of what constitutes rurality, a rural community and the identity rural women. This is encapsulated in the following recollection from a female farmer who attended the meeting.

> Cheryl: And one woman stood up and said, "I want a movie theatre. I want an arcade, amusement arcade for the kids. I want to have Paddy's Market every month. I want this, this, this and this." And Louise said, "Are you saying you want people to entertain your children for you?" And she said, "Yes." And Louise said, "Well, I'm afraid in a country community, if you want something to

happen, you've got to get in, get involved and make it happen." And the woman said, "Well I'm not prepared to do that" and she sat down.

The view that a desire for a childcare centre was a breach of the norms and values of a rural community was similarly expressed by other farming women who recalled the heated discussions at the meeting. Particular contention circulated around the issue of sport, which, as in many country towns of Australia, is seen as central to 'community' (Tonts 2005). When one of the mining women suggested that she was looking forward to a childcare centre being in operation as it meant her children could be escorted to sport from school and she could simply pick them up when it was finished at the end of her shift a number of the long term agriculturally based women reacted angrily. One argued that, 'This was not sport', rather 'sport was mothers getting involved and helping'.

Given the morally charged descriptions the farming women used about the mining women it is important to give particular consideration to the group of four women who had relationships with both farming and mining. For two of these women, however, there was little tension as they identified themselves primarily as farming women and their husbands as farming men despite their partners' employment at the mine. Their involvement in the mine was seen as a short-term solution to address the financial security of the farm. In fact, these women were vocal in reiterating many of the allegedly morally defective aspects of mining employment, such as the excessive pay and limited need for industry, which they believed could be harnessed for the morally legitimate task of safeguarding the farm. They were clear that if given a choice their husbands would much prefer to be farming full time. For the other two women the situation was more complex as they themselves were employed at the mine. These women were extremely happy in their employment explaining that they had been much less fulfilled when working on the farm. They not only enjoyed the income, but the new social networks and personal and professional development. At the same time, they were highly aware of the negative discourses circulating about mining people in the community and cognizant of the fact that any shift in identity from 'farming woman' to 'mining woman' could result in them being situated within such discourses.

> Tammy: When I first applied for this job [at the mine] I went to a Parents and Citizens meeting and had a mother say, "Oh gee, I hope we don't get any mining brats at our school when all the changes happen." And I was kind of sitting back thinking to myself, "Well, if I get this job does that then change my children to mining brats?"

In contrast to the 'farming women' the 'mining women' were much less vocal and certainly not disapproving as they spoke about the agricultural women in the community. Many stated that they did not socialize with farming women and could not comment on their experiences with them. Others made references to the 'farming women' being 'strong', 'hard working' and 'committed'. The only comment made that was negative was that farming women tend to be 'conservative' but this was erased as it was claimed that this was understandable given their life trajectories. This unevenness is reflective of the key role farming has had as a signifier for rural communities, and the ongoing dominance of widely circulating discourses which associate moral value, such as honour, respectability and endurance, with being a farmer (Chavez 2005, Bryant 1999). Alongside farming people mining people are negatively assessed as 'other' and constructed as morally inferior (Gibson-Graham 1994: 207; Pini, Price and McDonald 2010).

Conclusion

In reporting on data from a study of the Ravensthorpe Shire in Western Australia this chapter has ulitized contemporary cultural class theory to investigate class relations and rurality. Moreover, it has brought a gender lens to the analyses exploring how community members negotiate the intersecting discourses, practices, and assumptions about femininity and masculinity, rurality and class.

Three different classed categories were examined in the chapter. The first, the classed differences between women involved with BHP Billiton either through their husband's employment or their own. In stark contrast to past scholarship which has reported on the critical importance of collective notions of class in resource affected communities (e.g., Williams 1981, Gibson-Graham 1991, 1994, 1996) participants in this study minimized or dismissed the place of class in their lives. This is no doubt indicative of the broader 'disidentification of class' which has been found to be prominent today (Skeggs 2004: 59), a desire to establish oneself as 'ordinary' and 'outside class' (Savage, Bagnall and Longhurst 2001: 875) as well as representative of the declining influence and power of unions in what is now largely a deregulated sector (Ellem 2004). While collective understandings of class may have diminished in mining, class is not necessarily irrelevant amongst the women who have an association with BHP Billiton. For example, it was clear that class informed social and leisure groups outside the workplace and was often signalled when introductions were made between women.

The second classed categorization examined in the chapter was between the 'BHP Billiton women' and 'the contractors' while the third was between 'mining women' and 'farming women'. The analysis of interviews demonstrated that the BHP Billiton women positioned contractors as responsible for a range of antisocial behaviour. Viewed as central to the contractor's moral degeneracy was the fact that they were just in the community to obtain an income; an assertion that was also made by the farming women when talking about the mining women. In making such assertions interviewees dismissed the economic capital of these groups and drew attention to what they were seen to lack in terms of cultural, social and symbolic capital. The different groups engaged in 'moral boundary drawing' (Sayer 2005: 952) delineating particular people, practices and attitudes negatively and others positively and, importantly, marking some as belonging in the rural and others as not belonging in the rural. This attribution of value, was, as this chapter has demonstrated, intrinsically gendered. It was, for example, not only that the women associated with mining were deemed by their agricultural counterparts as failing in their performance of normative middle-class rurality, but as failing in their performance of normative middle-class rural femininity. Integral to such a performance is an emphasis on home and family along with community and volunteer work.

Ravensthorpe provides a particularly rich case study for examining gender and class in the rural as it is a township which continues to undergo significant change. At the time of our interviews the classed and gendered conventions of this rural area were being opened up to challenge, debate and question by the presence of a new cohort of residents associated with the mine. It was, however, very early in the town's evolution from a predominantly farming community to a predominantly mining community, and as time has progressed it is likely that the story reported here has shifted considerably; such is the dynamic nature of gender and class.

References

Agg, J. and Phillips, M. 1998. Neglected gender dimensions of rural social restructuring, in *Migration into Rural Areas: Theories and Issues*, edited by P. Boyle and K. Halfacree. West Sussex: John Wiley, 252–79.

Australian Bureau of Agricultural Economics. 2009. *Minerals and Energy: Major Development Projects*. Canberra: Australian Government Publishing.

Australian Bureau of Statistics. 2007. *2006 Census QuickStats: Ravensthorpe (S) (Local Government Area)*. [Online: Australian Bureau of Statistics]. Available at: http://www.censusdata.abs.gov.au [accessed: 27 August 2010].

Bottero, W. 2004. Class identities and the identity of class. *Sociology*, 38(5), 985–1003.

Bowden, B. 2003. Regulating outsourcing: the use of contractors on the Central Queensland coalfields, 1974–2003. *Labour and Industry*, 14(1), 41–56.

Bryant, L. 1999. The detraditionalization of occupational identities in farming in South Australia. *Sociologia Ruralis*, 29(2), 236–61.

Chavez, S. 2005. Community, ethnicity and class in a changing rural California town. *Rural Sociology*, 70(3), 314–37.

Cloke, P. and Thrift, N. 1987. Intra-class conflict in rural areas. *Journal of Rural Studies*, 3(4), 321–33.

Cloke, P. and Thrift, N. 1990. Class and change in rural Britain, in *Rural Restructuring: Global Processes and their Responses*, edited by T. Marsden, P. Lowe and S. Whatmore. London: David Fulton, 165–81.

Dempsey, K. 1992. *A Man's Town. Inequality Between Men and Women in Rural Australia*. Melbourne: Oxford University Press.

Dicks, B. 2008. Performing the hidden injuries of class in coal-mining heritage. *Sociology*, 42(3), 436–52.

Ellem, B. 2004. *Hard Ground: Unions in the Pilbara.* Pilbara: Pilbara Mineworker's Union.

Gibson-Graham, J.K. 1991. Company towns and class processes: a study of the coal towns of Central Queensland. *Environment and Planning: Society and Space*, 9(3), 285–308.

Gibson-Graham, J.K. 1994. 'Stuffed if I know!': Reflections on post-modern feminist social research. *Gender, Place and Culture*, 1(2), 205–24.

Gibson-Graham, J.K. 1996. *The End of Capitalism (as we knew it): A Feminist Critique of Political Economy.* London: Blackwell.

Gier-Viskovatoff, J. and Porter, A. 1998. Women and British coalfields strikes: 1926 and 1984. *Frontiers*, 19(2), 198–230.

Gillies, V. 2006. Working-class mothers and school life: exploring the role of emotional capital. *Gender and Education*, 18(3), 281–93.

Hall, V.G. 2004. Differing gender roles: women in mining and fishing communities in Northumberland, England, 1880–1914. *Women's Studies International Forum*, 27(3), 521–30.

Hebson, G. 2009. Renewing class analysis in studies of the workplace: a comparison of working-class and middle-class women's aspirations and identities. *Sociology*, 43(1), 27–44.

Hey, V. 2003. Joining the club? Academia and working-class femininities. *Gender and Education*, 15(3), 319–35.

Lawler, S. 1999. 'Getting out and getting away': women's narratives of class mobility. *Feminist Review*, 63(1), 3–24.

Lawler, S. 2005. Disgusted subjects: the making of middle-class identities. *The Sociological Review*, 53(3), 429–46.

Maguire, M. 2005. 'Not footprints behind but footsteps forward': working class women who teach. *Gender and Education*, 17(1), 3–18.

Mayes, R. 2007. *Contemporary Rural Change: The Complex Case of Jerdacuttup.* Paper to The Australian Sociological Association and Sociological Association Aotearoa New Zealand Conference: Public Sociologies: Lessons and Trans Tasman Comparisons. Auckland: 4–7 December 2007.

Mayes, R. and Pini, B. 2010. The 'feminine revolution in mining': A critique. *Australian Geographer*, 41(2), 233–45.

Oliver, D. 2008. Unions in 2007. *Journal of Industrial Relations*, 50(3), 447–62.

Pahl, R. 1965a. Class and community in English commuter villages. *Sociological Review*, 5(1), 5–23.

Pahl, R. 1965b. *Urbs in Rure: The Metropolitan Fringe in Hertfordshire.* London: Weidenfeld and Nicholson.

Panelli, R. 2006. Rural society, in *Handbook of Rural Studies*, edited by P. Cloke, T. Marsden and P.H. Mooney. London: Sage, 63–90.

Phillips, M. 1998a. Investigations of the British middle-classes – part 1: from legislation to interpretation. *Journal of Rural Studies*, 14(4), 411–25.

Phillips, M. 1998b. Investigations of the British middle-classes – part 1: fragmentation, identity, morality and contestation. *Journal of Rural Studies*, 14(4), 427–443.

Pini, B. Price, R. and McDonald, P. 2010. Teachers and the emotional dimensions of class in resource-affected rural Australia. *British Journal of Sociology of Education*, 31(1), 17–30.

Poiner, G. 1990. *The Good Old Rule: Gender and Power Relations in a Rural Community*. Sydney: Sydney University Press and Oxford University Press.

Reay, D. 2003. A risky business? Mature working-class women and students and access to higher education. *Gender and Education*, 15(3), 301–17.

Reay, D. 2005. Beyond consciousness? The psychic landscape of social class. *Sociology*, 39(5), 911–28.

Reay, D. 2006a. The zombie stalking English schools: social class and educational inequality. *British Journal of Educational Studies*, 54(3), 288–307.

Reay, D. 2006b. 'Unruly places': Inner-city comprehensives, middle-class imaginaries and working-class children. *Urban Studies*, 44(7), 1191–201.

Rhodes, L. 2005. *Two for the Price of One: The Lives of Mining Wives*. Perth: API Network.

Savage, M. 2000. *Class Analysis and Social Transformation*. Buckingham: Open University.

Savage, M., Bagnall, G., and Longhurst, B. 2001. Ordinary, ambivalent and defensive: Class identities in the northwest of England. *Sociology*, 39(5), 965–82.

Sayer, A. 2005. Class, moral worth and recognition. *Sociology*, 39(5), 947–63.

Shaw, M. and Mundy, M. 2005. Complexities of class and gender relations: Recollections of women active in the 1984–1985 miners' strike. *Capital and Class*, 29(3), 151–74.

Skeggs, B. 1997. *Formations of Class and Gender: Becoming Respectable*. London: Sage.

Skeggs, B. 2004. *Class, Self, Culture*. London: Routledge.

Strangelman, T., Hollywood, E., Beynon, H., Bennett, K., and Hudson, R. 1999. Heritage work: Re-representing the work ethic in the coalfields. *Sociological Research Online*, 4(3), 1–18.

Tonts, M. 2005. Competitive sport and social capital in rural Australia. *Journal of Rural Studies*, 21(2), 137–149.

Walkerdine, V., Lucey, H. and Melody, J. 2001. *Growing Up Girl: Psychosocial Explorations of Gender and Class*. New York: New York University Press.

Warwick, D. and Littlejohn, G. 1992. *Coal, Capital and Culture*. London: Routledge.

Williams, C. 1981. *Open Cut: The Working Class in an Australian Mining Town*. Sydney: Allen and Unwin.

Williamson, B. 1982. *Class, Culture and Community: A Biographical Study of Social Change in Mining*. London: Routledge and Kegan Paul.

Chapter 7

Jobs for Women? Gender and Class in Ontario's Ruralized Automotive Manufacturing Industry

Belinda Leach

Rural communities in many parts of Ontario, Canada have long been sustained by jobs in the manufacturing sector, contrary to the many depictions of rural communities as reliant solely on primary agriculture and resource extraction industries. The histories of manufacturing in these places, and the jobs and social relations that flowed from those histories have resulted in a particular class character for these communities, one shaped also by the ways that gender intervenes into the labour market practices of both employers and workers.

For most of a century women in Southwestern Ontario have found work in the automotive parts industry. This industry has been growing in Ontario and despite the recession of the past couple of years it continues to be very significant in many communities, including rural ones. It would seem reasonable to expect that the long history of women's employment combined with the growth of the sector, would lead to expanded opportunities for women to obtain these relatively good rural jobs. This has not been the case. In this chapter I argue that volatility in the automotive industry, manifesting in the threat and reality of layoffs, combines with a powerful form of rural industrial masculinity, at the intersection of class and gender, to exclude women from the benefits of the best working-class jobs in rural Ontario communities. While previous scholarship has examined rural masculinities and industrial masculinity separately, rural Southwestern Ontario provides a context where elements of both combine to construct a locally specific form. The research contributes to debates on rural gender identities by treating rural masculinities and femininities as classed constructions. The question is what happens to entrenched gender identities when relatively well paid jobs in the automotive industry are available. The clashes that arise as these identities are pushed and pulled in different ways are the focus of my attention here.

The automotive sector's current volatility is closely associated with the crisis in Canadian manufacturing that resulted from the combination of fierce international competition over several years; the more recent quite dramatic decline in strength of the United States (US) dollar and the concomitant rise of the Canadian dollar; and of course a US credit crisis with global consequences. This crisis has led to dramatic losses of manufacturing jobs. In Ontario, where most of Canada's manufacturing is concentrated, tens of thousands of people have lost jobs as plants either downsize or close altogether. Using Statistics Canada data, the Canadian Auto Workers Union estimates that 350,000 manufacturing jobs were lost across Canada between 2002 and March 2008 (Canadian Auto Workers 2008), illuminating the extent of the employment shrinkage. This reduction in access to jobs in the manufacturing sector has particular gendered and classed effects.

It is often assumed that it is men who are most seriously affected by manufacturing job losses, but in fact, the sectors where women work: food manufacturing, fish processing, automotive assembly and parts, aerospace, and so-called light manufacturing (such as garments, novelties, plastics); have all experienced particular difficulties, affecting both women and men. The crisis in Canadian manufacturing then represents a particular kind of economic predicament for women. For a very long time, employment in the manufacturing sector in both urban and rural areas has offered working-class women some of the best jobs available because they are more likely to be full-time, to command higher wages, and to be associated with a greater chance of unionization, bringing with it benefits and greater job security. The crisis thus disproportionately threatens the loss of good working-class jobs for women, and given the significance of manufacturing to employment in rural Ontario communities, this has particular implications for rural women.

This chapter is based on my research over 15 years focusing on work and workers in Ontario's automotive industry. The research has examined the geographic shift into rural Ontario communities that has accompanied the restructuring of the automobile industry in the past 30 years and the particular gendered implications associated with this shift. The argument advanced here emerges from ethnographic research and interviews with automotive parts and assembly workers and with key informants in six rural communities, which provides the context for considering how gender intervenes in the highly volatile rural labour market for automotive work. This analysis contributes to the growing body of scholarship that nuances the analysis of gender relations and gender identities in specific places and under particular conditions through consideration of both history and contemporary economic change.

The Ontario Context for Manufacturing Work

Jobs in manufacturing have historically been crucial to the Canadian economy, especially in the industrial regions of Ontario. They have provided decent wages, good benefits and until the past couple of decades reasonable stability for people in both urban and rural communities. In the second half of the nineteenth century, many of the smaller communities to the north and west of Toronto emerged as centres of diversified small industry, much of it serving the needs of the agrarian economy as well as individual households. The grist mills and cheese factories that were among the earliest rural Ontario industries were joined in the nineteenth century by factories making agricultural implements, furniture, shoes, and garments, and preserving and processing food. The entrance of American branch plant operations in the mid-twentieth century, followed by later trends in capitalist restructuring and government policy, led to a dramatic decline in rural manufacturing operations. Yet some manufacturing industries managed to hang on and other new ones to emerge during these years (Winson and Leach 2002). Bucknell, Paulmer and Fuller (2005:8) report that almost 13 per cent of manufacturing jobs in Ontario in 2004 were in rural areas.

The automobile industry has been a significant component of manufacturing change in Ontario. Originally the industry was based around Big Three assembly operations and subsidiary parts suppliers located in urban and rural areas, and protected through the 1960s AutoPact.[1] The entry of Japanese assembly plants (two rural and one suburban) in the 1980s, and another new rural assembly plant in 2008, combined with the decline of subsidiary makers in favour of specialized parts manufacturers have quite dramatically changed rural labour markets. The rural assembly plants, in particular, present opportunities for jobs in rural communities that are unmatched in terms of pay. Rural *and* urban workers drive hundreds of miles, literally to line up for the chance to work at a rural assembly plant where starting pay is about C$28 an hour. At the rural CAMI Automotive (CAMI) assembly plant, a hiring process for 200 new positions in early 2010 attracted 10,000 applicants. As the industry has restructured internationally to respond to multiple challenges, Ontario parts and assembly plants have been variously buffeted and buoyed, resulting in tremendous instability, volatility and unpredictability across the sector. Recalls of laid off workers and new hiring in assembly trickle down to the parts sector, and provide greater security there, but the cycle of layoffs accordingly reverses that process.

Charlotte Yates and I (2007) have argued recently that manufacturing continues to be critical to the Canadian economy and labour market, especially in Ontario, despite the prevailing rhetoric of the information economy. In Ontario, while some of the older manufacturing industries, like furniture, footwear, some food processing and most clothing and textiles, have been lost to locations with cheaper labour, new manufacturing investment *has* taken place in recent years, and that has been largely in the automotive industry.

One of the interesting things about investment in the Ontario automobile industry is that it is associated with rural location decisions. This is clearly based on more factors than the well-known advantage of lower Canadian costs in comparison to those in US plants. It has been driven also by abundant low cost land, by available workers[2] who are willing to work for less than urban workers, and by attractive incentives from rural municipalities such as infrastructure provision and tax

---

1   The AutoPact established a limited free trade framework between Canada and the US intended to ensure that the number of vehicles produced in Canada remained related to the number of vehicles being sold there.

2   The availability of rural labour for activities other than agriculture is linked to the restructuring of the agriculture sector, notably the entry of large scale commercial farming that both consolidates smaller family-operated farms and requires far fewer agricultural labourers.

holidays. But it is also driven by not always successful union avoidance strategies in which rural people are perceived as less likely to join unions (Yates and Leach 2007: 172–173, see also High 2003, Winson 1997). In the last couple of decades, then, there has been a respatialization of the industry as it reprises some of its early twentieth century practices of pushing into rural Ontario.

Capital, Labour and Place: Constructing Rural Gender Identities

Cultural geographers have pointed out that, as Pred and Watts (1992: 11) argue 'how things develop depends on where they develop'. Thus, how and why the automobile industry has claimed rural space is significant. A major reason certainly concerns the industry's labour needs, and Jamie Peck's (1996) approach to the study of labour markets, that considers the ways in which they are *embedded* in local cultural values, norms and institutions is useful for trying to understand how rural labour markets operate. As Peck (1996: 11) puts it 'the geographic distinctiveness of labour markets stems from variability in the social and institutional fabric that sustains and regulates capitalist employment relations'.

Jane Collins and Amy Quark (2006) have applied Peck's (1996) argument regarding the locally constituted nature of labour markets to a rural context, positing that embeddedness is a complex phenomenon that cannot simply be read off factors such as the length of time a firm has been established in a particular location. Further specifying the place based nature of labour markets, Collins and Quark (2006) argue, from a study of rural apparel firms in Wisconsin, that employers are constrained by corporate demands from outside as well as local issues. Multiple factors operate in combination, then, to generate the 'locally-specific power configurations within which workers, employers and community members meet' (Collins and Quark 2006: 286). These include corporate decisions made far away as a consequence of global economic pressures, and provincial and national industrial and other policies, such as immigration.

Other factors that come into play include the local environment for corporate investment in terms of natural resources and transportation infrastructure. These combine with the decisions and practices of local management, employment agencies, social movement actors such as unions, as well as workers themselves. Catherine Rankin (2003: 724) suggests that 'enduring local particularisms' persist in shaping the social world, including capital's efforts to restructure firms and local economies. The ruralization of the automobile industry and automobile work suggest a particular configuration of relationships among capital, labour and place, which require more thorough and systematic investigation. These relationships then shape gendered (and racialized) class outcomes.

I argue that the gender relations and gender ideologies that prevail in a particular place contribute as much as these other factors to how labour markets operate. Gender denotes unequal relations between men and women, relations that are socially constructed through gendered meanings and practices. Men and women actively participate in reinforcing and resisting these constructions, but on different terms. As actors women and men can initiate change, though under gender related constraints. Recently rural scholars have paid attention to the construction of particular rural identities in specific places. Rural gender scholar Bettina Bock (2006: 279) argues that identities are not defined solely by social and economic characteristics, but are 'continuously re-constructed by people, embedded in and informed by culture in a specific context in time and place' (see also Little and Morris 2005). Consequently, identities are not fixed or stable, but rather variable and flexible, although constrained by structural factors. Rural identities are then based in power differences while simultaneously operating to reconfirm and legitimate existing power differences.

Feminist rural researchers have argued that traditional gender ideologies are more secure in rural areas than they are in urban ones. In rural areas ideas about what women and men should do and 'be' are relatively clear cut and are less subject to contestation than they are in urban areas. Rural femininity and masculinity as such are powerful constructions that shape the experience and practice of rural life. Feminist rural scholars have examined the construction and reinforcement of gender identity through the media and in popular discourse. Along these lines I have argued (Leach 1999) that in Ontario rural femininity and masculinity are reinforced though events like fall fairs that represent rural women as excellent bakers and canners in sales and competitions, and rural men as strong and technologically savvy through competitions like tractor pulls. I have argued that in the face of these regular performances of masculinity and femininity, it is difficult to pursue occupational, or leisure, choices not regarded as appropriate for women, especially when those choices seem to compromise women's traditional role and attached responsibilities of caring for children, husbands and home based enterprise.

In the popular imagination rural space is often associated with particular social, moral and cultural values. Feminists have argued that the '*rural idyll*' (Little and Austin 1996) is a popular lens through which the rural is viewed, with particularly negative consequences for women. Here the positive and idyllic side of the rural, where qualities like safety, peace and quiet, beautiful landscapes and a caring community, are in focus. This construction has been challenged by feminists and others (see for example Little and Panelli 2003). Feminists have pointed out that the traditional definition of rural femininity casts women as mothers and caretakers of the community, rooted in heterosexuality and the conjugal family as its 'natural' basis. Ontario fall fairs merge all these ideas into a tidy package for internal and external consumption.

Lia Bryant (1999), working in Australia, has recently argued that changes in the practice of agriculture have led to new occupational identities, which for men lean more towards managing and entrepreneurship rather than hard work and physical labour. In turn women are increasingly responsible for sustaining the farm economically and this is reflected in more recognition of their professional identity in place of their traditional identities as wives and mothers. Bryant argues that these new identities have contributed to shaping more equal gender relations defined by partnership rather than male domination. But this is contested by other analysts. Morris and Evans (2001) argue that while women may be engaging more professionally in agriculture, their reproductive role is still represented as their primary responsibility. Further complicating farm women's identities, Susan Machum (2011) has demonstrated the ways in which agriculture is itself cross-cut by class distinction. Certain kinds of agriculture produce far less income than others, and in the process shape the on-farm work of women in very particular ways. In her Canadian case, potato farming generated relatively low revenues, but the seasonal nature of the work allowed women to work off farm in the winter and bring in valued additional income. In contrast, dairy farming was year-round work, generated far higher revenues, and required far more managerial work often carried out by women (See Machum 2011 and Chapter 3 this volume).

The class dimensions of rural gender identities demands more thorough investigation by rural gender scholars. The value of analysing the lived experience of class as it interlocks with gender has been demonstrated by Reay (2005) and Skeggs (1997, 2004). In a rural context this idea takes on a particular character. Jo Little (1997) has shown how the combination of rural labour market structure with rural ideology marginalizes women from the employment paths they might otherwise pursue. Morris and Little (2005) conclude from their study of three English counties that an occupational polarization is emerging for women within and between rural areas. While some women are employed professionally, others' job choices are extremely limited. Interestingly, all the women in their study claimed that there was widespread acceptance that women would work. Yet despite a broader range of rural femininities now available to women, the enduring nature of traditional ideology continues to place particular constraints on women's engagement in paid labour, as Morris and Little (2005) also suggest. This does not mean that they are excluded altogether from paid work. Rather it means that while it is acceptable for women to work in nursing homes or garment factories, it is much less so for them to work in automobile factories. This has classed consequences. Women's pay, conditions of work, and how they can care for their families are all limited as women are steered toward low paying jobs characteristic of the growing service sector. When women seek jobs in the auto sector they are hoping for economic security, but they are also challenging traditional notions of what it is to be a woman in a rural community.

As a corollary, the construction of rural masculinity incorporates a number of dimensions that are challenged by women's entry into auto jobs. One element of rural masculinity is physical strength and the ability to endure and dominate the forces of nature. These characteristics are put to work through engagement with the heavy machinery that is required to farm inhospitable land, clear forests and locate and remove valuable resources. Many analysts note the association of men with farming technologies and the symbolic value that continues to be imbued in tractors (Brandth 1995, Ni Laoire 1999, Saugeres 2002). Finney, Campbell and

Mayerfield Bell argue that rurality and masculinity are mutually constructed. For them:

> The majority and the most culturally-ratified of "country boy" narratives ... reinforce the masculine as strong, capable, tough and powerful, and the rural as sincere, reliable, trustworthy, authentic and (quite literally) "down to earth" (Finney, Campbell and Mayerfield Bell 2004: 2 cited in Bock 2008).

Other dimensions of rural masculinity are the rejection of formal education, seen to be associated with the experience that most rural jobs for men do not require it (Bye 2009, Corbett 2007). Jobs requiring physical capabilities rather than educational skills are then given particular value in rural communities, while as Campbell (2006) found, office jobs among others are identified as lacking appropriate masculine traits. Campbell's (2006) work also identifies the ways in which rural men claim and appropriate certain kinds of rural space. In his example local pubs operated as informal hiring halls for casual male labour. For other analysts hunting grounds were identified as primarily masculine space (Bye 2007). Rural masculinity has also been examined in terms of rural men's privileged access to political power and representations, such as through farmer organizations (Pini 2008). Finally, men's access to the domestic services provided by women extends further than in urban areas, where at least in contemporary times, that is limited mainly to 'housework'. In rural areas domestic work continues to encompass caring for animals, tending gardens, preparing food for storage, and caring for seasonal and long-term workers in agricultural and extraction industries.

How rural masculinities change in association with broader economic shifts affecting agriculture and other rural economic dynamics, such as tourism, is a central concern of much of the literature on the topic. Change is also a key aspect of scholarship on working-class and industrial masculinity in North America. Here, and especially in industrial regions like Ontario, hegemonic masculinity (Connell and Messerschmidt 2005) has been strongly correlated with industrial factory work and the power of a breadwinner ideal. Breadwinning was a critical piece of industrial male identity that prevailed through much of the twentieth century, but chronic job insecurity and growing social inequality have had serious consequences for individuals' capacity to uphold it (Broughton and Walton 2006, Newman 1993). As a section of the broader category of industrial work, labour in the automobile industry has been central to the construction of the paradigmatic male worker in the twentieth century: unionized and militant, well paid, and thus able to support a wife at home. This specific industrial worker identity was bolstered by the cultural importance of the automobile (Kay 1997) in constructing masculinity more generally.

In the rural context, then, I am arguing that a particular form of *industrial* masculinity is enhanced and reinforced through prevailing rurally specific ideas about gender. Most of the research on rural gender identities has focused on a context of agriculture or extraction industries, such as forestry. Here I examine a rather different context, rural manufacturing, with different consequences for the construction of masculinity and femininity in specific rural places, and with an explicit class component that is often left unanalysed in other studies.

Jobs for Women: Contradictory Imperatives

Feminist scholars have lamented the lack of employment opportunities for women in rural communities, especially with decent pay and conditions (Morris and Little 2005, Hughes and Nativel 2005). Further studies have linked this to the forms of subordination of women found in rural communities and to issues of violence against women, women's and children's poverty and outmigration (Bjarnason and Thorlindsson 2005, Wendt 2009). Thus clearly class affects other aspects of women's lives in serious and disturbing ways. In this context, the mobilization of women's labour in the Ontario rural automotive parts sector is significant. Historian Steven High (2003) describes how American automakers have historically sought cheaper workers, usually meaning non-union workers, to make component parts. In the early decades of last century they established rural factories in the US south and in the rural Ontario hinterland east of Detroit and Windsor, Ontario. Here women workers were seen to have advantages over male workers, for all of the reasons that are familiar from the studies of women workers in multinational factories internationally: low wage expectations, dexterity in working with small parts, and docility. They were anticipated to be a compliant and non-militant labour force.

Steven High (2003: 103) reports that in the 1950s and early 1960s wages for women in rural communities were less than half of those for men and women in Windsor, despite the fact that they were working for the same companies. Most of the work women did involved tasks associated with their so-called 'natural' talents and domestic work, such as sewing. For example, women were employed sewing seat covers or threading wiring harnesses, while men were more likely to work in engine and brake factories. These occupational divisions clearly reflected prevailing gender ideologies in relation to physical strength and abilities. And despite the hoped for docility, rural parts factories soon followed the pattern of Windsor and Detroit, as workers joined the United Auto Workers union. In some cases when this happened, as High (2003) reports, companies closed shop and moved yet deeper into rural Ontario.

As a result of this early ruralization of the parts industry, in communities like Stratford, Chatham, and Bracebridge, among many others in Ontario, the industry provided decent jobs for women. And unlike most jobs in rural communities, over time these jobs were unionized. As well as providing women with comparable wages and benefits to men in their communities (some of whom worked alongside them), these jobs put pressure on neighbouring factories to offer competitive wages.

The longstanding availability of unionized factory work in rural Ontario, especially through the dispersal of the heavily unionized automotive industry, led to a particular character for gender relations in these manufacturing based rural communities. Gender inequality continued to subordinate women in many ways, and as scholars have repeatedly argued, has been slow to change in Canadian rural areas (Leach 1999, Carbert 1995, Avakova 2008), as feminist scholars have similarly noted for rural gender relations globally (Sachs 1996, Bock and Shortall 2006). Yet overlaid with traditional ideas about women's place in their societies, which were deeply held by both women and men, were contradictory class practices that were possible in communities with automotive industry jobs because of women's access to a decent wage and the benefits of unionization.

My research with unionized women workers in rural Ontario communities indicates that for several decades they have been able to maintain what has been an unusual level of independence for rural women, as a result of their relatively more secure financial position. This has permitted them access to larger sums of discretionary money. With this they have been able to do a number of things that women with lower incomes and less job security, that is most women in rural communities, could not. They could support children separately from the father, and continue to do so as children became young adults. Without the need to depend on a partner, they could leave those they no longer wanted to live with. It also allowed them to purchase consumer goods. Some of these would be labour saving items, like freezers, or clothes driers, which have a direct impact on their work in the home. But another item is especially important: a car. Given the absence of public transportation in Ontario rural communities (Fuller and O'Leary 2008) car ownership provided another basis for independence. As Cheryl Morse-Dunkerley (2003) has shown, young men have priority access to private automobiles in rural communities. Thus car ownership allows control over where women live in relation to where they work and where their children are cared for. It gives them control over their movements more generally, including the ability to leave a violent partner with their children and some belongings.

This kind of economic independence for rural women was often hard won and involved them in decidedly non-traditional actions. In 1978 women at a rural automotive parts firm called Fleck, in Huron County, Ontario, engaged in a strike that has been celebrated in the feminist literature. The Fleck women were on strike for 23 weeks fighting for a first contract, against an employer who refused to collect union dues and to pay more than minimum wage. The strike is notorious for the way the provincial police attempted, and failed, to intimidate the women strikers. On 13 April 1979, for example, reporters noted 950 Ontario Provincial Police officers, 80 cruisers, five paddy wagons, dogs and trainers and two special weapons and tactics teams set up to 'police' 30 picketers (Musson 2008). The contract was eventually signed, and issues around pay, safety and harassment were all dealt with.

In a more recent example, in 1999 women led an occupation of the Johnson Controls seat cover plant in Stratford to protest the company's plan to move

200 jobs to Mexico. Twenty-five workers, led by women, barred the entrances to the plant during the night following the afternoon shift, and refused to allow management back in until layoff notices had been rescinded and an agreement reached that the plant would continue to operate for the next 2 years (Leach and Yates Forthcoming).

Both of these examples of women's militancy in the rural automotive parts industry occurred in unionized plants. In the past 10 years or so many new parts plants have opened but relatively few have become union plants. Nevertheless, given the dearth of jobs for women in rural areas, and the fact that in the automotive parts sector hourly wage rates range from C$12 to C$25 per hour (minimum wage in 2010 is C$10), women have sought work there. Overall rural labour market participation rates for women continue to be lower than in urban areas (56 per cent in non-harvest months, compared to about 72 per cent for urban women), but are higher in those communities with more manufacturing jobs. This trend suggests the value of the manufacturing sector for providing women with employment opportunities with good wages. Yet issues remain that prevent women from relying on consistent employment in this sector.

Challenging Rural Industrial Masculinity

Despite the history of women's employment in the manufacturing sector along with its more recent growth, rural women still dare not count on the automotive industry for decent, stable jobs. The research suggests that two kinds of problems have beaten them back when they try to do so.

The first problem is the volatility of the automotive industry in general, and the parts sector especially. International wage competition, changes in consumer taste, including the impact of oil prices and concerns about the environment, and aging technology in plants have all operated to disadvantage Ontario automotive plants. This has destabilized labour markets for automotive work. As Collins and Quark (2006) point out, such issues are beyond local solutions but they inevitably disrupt the ways firms have accommodated, and been accommodated by, local social and cultural practices. Upheaval in the highly competitive parts sector has meant that in the last 10 years many of the older plants (those that were more likely to be unionized) have closed, some relocating to Mexico, the southern US, or elsewhere. Even in the case of Johnson Controls, where women occupied the plant, the plant was closed soon after the guarantee expired. Rural workers laid off from longstanding firms are frequently surprised at the apparent lack of loyalty to the community and their employees, or what they see as a betrayal of local cultural norms. While new parts plants have hired women, these too have proven to be unstable employers in the highly fickle contracting environment. Parts plants closures have been almost a daily news item in Ontario, and workers in non-union plants fare even worse when this happens.

Assembly plants have historically presented even more firmly closed doors to women. Sugiman (2001) documents the difficulties women confronted when they attempted to get such jobs in the early decades of the industry. The newer rural assembly plants, most of them Japanese owned or organized around Japanese production systems, have seemed more open to women assembly workers than the older Ford, General Motors and Chrysler plants that were established under early twentieth century gender ideologies. Through the efforts of the small number of women who got their foot in the door at the newer plants, more women have been hired into assembly jobs in recent years. Where unions exist, women have taken on leadership roles, and as an extension of that work, have tried to ensure more women are hired. But volatility in assembly plants, especially evident in the past 2 years, is also a major issue. Short-term or long-term layoffs, and/or the elimination of shifts have affected women disproportionately in both parts and assembly plants, since as more recent hires they have less seniority. The rural CAMI automotive assembly plant in Ingersoll laid off 550 people in 2008, everyone with 3 years of seniority or less. Of those 45 per cent were women, a vastly higher proportion than the 20 per cent of the overall workforce in 2007 who were women. After the layoff, this figure reverted to about 16.5 per cent. At the time of writing in 2011, most of those laid off had been recalled, although the recall was pushed forward several months because of the financial crisis. Closures, downsizings and layoffs all affect, and in some cases totally rescind, the gains women have made in getting jobs in parts and assembly. Even those who are laid off and recalled again have had their seniority and pay rates affected.

The second problem women confront is structural and day-to-day sexism on the job, both from their co-workers and from management. When women have entered automotive assembly plants they have had to face blatantly sexist behaviour: pin-ups exhibited at workstations, wolf whistles as they cross the floor, comments on their appearance, and even unwanted touching. This may create little surprise for the reader, since such behaviour is well-known in male dominated workplaces. But it is important not simply to acknowledge common phenomena, but rather to recognize that the same or similar practices in fact emerge from specific and often different historical antecedents. I argue that because there is little history of women entering Canadian automotive assembly plants *except* in rural areas, this kind of workplace behaviour takes on a particular meaning in the rural assembly plants. I identify four particular areas where women's attempts to enter the automotive industry as workers, especially in assembly plants, challenge the historically constituted form of rural industrial masculinity.

First, the specification and overvaluing of men's work with heavy machinery such as tractors, but also logging machinery, combines with longstanding ideas that link masculinity with the operation of heavy machinery more generally. This is directly challenged when women present themselves to operate such machinery in automotive plants. Women who have worked at the CAMI plant describe male co-workers who have gone to great lengths to demonstrate that women are unsuitable for these kinds of jobs. Men have failed to train women in safe practices, even when it was their job to do so. They have failed to provide women with assistance in handling unwieldy jobs, when typically more than one man would perform the task. And they sustain a shower of remarks that women are either unable or unlikely to perform a job as well as a man.

Second, when women become active in unions, or if they choose the route towards supervisory roles and managerial positions, they challenge men's privileged access to political power and representation. Kathy Austin, who was elected President of the union local[3] at the CAMI assembly plant in 2006, says that she knew she would get only one term in that position. Women active in the union women's committee say they know that behind their backs, and occasionally to their faces, they are referred to in the most misogynistic terms.

In many of these efforts to make women feel unwelcome in the automotive workplace men have been supported, either tacitly or through particular practices, by management *and* their union leadership. Both of these, as I heard from women workers, failed to take action to condemn or to bring about change. This cross-class alliance within automotive plants has been identified by Lisa Fine (1993) as a key aspect of automotive industry masculinity. This promises privileges for working-class men and reciprocally their compliance for managers and corporate owners. As Fine (1993) explains, this alliance plays into management attempts to promote paternalism as an alternative to unionism. Given management's ongoing attempts to undermine union strength, it is likely to be ever present in unionized environments. This connects easily to paternalistic cross-class relationships in rural areas between those men who own land and those who work it, as described in the literature on rural masculinities.

Third, rotating shifts and mandatory overtime requirements in both parts and assembly plants, overtime often following an afternoon shift (that is, working until two or three in the morning) all place difficult demands on women. In the rural context childcare provision is largely informal and consistent with traditional ideology women are considered primary caregivers. These issues have proven to be the breaking point for some women, as I've heard from women who left the CAMI plant. More explicitly, even as women entered the plant in greater numbers, until a human rights complaint was filed management had been unwilling to accommodate requests for lighter duties for pregnant women. When women take demanding shift work, men's accustomed access to women's usual domestic services is restricted. In rural areas, traditional gender ideology promotes women's skills in domestic tasks that urban women have exhibited only rarely in recent generations. When women are no longer demonstrating these skills because they have competing work demands, I would argue that they are demonstrating a shift in gender ideology and identity.

Fourth, all of these aspects of women in automotive work challenge another significant aspect of masculinity, the claiming of masculine space. Until quite

---

3   The union local is Canadian Auto Workers Local 88 at the CAMI assembly plant in Ingersoll, Ontario. The Local represents about 2,500 workers.

recently, certain kinds of automotive parts plants, and all assembly plants have represented what could be safely seen as masculine space. Women's presence there presents a serious challenge to that, met by all of the practices of men as described above. One woman I talked to who had left the CAMI plant described it as a 'boys' world' and many women who felt they had entered an unwelcoming and even poisonous work environment did not stay around to fight it.

Conclusion

Women were permitted access to rural industrial workplaces in the twentieth century in Ontario as long as their presence was restricted to jobs that could be constructed as women's work. But when women intended to build car bodies or engines, or to assemble vehicles, they challenged the powerful and complex form of rural industrial masculinity that has developed. The research indicates that this masculinity is especially resilient to such challenges, and the considerable ideological and economic resources of the cross-class alliance can be mustered when necessary. When that has failed (due for example, to insistence on the local implementation of human rights policies) industrial volatility, driven by global markets in automobiles and in oil that are beyond the power of local firms, has in recent years finished the job of purging women from the workplace.

Rural women face economic conditions like urban women in many ways, but with added disadvantages such as limited employment opportunities and restricted access to training, transportation and childcare. When all of these occur in the context of an extraordinarily powerful construction of masculinity that demonstrably cuts across class boundaries, getting a foot in the door of the automotive plants is clearly not going to be enough.

Acknowledgements

The research has been supported by the Social Sciences and Humanities Research Council of Canada. I thank Barbara Pini and Clare Morgan for their assistance in the preparation of this chapter.

References

Avakova, N. 2008. *Rural Households, Livelihood Strategies and Reproductive Labour in the Era of Neoliberal Restructuring*, unpublished PhD thesis. Guelph, Ontario: University of Guelph.

Bjarnason, T. and Thorlindsson, T. 2005. Should I stay or should I go? Migration expectations among youth in Icelandic fishing and farming communities. *Journal of Rural Studies*, 22(3), 290–300.

Bock, B. 2006. Rurality and gender identity: an overview, in *Rural Gender Relations: Issues and Case Studies*, edited by B. Bock and S. Shortall. Wallingford: CABI Publishing, 279–87.

Bock, B. and Shortall, S. 2006. *Rural Gender Relations: Issues and Case Studies*. Wallingford: CABI Publishing.

Brandth, B. 1995. Rural masculinity in transition: gender images in tractor advertisements. *Sociologia Ruralis*, 34(2–3), 127–49.

Broughton, C. and Walton, T. 2006. Downsizing masculinity: gender, family and fatherhood in post-industrial America. *Anthropology of Work Review*, 27(1), 1–12.

Bryant, L. 1999. The detraditionalization of occupational identities in farming in South Australia. *Sociologia Ruralis*, 39(2), 236–61.

Bucknell, D. Paulmer, H. and Fuller, T. 2005. *Manufacturing in Rural Ontario*. Rural Development Division, Ontario Ministry of Municipal Affairs and Housing.

Bye, L.M. 2009. 'How to be a rural man': young men's performances and negotiations of rural masculinities. *Journal of Rural Studies*, 25, 278–88.

Campbell, H. 2006. Real men, real locals, real workers: realizing masculinity in small town New Zealand, in *Country Boys: Masculinity and Rural Life*, edited by H. Campbell, M. Mayerfeld Bell and M. Finney. University Park: University of Pennsylvania Press, 87–103.

Canadian Auto Workers. 2008. *Manufacturing Matters: Jobs Fact Sheet* [Online: Canadian Auto Workers]. Available at: http://www.caw.ca/en/campaigns-issues-manufacturing-matters-manufacturing-jobs-fact-sheet-2008.htm. [Accessed: 9 June 2010].

Carbert, L. 1995. *Agrarian Feminism*. Toronto: University of Toronto Press.

Collins, J. and Quark, A. 2006. Globalizing firms and small communities: the apparel industry's changing connection to rural labor markets. *Rural Sociology*, 71(2), 281–310.

Connell, R.W. and Messerschmidt, J.W. 2005. Hegemonic masculinity: rethinking the concept. *Gender and Society*, 19(6), 829–59.

Corbett, M. 2007. *Learning to Leave: The Irony of Schooling in a Coastal Community*. Halifax: Fernwood Publishing.

Fine, L. 1993. 'Our big factory family': masculinity and paternalism at the Reo Motor Car Co. of Lansing, Michigan. *Labor History*, 34(2–3), 274–291.

Finney, M., Campbell, H. and Mayerfield Bell, M. 2004. *Rural Masculinities: Towards a New Research Agenda*. Paper to the XI World Congress of Rural Sociology: Globalisation, Risks and Resistance, Trondheim, Norway, 25–30 July 2004.

Fuller, A. and O'Leary, S. 2008. *The Impact of Access to Transportation on the Lives of Rural Women* [Online: Rural Women Making Change]. Available at: http://www.rwmc.uoguelph.ca/document.php?d=181 [Accessed June 9, 2010].

High, S. 2003. *Industrial Sunset: The Making of North America's Rust Belt, 1969–1984*. Toronto: University of Toronto Press.

Hughes, A. and Nativel, C. 2005. Lone parents and paid work: evidence from rural England, in *Critical Studies in Rural Gender Issues*, edited by J. Little and C. Morris. London: Ashgate, 27–44.

Kay, J.H. 1997. *Asphalt Nation: How the Automobile Took Over America and How We Can Take It Back*. Berkeley and Los Angeles: University of California Press.

Leach, B. 1999. Transforming rural livelihoods: gender, culture and restructuring in three Ontario Communities, in *Restructuring Caring Labour*, edited by S. Neysmith. Toronto: Oxford University Press, 209–25.

Leach, B. and Yates, C. Forthcoming. *Negotiating Risk, Seeking Security, Losing Solidarity.*

Little, J. 1997. Employment, marginality and women's self-identity, in *Contested Countryside Cultures: Otherness, Marginalisation and Rurality*, edited by P. Cloke and J. Little. London: Routledge, 167–87.

Little J. and Austin, P. 1996. Women and the rural idyll. *Journal of Rural Studies*, 12(2), 101–111.

Little, J. and Morris, C. 2005. Introduction, in *Critical Studies in Rural Gender Issues*, edited by J. Little and C. Morris. London: Ashgate, 1–8.

Little, J. and Panelli, R. 2003. Gender research in rural geography. *Gender, Place and Culture*, 10(3), 281–89.

Machum. S. 2011. *Farm Wives' Work: A Comparative Study of Dairy and Potato Farming in New Brunswick, Canada*. Lewiston: The Edwin Mellen Press.

Morris, C. and Evans, N. 2001. Cheese makers are always women: gendered representations of farm life in the agricultural press. *Gender, Place and Culture*, 8(4), 375–90.

Morris, C. and Little, J. 2005. Rural work: an overview of women's experiences, in *Critical Studies in Rural Gender Issues*, edited by J. Little and C. Morris. London: Ashgate, 9–26.

Morse-Dunkerley, C. 2003. Risky geographies: teens, gender and rural landscape in North America. *Gender, Place and Culture*, 11(4), 559–79.

Musson, P. 2008. *Fleck Strike* [Online: OPSEU Local 110 Faculty Union, Fanshawe College]. Available at: http://www.opseu110.ca/Newsletters/Web_Feature_Fleck.htm [accessed: 7 May 2010].

Newman, K. 1993. *Declining Fortunes: The Withering of the American Dream*. New York: Basic Books.

Ni Laoire, C. 1999. Gender issues in Irish rural out migration, in *Migration and Gender in the Developed World*, edited by P. Boyle and K. Halfacree. London: Routledge, 223–37.

Peck, J. 1996. *Work-Place: The Social Regulation of Labour Markets*. New York: Guilford Press.

Pini, B. 2008. *Masculinities and Management in Agricultural Organizations Worldwide*. London: Ashgate.

Pred, A. and Watts, M. 1992. *Reworking Modernity: Capitalism and Symbolic Discontent.* New Brunswick: Rutgers University Press.

Rankin, C. 2003. Anthropologies and geographies of globalization. *Progress in Human Geography*, 27(6), 708–34.

Reay, D. 2005. Beyond Consciousness? The psychic landscape of social class. *Sociology*, 39(5), 911–28.

Sachs, C. 1996. *Gendered Fields: Rural Women, Agriculture and Environment.* Boulder: Westview.

Saugeres, L. 2002. Of tractors and men: masculinity, technology and power in a French farming community. *Sociologia Ruralis*, 42(2), 143–59.

Skeggs, B. 1997. *Formations of Class and Gender: Becoming Respectable.* London: Sage.

Skeggs, B. 2004. *Class, Self, Culture.* London: Routledge.

Sugiman, P. 2001. Privilege and oppression: the configuration of race, gender, and class in Southern Ontario Auto Plants, 1939 to 1949. *Labour/Le Travail*, 47, 1–83.

Wendt, S. 2009. *Domestic Violence in Rural Australia.* Annandale, New South Wales: The Federation Press.

Winson, A. 1997. Does class consciousness exist in rural communities? The impact of restructuring and plant shutdowns in rural Canada. *Rural Sociology*, 62(4), 429–53.

Winson, A. and Leach, B. 2002. *Contingent Work, Disrupted Lives: Labour and Community in the New Rural Economy.* Toronto: University of Toronto Press.

Yates, C. and Leach, B. 2007. Industrial work in a post-industrial age, in *Work in Tumultuous Times: Critical Perspectives*, edited by V. Shalla and W. Clement. Kingston and Montreal: McGill Queen's University Press, 163–19.

Chapter 8

Digging Deeper: Rural Appalachian Women Miners' Reconstruction of Gender in a Class Based Community

Suzanne E. Tallichet

During the late 1970s hundreds of rural women in the Appalachian region of the United States, taking full advantage of a successful class action suit over sex discrimination in the coal industry, began working in large underground coal mines throughout central Appalachia (Hall 1990). However, by the end of the following decade as the coal industry went into decline, women were also disproportionately and permanently laid off from their mining jobs. Simultaneously as traditionally male dominated mining employment declined in the region, the central Appalachian economy began an unprecedented restructuring as female dominated service employment expanded (Maggard 1994, Miewald and McCann 2004). Unfortunately, there is little scholarship examining the gender struggles that ensued at work and in their homes and communities for women workers. As Miewald and McCann (2004) assert there needs to be a greater focus on the microsites where these gender role struggles have occurred. This chapter addresses this gap in the literature by reporting on a study of Appalachian women miners in the latter part of the twentieth century. These women, whose stories are reflected in other studies of women engaged in non-traditional employment in other male dominated class centric rural extractive industries in the West (Brandth 1994, Eveline and Booth 2002, Keck and Powell 2006, Mayes and Pini 2010, Pini 2005), represented an early challenge to capitalist patriarchy in the emerging post-colonialism of the Appalachian region.

Because studies of rural women's interests are more typically located in the domestic sphere (Bryant and Pini 2008), rural women's entry into a classed and intensely masculine identified occupation, such as underground coal mining, sheds further light on the incremental changes that occur at the intersection of gender and class. The present study focuses on how Appalachian women miners negotiated and reconstructed their identities as they challenged the masculine hegemonic discourses similar to those encountered by women working in other non-traditional occupations. In particular, it examines the various gender management strategies women miners developed for both resisting and accommodating the highly masculinized subculture of underground coal mining during their ongoing struggle to be considered legitimate. In parallel fashion, their gender management strategies are viewed in terms of both the 'undoing' and 'doing' of gender (Butler 2004, Risman 2009, West and Zimmerman 1987). Data for this study are based on my in-depth interviews with 14 women, seven men miners and the mine superintendent working at a large underground coal mine in southern West Virginia during the peak of the region's coal production in mid 1990s. Specifically, this chapter is divided into several sections centring on how the women resisted men's constructions of their entry into mining but accommodated to dominant discourses, attempting to replace men's sexualization of work relations with their claims to be 'the breadwinner' and men's attention to their inadequacies by becoming 'a good miner'.

Theoretical Framework

Historically, women's roles have been sharply defined and circumscribed by rural Appalachians' more traditional gender role ideology (Maggard 1994, 1999, Pudup 1990). Feminist scholars have noted that rural women's roles and corresponding beliefs about 'a woman's place' have been notoriously slow to change particularly in mining communities (Gibson-Graham 1992, 1996, Mayes and Pini 2008, Tickamyer and Henderson 2003). These traditional notions about men's and women's work are more strictly defined and ultimately reinforced by the interests of capital in the region.

To review briefly, previous scholarship on Appalachia has defined the region as an 'internal colony', focusing on the acquisition of natural resources and the exploitation of labour by absentee corporate owners and local elites, along with the destruction of Appalachian culture via the substitution of outside institutional and administrative control of the region's indigenous populace, particularly through the establishment of 'coal camps' (Caudill 1962, Eller 1982, Lewis and Knipe 1978). These paternalistic forms of control precluded miners from having a voice in community affairs, as Appalachians lost of control over their regions' natural resources and local institutions. Having suffered both economic and cultural exploitation, generations of central Appalachians continue to bear the scars of real poverty and the stigma of perceived inferiority. These scholars further argue that a 'condition of racism' is evidenced by the stereotyping of Appalachians as lazy and backward, even by small independent coal operators who constitute a separate class of local elites. Thus, two basic social classes and their mutually antagonistic relationship have evolved from these oppressive practices.[1]

---

1. As capitalists rapidly industrialized central Appalachia from 1880 until 1930, they established coal camps featuring 'stabilizing' institutions such as churches, schools, stores, and their own local law enforcement (Eller 1982). Miners were paid by credit or in company scrip, not cash, which could only be used at the company store and miners lived in company housing insuring a stable labour supply. Company officials also hired diverse racial and ethnic groups meant to divide the labour force and preclude unionization via segregated housing and job discrimination (Eller 1982). In sum, the coal operators created a culturally

Feminist scholars have also contended that the colonization of central Appalachia not only created two different and distinct economic classes, but it also established a division of labour in the family and sex segregation in the workplace (Maggard 1994, 1999). As the coal industry came to dominate the region's economy by turning the male members of subsistence farm families into wage dependent miners, the type of working-class masculinity associated with coal mining, mobilizing around notions of physicality, strength and technological expertise came to be privileged (Scott 2007). As women became more dependent on their husband's mining wages, patriarchal mining families came to resemble the 'little white man's colony' where working-class men could now more easily dominate their unpaid labouring wives and children (Mies 1986, Seitz 1995) or what Campbell (1986) has called 'proletarian patriarchy'. This was accompanied by a 'two-pronged, gendered ideology [that] emerged to justify this division and unequal valuing of labour' (Maggard 1994: 16) which also served the interests of capitalists (Barry 2001, Eviota 1992, Gibson-Graham 1996, Woods 1995). For generations, the resulting hegemony has supported what Scott (2007) calls a 'dependent' construction of masculinity strengthened by the intertwined notions of male breadwinning via legitimate work, patriotism and moral worth similar to that found by Bryant and Pini (2008) also located at the intersection of rurality, class and gender among members of Australian farming communities.

Looking through a post-colonial lens, Appalachia is viewed in a global context, as similar to other rural regions around the world that are similarly affected by expanding empires, the appropriation of land and other resources, ecological destruction and the 'othering' of its inhabitants. Typically, colonized people are those whose voices have been swallowed, their true faces and hearts hidden, their realities unrecorded because they mar the image of progress and prosperity that modernity and its corresponding growth brings to 'unfinished' rural areas (Harris 2001). In the post-colonial view, rural Appalachian women miners are not deemed to be 'super exploited' by the structural frame of a capitalist patriarchy (Levi and Dean 2003, Scott 2003).

Rather a post-colonial approach recognizes that subordinated individuals should not be categorized as powerless and views them as determined to survive and empower themselves in light of dominant colonial discourses via self assignment. Specifically then, rural working-class women are seen as actors in passive and active defiance of the corresponding dominant gendered discourses by which working-class women in particular, have been typically defined and presumed to be controlled. Thus, in the present study, women as miners are regarded as breaking the mould of essentialist assumptions about working-class Appalachian women as miner's wives, daughters and auxiliary members of the union. This study seeks to show how women miners struggled to define themselves as women while doing a 'man's job'.

This research draws attention to the agency of women miners. As Bennett (2004: 149) has argued, 'Women are not just the products of controlling structures and not simply the recipients of powerful actions because workings of power are complex

---

divided, institutionally captive labour force that was dependent upon and, to some degree, relatively powerless against their domination.

and individuals negotiate power relations in subtle ways'. In the constructivist sense, as established by previous scholars, gender is performed (Butler 2004, Risman 2009, West and Zimmerman 1987). Women's actions can be considered in terms of the more accommodating 'doing gender' (West and Zimmerman 1987) or as resistance when they are 'undoing gender' (Butler 2004, Risman 2009). Men do gender because they have a status stake in doing so (Ridgeway 2009), but when they undo gender, egalitarianism results (Risman 2009). The gendered navigations men and women make in this regard are, of course, mediated by other social locations, such as, for example, class.

Women facing conflicting demands to do femininity and yet perform their masculinized work roles must practice gender management strategies of doing and undoing of gender (Butler 2004, Risman 2009, West and Zimmerman 1987). This allows them to establish their legitimacy as women and miners without suffering the more severe consequences of seriously disrupting the highly masculine hegemonic discourses of the workplace. Resistance itself is a demonstration of these power structures and their hegemonic control. At the same time, women may also act in ways, either consciously out of a loyalty to cultural traditions or unwittingly, that reproduce controlling gendered discourses (Bennett 2004). Undoing gender has implications for changing the culturally maintained gender frames (Ridgeway 2009), while doing gender may help explain why dominant discourses are so resistant to change. When women attempt to undo gender, how they reconcile the discrepancies between gender as hegemonically defined and their own deviations from it constitute their reconstruction of their gendered identity. Therefore, the aim of the present study is to identify various gender management strategies used by Appalachian women miners and to assess the extent to which these strategies may have altered the masculinist discourses meant to either exclude or dominate them.

Methodology

The large operating coal mine under study is located in a relatively isolated rural area in southern West Virginia. While employing only about half as many miners today, during the late 1970s the company employed around 800 miners, including 97 women most of whom were hired as a result of a successful lawsuit.[2] Work crews performed either maintenance duties on 'down' sections or they were 'running' coal on coal producing sections. Sections were supervised by a foreman

---

2   Before 1977, women in the Appalachian coal fields were hired on their own often by filing complaints with state equal employment agencies (Hall 1990). In May of 1978, a successful class action lawsuit filed by the Coal Employment Project women's advocacy group ushered hundreds of rural Appalachian women into underground coal mining jobs. The suit, filed against 153 coal companies so accountable because they had federal government contracts, mandated the hiring of women previously denied mining jobs with back pay and to begin hiring more women on a quota basis.

or 'boss', who was a non-union, salaried company employee. These supervisors made the day-to-day decisions regarding production activities, safety and each crew member's work assignment. All the miners were members of the United Mine Workers of America (UMWA). According to the miners' contract, mining jobs were classified among five job grades. Grade 1 jobs required fewer skills and more physical strength while jobs in Grades 2 to 5 required specific operative skills or certification.

Data for this study were collected during the fall of 1990 and the summers of 1995 and 1996 using in-depth interviews, observation and document study. In total, I spent two months in the field interviewing 14 coal mining women, seven men miners and the mine superintendent. I also had informal conversations with additional women and several more men miners and members of the local community. Seven of the 1990 interviews with the women and mine superintendent were repeated during 1995 or 1996. Three of the men miners I interviewed were also local union officials at that time. Virtually all of the miners I interviewed were life long residents of southern West Virginia who were born into coal mining families.

Both purposive and snowball sampling techniques were used. Women were selected to insure a diverse sample in terms of age, seniority, job rank and experiences with harassment and discrimination. Most of my interviews with miners, especially the women, lasted at least three hours and usually took place in my motel room or in miners' homes. A few other interviews took place in the women's bathhouse, in a local diner, or in isolated places on the company's property. These more private locations were selected so that informants felt less inhibited about discussing sensitive topics. Observation was done during my almost daily visits to the women's bathhouse and occasional visits to the mine office, during my underground mine tour, or out in the local community. Document study was limited to recording data from open records posted in the lamp house where miners get their equipment and often congregate between shifts.

In the fall of 1990 when I began my study, the company employed a dozen foremen, all white males, and almost 500 miners, including 23 women. By 1996, there were 18 women working at the mine. Although a few women worked in pairs on their crews, most of the women worked alone on all male crews. The women I interviewed were diverse in age, race, education, marital status, childbearing, mining experience, and current job. Most of them were hired between 1978 and 1980. In 1996 most were in their late thirties and forties, two were aged 56 and 62. Three had less than a high school education, nine had high school diplomas, and two had gone to college, but never graduated. Most of the women were single mothers when they began mining. Only two were single and childless and only one was married. All of them said they need a coal mining job to support either themselves or their families. In 1996, their years of mining experience ranged between 12 and 21.

Woman Miner as Breadwinner

As the women miners in this study began to work underground they soon realized the depths of resentment for them both above and below ground. In the community, an older man miner declared that 'as a general rule, people believe that women don't need to be in the workplace anywhere, let alone a coal mine'. Similar to some men miners, the non-mining men said they disapproved of women in the mines believing that women were not capable of doing the work, that the men would have to take up the slack and that women were 'taking a man's job'. In contrast, women working for pay in the local community tended to be sympathetic towards the women miners. Because at one time women were almost 10 per cent of the total underground workforce, one woman working at a local diner declared 'that's a woman's mine and if I was younger, that's where I'd be working'. It is noteworthy that such a small percentage of women constituted such a substantial challenge to the dominant discourses about underground coal mining in the community.

Generally, with few exceptions, miners' wives showed the deepest resentment toward women miners. One woman miner recalled that after 'a woman [miner] was killed in one of the other mines, this guy said, that his wife said she wished that every one of us [women] at [the mine] got killed'. Some women miners felt that the wives were jealous of them simply because they 'were out working, making a living and independent' or, as Keck and Powell (2006) found in a Canadian mining community, miner's wives feared that women miners would take either their husband's job or their husbands.

Most of the women miners blamed the wives for the men's attitudes towards them making it more difficult for the men to accept them as coal miners. 'The wives were so jealous', said one of the women miners, 'that the husbands would actually go home and tell their wives that they didn't work with women'. Moreover, men miners often avoided women coworkers when with their wives in public. One woman concluded, 'I think they relate back to their wives griping, raising Cain at home. Well, you're in here with him and automatically we're whores. When we enter the coal mines, we're whores'.

Within the norms of the patriarchal family dominant in this working-class community, men work to support their families while women are expected to work in the home caring for them. It is in the class based interest of miner's wives to support working-class masculinist discourses that define men's and women's respective statuses according to their 'essential natures'. Men are assumed to be rational, competitive, assertive, and goal oriented, while women are assumed to be what men are not, meaning they are expected to be more emotional, cooperative, nurturing, and passive. Therefore, men are suited for coal mining and women are not. Working-class women who violate this controlling discourse are held accountable and become stigmatized according to their most salient characteristic; their sexuality (West and Zimmerman 1987).

In a study by Eveline and Booth (2002), Australian women were welcomed by managers who presumed they would have a 'civilizing influence' through their 'minding' work which only served to reinforce masculine discourses underground. In contrast, Appalachian women were hired based on a legal mandate. The mine superintendent saw this as his loss of managerial control over the workforce saying that the company 'had to pay the price for social change'. Like many men miners, he envisioned the irreparable erosion of working-class men's privilege. He believed that most of the women hired then were neither capable of nor serious about being coal miners because they were either 'looking for adventure or a sugar daddy'. Men miners echoed his sentiments by labelling 'all of [the women] troublemakers right off', said one man miner, '[because] they were taking men's jobs needed to feed their families'.

As the women began working underground, they said some men were supportive and showed them the 'tricks of the trade' representing an undoing of gender that rejected masculinist hegemony for more egalitarian discourses. By accepting the women as legitimate workers they also acknowledged that the women had a right to work underground. However, other men miners were uncooperative and openly hostile telling women they 'ought to get out of here and let a good man have this job. They said we should be home cleaning house, raising kids. That it's no place for us'. Some foremen assigned women to the most physically demanding jobs intending to force the women to quit.

As numerous other feminist scholars have asserted, men's 'sexualization of work relations' depicting women as sex objects created the greatest difficulties for women miners because it underscored the hegemonic notion that women were not capable of working as miners (DiTomaso 1989, Enarson 1984, Eveline and Booth 2002, Keck and Powell 2006, Swerdlow 1989). During their first few years on the job, the women estimated that up to at least half of the men miners and foremen demonstrated several forms of sexualized behaviours: verbal innuendo, body language, social derogation, sexual propositioning and sexual bribery (Gruber and Bjorn 1982). Sexual propositioning by men coworkers posed no particular problem for some women because, as one woman said, 'a man is too proud to keep asking if you're not going to go. If you made it known, they're not going to come back and keep begging you to go out'.

However, as in Keck and Powell's (2006) study of Canadian women miners, both women and men in the present study knew that a boss's sexual propositioning usually led to sexual bribery. In her study of organizations, DiTomaso (1989) found that supervisors in particular misused their authority to delegitimize and stigmatize women workers as unsuccessful. Particularly during the women's first few years underground, some bosses made women's work assignments contingent upon sexual favours. As one older man miner admitted, 'if the guys asked her out, and she wouldn't go out, why they wouldn't help her as much as they normally would. If the foremen asked her out, and she wouldn't go, the foremen would make sure she got a dirty work assignment'. The superintendent resented having 'to teach the miners what harassment was' indicating that having women working underground defied the 'natural' hegemonic order at the mine. At the same time he handled these cases involving management swiftly by firing several offending foremen.

Generally women resisted the men's verbal harassment and more extreme sexualized behaviours by developing a new gender management strategy designed to draw new gendered boundaries. Similar to farm women's use of 'the farm as business discourse' in Pini's (2005) study, the women miners in the present study developed a 'women miner as breadwinner' discourse. For example, when a man coworker questioned why she was taking a man's job, one newly divorced woman miner quipped, 'It was a man that put me here. It's my job and I'm keeping it'. In addition, there was a narrative shared among the women that further reinforced women's 'breadwinner' status. One of the women was confronted by a group of miners' wives at the dentist's office. In response to their disapproval, she invoked her newly gendered breadwinner status adding 'or would you rather I go on welfare?' Notably, her legitimacy was based on her financial independence and avoidance of the welfare stigma.

Regarding men's sexual advances, one woman said, 'When I first came here I've made it known: Don't bother me. I'm here to work, I'm not here for romance, [but for] finance'. Another woman said 'Don't get in my path, I won't get in yours. Once you establish yourself, they know your boundaries'. Generally, invoking the woman miner as breadwinner discourse led to the men's dismissal of the women's symbolized sexuality. Conversely, it was relatively easy to ruin a woman's legitimacy based on her 'sexualized' status at the mine via innuendo alone. Thus, most of the women disassociated themselves from these women by adopting the men's discursive standard for evaluating a woman's worthiness as a miner. 'The majority of the men up there are good to you if you let them', said one woman. 'But they'll treat you how they see you act.' Women were very aware that each one of them was taken to represent her gendered category.

In sum, by invoking the 'women miner as breadwinner' discourse the women successfully avoided the attribution of moral degeneracy and their marginalization according to the prevailing class based masculinist discourses. As found in other studies about women miners in Canada (Keck and Powell 2006) and Australia (Eveline and Booth 2002), having at least modified the men's sexualization of them, now the women in the present study could focus on becoming 'good miners'.

Becoming a Good Miner

Like most of the men in the sample, many of the women were from mining families so they understood what it meant to be a 'good miner' and they knew they needed to prove themselves by building a solid work reputation and accommodating to various aspects of the gendered subculture of mining. These two tasks were key to developing cooperative work relations with both women and men miners.

Most of the women adopted the men's standards for hard work and for evaluating the work performances of other men and women miners. As one woman told me, if a woman wanted to establish a reputation for being a good miner she should 'get the toughest job underground and go at it'. In this sense women adopted the tenets of an embodied and physical discourse of working-class masculinity predominant amongst them. Another woman with a similarly solid work reputation said that the men on her crew often made her work harder not to discourage her, but to 'make a miner out of you'. However, other men sometimes volunteered to help the women with their work which put them in a double bind for proving themselves according to the masculinist hegemonic work standards. Most women refused their help and were occasionally criticized for being 'too independent'. But those women who either asked for help or accepted men's help were ridiculed by other men and women miners alike for failing to conform to the dominant discourses regarding work underground. But regardless of how hard they worked, the women in the present study continued to feel anxiety and pressure over their everyday work performances attributable to a persistent sexual division of labour at the mine as found among other women in mining (Mayes and Pini 2010).

As with the Australian women miners in Eveline and Booth's (2002: 565) study, some women in the present study felt that because they were 'latecomers in the world of mining', they should conform to the gendered ordering and the more feminized behaviours men expected. While most of them refused to play the feminine role as they worked underground, most of them to varying degrees engaged in sexualized behaviours themselves. Minimally, this included occasionally using profanity or 'men's language', telling jokes and even engaging in mock flirtations. One woman declared that 'I loosened up after three or four years. Now my workplace? I enjoy it'.

The women also voiced sympathy for the men at the mine. For example one woman declared 'It's a man's world and I knew that when I went into it. Things have changed so much and men had to change their ways'. Like the Australian women miners (Eveline and Booth 2002), some women viewed the mine as a man's workplace where women simply had to learn to fit in, but such accommodations had limits. They knew they had not significantly changed men or the gendered hegemonic discourses at the mine. Referring to men's sexualization of women, one woman declared 'it's not gone, it's just more subtle now'. Another said that gender boundaries at the mine, 'ain't never going to erase'. In sum, while men's more severe forms of sexualization exaggerating gender differences was a reminder that women had no place in the mines, the more subtle forms eventually defined women's place underground.

At the case study mine, the resetting of gendered boundaries and gendered relationships mirrored those hegemonic discourses typical of the patriarchal family. Every woman in the sample said their work crew was like 'being in a family'. They acknowledged their crew's cooperative spirit and individual feelings of loyalty. 'We're like family, it's just like we go there with our own section and we're not around nobody else, we're just around each other', said one woman, 'I got used to working with a certain group of people. I don't like the idea of being changed off and working with other people now'. Crew members looked to each other for emotional support, often confiding in each other about their problems with spouses and/or children.

However, the emergence of various familial styles of interaction between the women and men at the mine marks the terms upon which the men were willing to accept women as workers. Within the Appalachian region, the working-class family has endured as a solidly patriarchal social unit in which gender relations and women's subordinate status have been relatively slow to change (Scott 1995, Seitz 1995). The survival of subordinate group members relies on their knowledge and understanding of those who dominate them, while simultaneously adopting new identities for redefining themselves (Collins 1990). Although the women had established their reconstructed 'woman miner as breadwinner' identity, men at the mine acted to curtail its application as a sexual division of labour emerged underground.

Reflecting Burton's (1991) 'masculinity protection strategies', foremen and some men miners began to redefine and reset gender based boundaries underground. Generally, men expected the women to function in a housewife role underground as an extension of the patriarchal family discourse much like women miners in Australia (Eveline and Booth 2002) and Canada (Keck and Powell 2006) and women in other traditionally male dominated occupations such as farming (Pini 2005). In Eveline and Booth's (2002) study, women were expected to do 'minding work' corresponding to what other feminist scholars have called 'housewifization' (Mies 1986, Seitz 1995).

Among Canadian miners, Keck and Powell (2006) found that the myth that men had a right to mining jobs because they were physically stronger and still better suited for it persisted. Similarly and ironically men miners in the present study claimed that women weren't physically strong enough to be coal miners, yet the majority of women at the mine had been doing jobs requiring 'brute labour' for years which could also explain why they felt constant pressure to prove themselves in these capacities. At the same time, men at the mine asserted that 'there are some jobs women can do'.

One man miner explained that 'women are most suited for gang work where they've got a man there to do the heavy lifting and the women do what they can'. Likewise, women also readily identified 'women's jobs' underground, saying 'you got yourself on the belt, that's a woman's job. You go shovel the belt, you help the mason. Most of the time if I'm not by myself, I am helping one person'. Another woman said that unlike the men on her crew, she was always expected to clean up the dinner hole until one day she refused. And another woman who likened herself to a 'mining housewife' told me:

> I carried cinder block and rock dust, I put belt together, I cleaned up the garbage, I carried their junk to them if they wanted to work with it. It's go get me this, go get me that. You just do all the tasks that they don't want to do. Like the

men, when they set up a belt head, they throw down everything. They never put nothing away. Well, it's up to us to go clean up their mess.

However, more than men miners, it was usually the foremen who demonstrated their lack of confidence in the women's abilities to perform even the simplest of mechanical tasks. With a note of bitterness in her voice, one woman said that her men coworkers 'don't think women are smart enough to put something together, which I can do. I've done a whole lot. And the boss goes right along with it. It's hard [when] he's got the men putting [machinery] together. I don't think it is right'. Usually, foremen simply ignored women when assigning operative tasks to miners or providing on the job training opportunities. Finally, during our interview I asked the superintendent why women at the mine were disproportionately concentrated in the general labouring, entry level jobs. He attributed this to 'the natural settling of their skills and their application'.

In the Australian case men found that women kept the mine cleaner, more readily took orders and listened to the men's problems (Eveline and Booth 2002). What the two case studies have in common is that regardless of their hiring circumstances, women were expected to function as 'mining housewives'. Moreover, both the Australian and Appalachian women experienced the sexualization of work relations and the workplace, a sexual division of labour related to mechanized skills, and were generally denied on the job training; all for the sake of keeping hegemonic masculinity intact. Moreover, as Wainwright (2007) found among weavers' and millworkers' workplaces, spaces in the mine became gendered. Women were relegated to maintenance jobs in support of and in service to men in 'down' sections of the mine while men were disproportionately found in jobs requiring machine running skills producing coal. As other feminist scholars have found machines are still a 'masculine' boundary marker (Brandth 1994, Cockburn 1985, Pini 2005).

The overlay of dominant discourses prevalent in the working-class patriarchal family at the mine also supported men miners' greater legitimacy in the breadwinner role. As found previously, one of the major enduring elements of working-class masculinist hegemony was the belief that because men are presumably stronger, quicker and mechanically minded they are privileged as breadwinners and deserve better paying jobs running machinery (Keck and Powell 2006). Thus, the altered discourses at the mine allowed for the assimilation of women in 'minding' capacities and reserved more lucrative skilled jobs for men which was enforced according to formal contractual policies corrupted by these dominant discourses (Keck and Powell 2006, Tallichet 2006).

After working underground for over a decade, women and men no longer complained about each other. The women said that most men now viewed them as individuals rather than categorically as women. However, as the superintendent said, those women who remained working underground were 'the cream of the crop' or exceptions to the hegemonic rule leaving the working-class masculinist discourses of coal mining relatively undisturbed. The superintendent remarked

'We don't even think in terms of male and female anymore'. All the women felt they had the right to work underground, some felt they had a right to advance, and to a degree the women accepted a milder form of sexualized work relations as a gendered form of jocularity demonstrating the miners' everyday 'give and take' expected of all 'good miners'. It also represented a slight adjustment in working-class masculinist discourses and a hegemonic normalizing of women as miners.

Conclusion

Women miners' identity construction is formed by competing discourses that are infused by class and gender. Women who became involved in the Appalachian mining industry confronted a workplace in which a particular form of classed masculinity was predominant and around which they had to negotiate. They adopted a number of strategies to manage their vulnerable position, such as for example, positioning themselves within a 'breadwinner' discourse or taking up the nomenclature of the 'good miner', but ultimately these did not offer a serious challenge to the highly masculine identity of underground coal mining. This is no doubt because, in large part, this highly masculine identity is itself embedded in what are classed and masculinized identities; that of 'the breadwinner' and 'the good miner'.

Whether any further developments would have occurred can only be left to one's imagination as underground mining employment in central Appalachia began to sharply decline during the 1980s and into the 1990s. The type of pit closures that have been documented in research in Britain (Waddington et al. 2001), have been mirrored across Appalachia and as such since men have become less active in mining women have had to increase their wage work mostly by necessity rather than by choice. But it could also be argued that this newly constituted gender identity inspired and supported rural Appalachian women as they began to seek paid work outside their homes in the expanding service sector, chipping away at the male breadwinner discourse.

The restructuring of the Appalachian economy presents new opportunities and challenges for feminist and class based inquiry (Bennett 2004). While women have taken up the new role of breadwinners this is tempered by the fact that the nature of the available employment means that they are on very low wages and/or in part-time positions. Further, domestic violence has increased as laid off miners stay home assuming childcare responsibilities while women go to work (Maggard 1994, Miewald and McCann 2004). In this manner capitalism has seriously contested the traditional working-class gendered discourses within Appalachian families begging the question that if these economic changes persist, how might the restructuring of gender roles within working-class families and communities be reconditioned and forever altered.

According to Miewald and McCann (2004: 1060–1), 'as the dominance of the coal industry declines, some [women] have developed their own businesses and it is becoming more common for women, especially younger ones, to speak out about issues that affect them, such as domestic violence and welfare reform'. They note that the second generation of working-class rural Appalachian women are today spearheading the newer social, economic and environmental justice movements in the region's coal field communities by becoming politically and economically active in arenas which were previously an all male preserve.

Thus, despite their relatively smaller numbers, women miners have been more than a symbolic representation of gendered struggle. The hegemonic discourses found in the patriarchal family supported those found in the workplace. As long as the family was a model for workplace notions and practices, little was drastically changed in the workplace. Their attempts to redefine 'women's work' forged new pathways for the next generation of working-class women in rural Appalachian communities as many of these women also 'strive to redefine the traditional gender ideology and take advantage of new opportunities in waged work' (Miewald and McCann 2004: 1061). As implied in the present findings, the challenge for working-class women in rural Appalachia is for women to bond in ways that foster a more collective consciousness that could benefit them individually in the workplace and the home. All this represents women's continuing struggle to simply enjoy similar forms of hegemonic privilege when they enter male dominated and highly masculinized domains.

References

Barry, J. 2001. Mountaineers are always free? An examination of the effects of mountaintop removal in West Virginia. *Women's Studies Quarterly*, 29(Spring/Summer), 116–30.

Bennett, K. 2004. A time for change? Patriarchy, the former coalfields and family farming. *Sociologia Ruralis*, 44(2), 147–66.

Brandth, B. 1994. Changing femininity: the social construction of women farmers in Norway. *Sociologia Ruralis*, 34(2–3), 27–149.

Bryant, L. and Pini, B. 2008. *Rural Community Narratives of Self-worth: The Moral Value of Gender and Class*. Paper to the Annual Conference of The Australian Sociological Association: Reimagining Sociology, University of Melbourne, Australia, 2–3 December 2008.

Burton, C. 1991. *The Promise and the Price: The Struggle for Equal Opportunity in Women's Employment*. Sydney: Allen and Unwin.

Butler, J. 2004. *Undoing Gender*. New York: Routledge.

Campbell, B. 1986. Proletarian patriarchs and the real radicals, in *The Cutting Edge: Women and the Pit Strike*, edited by V. Seddon. London: Lawrence and Wishart, 249–82.

Caudill, H.M. 1962. *Night Comes to the Cumberlands: A Biography of a Depressed Area*. Boston: Little, Brown and Co.

Cockburn, C. 1985. *Machinery of Dominance: Men, Women and Technical Know-how*. Dover, New Hampshire: Pluto Press.

Collins, P.H. 1990. *Black Feminist Thought: Knowledge, Consciousness, and the Politics of Empowerment*. New York: Routledge.

DiTomaso, N. 1989. Sexuality in the workplace: discrimination and harassment, in *The Sexuality of Organization*, edited by J. Hearn, D. Sheppard, P. Tancred-Sheriff and G. Burrell. London: Sage, 71–90.

Eller, R.D. 1982. *Miners, Millhands, and Mountaineers: Industrialization of the Appalachian South, 1880–1930*. Knoxville: University of Tennessee Press.

Enarson, E.P. 1984. *Woods-Working Women: Sexual Integration in the U.S. Forest Service*. Birmingham: University of Alabama Press.

Eveline, J. and Booth, M. 2002. Gender and sexuality in discourses of managerial control: the case of women miners. *Gender, Work and Organization*, 9(5), 556–78.

Eviota, E. 1992. *The Political Economy of Gender*. London: Zed Books.

Gibson-Graham, J.K. 1992. Hewers of cake and drawers of tea: women, industrial restructuring and class processes on the coalfields of central Queensland. *Rethinking Marxism*, 5(4), 29–56.

Gibson-Graham, J.K. 1996. *The End of Capitalism (as we knew it), A Feminist Critique of the Political Economy*. Cambridge: Blackwell Publishers.

Gruber, J.S. and Bjorn, L. 1982. Blue-collar blues: the sexual harassment of women autoworkers. *Work and Occupations*, 9, 271–98.

Hall, B.J. 1990. Women miners can dig it, too!, in *Communities in Economic Crisis: Appalachia and the South*, edited by J. Gaventa, B.E. Smith, and A. Willingham. Philadelphia: Temple University Press, 53–60.

Harris, R.P. 2001. Hidden voices: linking research, practice and policy to the everyday realities of rural people. *Southern Rural Sociology*, 17, 1–11.

Keck, J. and Powell, M. 2006. Women into mining jobs at Inco: challenging the gender division of labor, in *Mining Women: Gender in the Development of a Global Industry, 1670 to 2005*, edited by J.J. Gier and L. Mercier. New York: Palgrave Macmillan, 280–95.

Levi, J.M. and Dean, B. 2003. Introduction, in *At the Risk of Being Heard: Identity, Indigenous Rights, and Postcolonial States*, edited by B. Dean and J.M. Levi. Ann Arbor: University of Michigan Press, 1–44.

Lewis, H.M. and Knipe, E.E. 1978. The colonialism model: the Appalachian case, in *Colonialism in Modern America: The Appalachian Case*, edited by H.M. Lewis, L. Johnson and D. Askins. Boone: Appalachian Consortium Press, 9–31.

Maggard, S.W. 1994. From farm to coal camp to back office and McDonald's: living in the midst of Appalachia's latest transformation. *Journal of the Appalachian Studies Association*, 6, 14–28.

Maggard, S.W. 1999. Gender, race, and place: confounding labor activism in central Appalachia, in *Neither Separate nor Equal: Women, Race, and Class in the South*, edited by B.E. Smith. Philadelphia: Temple University Press, 185–206.

Mayes, R. and Pini, B. 2008. *Women and mining in contemporary Australia: an exploratory study*. Paper to the Annual Conference of The Australian Sociological Association: Reimagining Sociology, University of Melbourne, Australia, 2–3 December 2008.

Mayes, R. and Pini, B. 2010. The 'feminine revolution in mining': A critique. *Australian Geographer*, 41(2), 233–45.

Mies, M. 1986. *Patriarchy and Accumulation on a World Scale: Women in the International Division of Labor*. London: Zed Press.

Miewald, C.E. and.McCann, E.J. 2004. Gender struggle, scale, and the production of place in the Appalachian coalfields. *Environment and Planning*, 36(6), 1045–1064.

Pini, B. 2005. Women tractors and gender management. *International Journal of the Sociology of Food and Agriculture*, 13(1), 1–12.

Pudup, M.B. 1990. Women's work in the West Virginia economy. *West Virginia History*, 49, 7–20.

Ridgeway, C.L. 2009. Framed before we know it: gender shapes social relations. *Gender and Society*, 23(2), 145–60.

Risman, B.J. 2009. From doing to undoing: gender as we knew it. *Gender and Society*, 23(1), 81–4.

Scott, C.V. 2003. From modernization and development to globalization and the new imperialism. *Development and Modernization*, 25(1).

Scott, R.R. 2007. Dependent masculinity and political culture in pro-mountaintop removal discourse: or, how I learned to stop worrying and love the dragline. *Feminist Studies*, 33(3), 484–509.

Scott, S.L. 1995. *Two Sides to Everything: The Cultural Construction of Class Consciousness in Harlan County, Kentucky*. Albany: State University of New York Press.

Seitz, V.R. 1995. *Women, Development, and Communities for Empowerment in Appalachia*. Albany, New York: State University of New York.

Swerdlow, M. 1989. Men's accommodations to women entering a nontraditional occupation: a case of rapid transit operatives. *Gender and Society*, 3(3), 373–87.

Tallichet, S.E. 2006. *Daughters of the Mountain: Women Coal Miners in Central Appalachia*. University Park, Pennsylvania: Penn State Press.

Tickamyer, A.R. and Henderson, D.A. 2003. Rural women: new roles for the New Century?, in *Challenges for Rural America in the 21st Century*, edited by D.L. Brown and L.E. Swanson. University Park: Penn State Press, 109–117.

Waddington, D., Critcher, C., Dicks, B. and Parry, D. 2001. *Out of the Ashes? The Social Impact of Industrial Contraction and Regeneration on Britain's Mining Communities*. London: The Stationary Office.

Wainwright, E.M. 2007. Constructing gender workplace 'types': the weaver-millworker distinction in Dundee's Jute Industry, c. 1880–1910. *Gender, Place and Culture*, 14(4), 467–82.

West, C. and Zimmerman, D.H. 1987. Doing Gender. *Gender and Society*, 1(2), 125–251.
Woods, E.M. 1995. *Democracy Against Capitalism: Renewing Historical Materialism*. Cambridge: Cambridge University Press.

Chapter 9

Class, Rurality and Lone Parents' Connections with Waged Labour: The Mediating Influences of Relational Assets and Human Capital

Annie Hughes

Contrary to the lack of a class based analysis of rural gender research, notions of class (and gender) pervade definitions of, and debates about, (lone) parenthood (Rowlingson and McKay 2002). There is an increasing body of literature which explores the sociality of lone parenthood and uncovers how lone parents are constituted in and by complex networks of power relations (Hughes 2004). These constructions are simultaneously gendered and classed. They are juxtaposed with the construction of good mothering (as opposed to good fathering) epitomized by the traditional idealized model of motherhood, derived from white, middle class society (Roseneil and Mann 1996, Song 1996, Wallbank 2001). In the latter part of the twentieth century, political discourses aligned the growing numbers of lone parent families with the development of an 'underclass' characterized by welfare dependency, societal breakdown, crime and deviancy (Atkinson 1998, Bullock, Wyche and Williams 2001, Murray 1990, 1994). In the United Kingdom throughout the first decade of the 21st century New Labour constructed lone parents as dependent and, to some extent, an underclass (Smith 1999, see also Driver and Martell 2002, Rake 2001, Rodriguez Sumaza 2001). As we leave the first decade of the new millennium, the political response to lone parents has remained negative. The new conservative/liberal coalition government in Britain has strengthened the view that marriage is the 'best environment for families', making clear overtones in support of a tax system which favours married couples. Similar political rhetoric can be identified across many neo-liberal democracies across the Western world (e.g., Van Acker 2005, Little 2001, Wimberly 2000).This chapter explores the links between lone parenthood, class and rurality through the examination of detailed case studies collected during field research in two rural settings in England. The chapter begins by briefly examining the diverse lived experiences of lone parents in rural England. It argues that the tendency to reduce lone parenthood to a narrow set of classed definitions characterized by similar material and social (classed) circumstances obscures the multiple realities underlying the lives of parents defined as 'lone'. The second part of the chapter explores the complex connections between lone parents, class and rurality as they relate to lone parents' involvement in paid work. It introduces the notions of relational assets and human capital to assert that lone parents' relationships with paid work cannot simply be mapped on to traditional class based conceptions of mothering and attitudes to paid work.

The arguments are explored by reference to questionnaires as well as 51 interviews with lone parents (four men and 47 women) in two areas of rural England: Somerset and Cumbria. Located in the south west of England, Somerset can be categorized as an intermediate rural area in which significant migration (from within the United Kingdom) has taken place in recent years, particularly in some of its attractive market towns such as Frome, Street and Glastonbury. However, some parts of the county still suffer from considerable pockets of rural deprivation. Cumbria represents a remote rural area. The case study area extends into two districts, Eden and South Lakeland. Eden is the most sparsely populated district in England. Its economy is largely dependent upon tourism, agriculture and the services that support these industries. Although there are still a few large manufacturing companies, particularly around its main centre of population, Penrith, it is the essentially rural nature of the area that dominates economic activity. South Lakeland is highly dependent upon tourism as it includes parts of both the Lake District and Yorkshire Dales National Parks. Both Cumbria and Somerset have unemployment rates below the national average. However, these low rates of unemployment conceal hidden or seasonal unemployment.

Class Perspectives on Waged Labour and Mothering

McDowell (2006) points out that perhaps the most significant transformation of the early twenty-first century is the movement in Britain to an economy in which employment participation is expected of all working age adults, regardless of their family status. This is especially true of lone parents who have been encouraged, through workfare policies, to participate in the labour market; as well as fulfil their caring responsibilities (Land 2002). A new discourse of mothering has emerged which revolves around ideas of success and personal achievement based around, but not exclusively on, participation in paid employment (Pitt 2002). Indeed, good parenting is parenting which combines the caring role of the parent with their ability to support one's family through participation in waged labour.

Women's increased entry into the relations of waged employment has reconfigured the nature of class connections as well as relations between women in different class positions (McDowell 2006). Middle-class women increasingly employ working-class women to cook, clean and undertake childcare tasks (Gregson and Lowe 1995). Class, then, is essential in understanding these new relations of gender. Moreover, Duncan (2005) recognizes the importance of class based differences in how parents combine employment and caring for their children. Similarly, McDowell et al. (2005) highlight how decisions about paid work are influenced by class position and complex gendered (and class based) understandings of caring responsibilities. The work of Duncan and Edwards' (1999) is particularly relevant here. They developed the concept of 'gendered moral rationalities' to account for the varying understandings lone mothers' (and, in subsequent work, partnered mothers) possess about their responsibilities as mothers and bringing up children and employment. In elaborating upon this Duncan (2005: 54) states 'They were gendered because they dealt with notions of mothering, they were moral in providing answers about the right thing to do, and they were rationalities in providing a framework for taking decisions'. Duncan et al. (2003: 313) characterized gendered rationalities into a threefold typology. That is, 'primarily mother' which gave primacy to the benefits of physically caring for their children themselves; 'primarily worker' where paid work was for themselves as separate to their identity as mothers and finally 'mother/worker integral' where full-time employment was viewed as part of 'good' mothering. The authors claim that 'gendered moral rationalities' are strongly classed. Generally, middle-class mothers tend more towards the 'primarily worker' position, whilst working-class mothers held a 'primarily mother' position.

This chapter argues that, despite the assertions of Duncan et al. (2003), lone parents' decisions about participation in paid employment in rural areas of England cannot simply be read off a class based typology. Rather, two key sets of factors, which in themselves relate to class in complex ways, are identified which act to shape lone parents' engagement with waged employment. The first is the 'relational assets' available to the lone parent. The second set of factors relates more directly to their own human capital most notably their health, employment biographies and educational attainment. These are explored in the following sections. However, before I go on to explore the complex relationships between rural lone parents, their participation in paid work and its class based associations, I wish to briefly outline the small but growing body of research which has focused on the lives and experiences of lone parents in rural locales.

Lone Parents in Rural Areas: A Review of Themes

There is a now embryonic literature which has begun to shed light on the lived realities of lone parents living in a variety of rural contexts. Indeed, policy organizations in the United Kingdom and elsewhere have begun to recognize the problems faced by rural lone parents; particularly with regard to securing and retaining paid employment (Gingerbread 2010, Gloster et al. 2010).

The majority of academic literature concerned with rural lone parent families has focused on their 'survival strategies' as they relate to three key themes; poverty, employment and welfare regimes. For example, Brown and Lichter (2001) compare the economic livelihood strategies amongst metropolitan and non-metropolitan lone mothers in the United States. While they noted that the survival strategies adopted by single mothers in these two different types of areas were remarkably similar, single mothers living in non-metropolitan areas were less likely to benefit economically from full-time employment. Powell (2005) adopts a similar argument in a study of lone mothers from rural Appalachia, also in the United States, arguing the women experience 'regionally specific obstacles to making ends meet'. He continues 'rural areas are more geographically remote and were more likely to have inadequate transportation. Also, jobs and daycare are harder to come by in rural areas' (Powell 2005: 79). Similarly, Marchant (2009) documents the barriers that rural single mothers face in securing access to education, employment, and community in rural Australia. All of these authors question the efficacy of 'work first' policies in non-metropolitan areas addressing the issue of the spatially differentiated outcomes of welfare reform.

A second research theme identifies common characteristics of lone parent households as they relate to participation in paid employment. Ward and Turner (2007), in their work in Northern New England in the United States, argue that young single mothers with lower educational attainment, who perceive themselves to have fewer social networks, are more likely to depend on welfare. This research is supported by more recent work which has identified the importance of informal social networks in enabling lone parents to retain paid employment. Son and Bauer (2010: 107) argue that mothers who have been consistently employed in the same jobs 'receive consistent support from families'. Similarly, Nelson (2005) highlights the importance of social support in the lives of rural single mothers. Nelson's work in rural Vermont highlights how white single mothers enter a social economy characterized by relationships of personal exchange, reciprocity and shared goods and services. She sets this against a back drop of a tough(ening) welfare system that stresses work, personal responsibility and self-sufficiency.

While all these studies contribute to our knowledge of the experiences of lone parents few directly explore relationships of class amongst rural lone parents. In contrast, the following sections of the chapter seek to bring class to the fore in discussions about lone parents.

Constructions of 'The Rural Lone Parent': Participant Perspectives

The experiences of respondents differed widely and their routes into lone parenthood were complex. However, the majority of respondents had become lone parents through a marriage breakdown, as opposed to the breakdown of a non-married partnership or situation of a never partnered parent. Contrary to the underclass thesis, over 53 per cent of respondents in this study were between 35–44, while 36 per cent were between 25–34. Only 2 per cent were younger than 25. Clearly the (under)classed stereotype of the lone parent in popular credence is a gross misrepresentation of the rural lone parents.

Many lone parents in the study were necessarily sensitive to the politics of representation. Lone fathers were particularly cognizant of the feminization of lone parenthood. However, of the one hundred and ninety respondents to the questionnaire, only ten were lone fathers representing less than 6 per cent of the sample. Lone parents' representations of themselves were often significantly at odds with the prevailing stereotypes. However, they were clearly aware of the stereotypes abounding in popular and political rhetoric. Kim, an unemployed lone mother with two dependent children (aged 14 and 12 years) living in South Lakeland in Cumbria stated, 'The worst problem is the political attitude towards single parents as though we are all 16 year old irresponsible parents. Most are divorced/separated/widowed and trying to give their children the best start they can have in life like any other parent'. Indeed Petra, an unemployed lone mother living in Somerset felt that popular constructions had very real implications for how lone parents are viewed in society. She argued, 'People tend to look down on lone parents. Because of this we do not seem to be treated with much respect as "proper" parents and if things go wrong with the child they immediately assume it's our fault for being "lone parents"'. Many of the respondents were at pains to distance themselves from (under)class based stereotypes of lone parents particularly with regard to the issue on state dependency. Indeed, there was evidence of a strong work ethic amongst the rural lone parents sampled and a higher than average employment rate despite the considerable constraints encountered in gaining employment (Hughes and Nativel 2005). At the same time, many involved in the research expressed an awareness that members of their own rural communities had negative views about lone parents and that these were embedded in constructions of them as welfare dependent and unemployed. As Jenny, a self-employed lone parent working full-time, comments 'I would imagine if I did not work or have my own business, people would resent my claiming monies and lack of input into the economy'.

Lone Parents, Rurality and Class: Connections Between Parenting and Paid Work

All of the lone parents articulated a desire to be 'good parents' to their children. During the interviews respondents justified their motivations and actions in terms of the fact that their central goal was the welfare of their children. Parents who were employed talked in terms of being 'good role models', 'independent', 'self-reliant' and 'providing for their children'; as well as nominated the importance of traits such as self-respect and self-worth. Parents who did not work talked in terms of 'being there for their children' and 'not palming them off'. Many parents did not view care simply as a constraint on paid work. Rather, they expressed a strong and resilient desire to care which they believed was non-negotiable. Nevertheless, most lone parents, both those not involved in paid employment at present and those who were employed, felt that it would be appropriate for them to be involved in paid work at some point; when they could do so without having a detrimental effect on their children.

The class divisions of the notion of 'gendered moral rationalities' (Duncan 2005) which contends that middle-class mothers adopt a 'primarily worker' position, whilst working-class mothers tend to embrace a 'primarily mother' position were less distinct in this research. There are several probable reasons for this. Firstly, rural labour markets do not afford a great deal of choice for middle-class well educated women. Semi-professional and professional employment is particularly difficult to attain. Kate who had found a reasonably well paid part-time position stated, 'I have thought about changing my job ... but I've never really seen anything other than cleaning jobs ... once you get to semi-professional levels there just aren't the jobs around'. Lone parents working in professional occupations possessed jobs with better pay, a higher degree of security, more work benefits and better promotion prospects and, as a result, found themselves financially much better off than other lone parents. However, with the exception of teachers, these lone parents worked relatively long distances from their homes as many had found it impossible to find suitable professional employment within the vicinity. Their long (and exhausting) commuting patterns were adding additional cost (relating to petrol and childcare) and placing increased strain on balancing work and family. This strain in some cases, became too much to bear as one lone parent relinquished her employment to prioritize her parental role. Emily, a professional middle-class lone mother working full-time described the pressure of combining her employment with her caring role as mother to her daughter. During her interview she stated that she is looking to rebalance her work and life arguing:

> I am aiming for ... reduced hours ... [so] ... I am not so tired, so stressed ... and to improve the quality of life ... I do an average of six or seven hundred miles a week. It's a lot on top of your working day ... I get home feeling stressed, and then go to bed feeling stressed, and I don't sleep and then wake up feeling tired and it just going on and on and on ... I actually left Bethan at school one afternoon ... it got to twenty past three and I had a phone call from the school ... I cried all the way to school. I'm a bad mother, why I'm doing this to her ... I have good mother days and bad mother days.

Elspeth, a middle-class mother of two children living in Somerset left her well paid job in the banking industry to work as a housekeeper in a local holiday park. She admitted 'it is a bit of a comedown ... but they are so flexible and the Kids Club is great' (employer provides childcare in the summer holidays in the form of a Kids Club). Similarly, Katherine, a middle-class lone parent who is a teacher by profession found combining a paid job with looking after her two children emotionally fraught and physically exhausting. She explained, 'It was awful, awful, awful, awful. I was worn out after school ... I remember doing it. I liked the extra money but I don't know how I managed it'. She ultimately gave up her job and believes she is far happier.

Katherine's observation gestures towards the second reason why a simple dichotomy of middle-class 'worker' and working-class 'mother' holds less credibility in rural locations where community is seen as a strong cultural characteristic, particularly amongst middle-class residents (see Hughes 1997, Little and Austin 1996). Little and Austin (1996) point out that the aspects of rural life that women most value are those that prioritize the community and the family (especially the caring of young children), over their waged labour. This view, they argue, is clearly 'dominated by middle-class professionals' (Little and Austin 1996: 110). These sentiments were shared by a number of middle-class lone mothers in this study. Monica moved to rural Cumbria from London because she wanted a 'better quality of life'. She stated on her questionnaire that, 'My main reason [for moving] was to give up work and be with my children ... a big factor was being able to survive financially without having to juggle work and my children'. For Monica, Cumbria offered a location where she had the space to prioritize her parental role.

Notwithstanding their cultural interpretations of life choices in their rural communities, middle-class women were also often obliged to prioritize their mothering role for the simple reason that the services required for them to continue working were simply not available in many rural locales. This is especially the case for childcare; which is freely available to urban women; if at a significant cost. Barbara, a middle-class mother of three very young children living on income support, found combining waged labour with her role as a lone mother impossible to reconcile in her local socio-spatial context. She was a teacher by profession and like many middle-class women, was in receipt of maintenance (financial support) from her her husband. However, she found it impossible to find local childcare for her three preschool aged children in order for her to return to work. She reflected 'I have the potential to earn a very good salary but there are just not the opportunities here and the childcare is non-existent'.

As discussed, the socio-spatial contexts in many rural areas render it virtually impossible to combine employment; particularly for women undertaking professional jobs. However, the extent to which lone parents' possessed (what I have termed here) 'relational assets' often mark the difference between a lone parent being able to combine paid employment (whether middle or working class) successfully with caring for their families. I discuss this concept in more detail in the following section.

Relational Assets

Relational assets include the resources, both material and emotional, that lone parents can draw upon from their immediate social environment. These resources include financial support from an ex-partner or family members, childcare provided by family or friends, emotional and practical encouragement from local social networks, employers, friends and family. These crucial attributes are particularly significant in rural locations where voluntarism and self-reliance are strongly valued cultural characteristics.

A diverse range of relational assets operate as mediating factors in lone parents' relationships with waged employment as they are shaped in and through rural locales. Many of these relational assets relate to class in disparate ways; but they are not reducible to class based relations; nor can they be explained by them. For example, middle-class women were more likely to have more robust financial arrangements with their ex-partners and were more likely to be in receipt of regular child and spousal maintenance. This meant that it was more economically advantageous for middle-class lone parents receiving maintenance to work as maintenance payments were not deducted from the tax credit calculations (unlike for income support claimants where maintenance is deducted). In this way, middle-class working mothers are better off than working-class lone parents in paid employment. On the other hand, there were no hard and fast rules as to a class typology related to fathers and their contact with their children who, in so doing, provided emotional and practical help to the resident parent. Kate, a working-class lone mother living in a small market town in Somerset and employed 24 hours a week, recalls, 'When they do go to their Dad's I get a complete break … He is still a very hands on dad … It makes life so much easier'. Similarly, Jemima, a middle-class mother of two agreed to share the care of her two children with her ex-husband when they separated. She observed, 'I don't feel like a lone parent because he is very supportive and good with the kids … I get more time for me now than I did when we were married'. Conversely, there was no strong evidence to suggest the existence of any class based differences between the practical support given to lone parents by their ex-partners.

Relational assets can also include financial, practical and emotional support from friends and family; such as the use of a car, payment of debts, and time away from the children. Lorna managed to train as a nurse after her divorce, and is now in a strong position to support her family financially. She attributes her success to the support of her parents who live in the same village. Without their financial, emotional and practical support, Lorna states that she would still be working in the local pub part-time and relying on government benefits. Indeed, her parents remain crucial to her ability to remain in employment. Lorna continues to rely on her mother for childcare in the school holidays. For example, during her interview she observed, 'I haven't even thought of the holidays. I have no idea what I will do with my children. I guess it will be down to my mum again. I hope!' Having the practical support of her parents has meant that Lorna does not have to worry about one of the major hurdles experienced by working lone parents: that is, what to do with the children in their school holidays. In addition to helping with childcare, Lorna's parents have also assisted her financially which allowed her to remain in her own home after her separation. In difficult times, her parents paid for her children's food and her petrol costs. While not undermining Lorna's achievements, it is clear that her success story relates directly to the extent of her relational assets.

Cynthia's story also highlights the centrality of the support of family for a lone parent to successfully combine paid work and their caring responsibilities. Cynthia, a working-class employed lone mother with one child (aged seven) moved closer to her parents who lived in a small village in Somerset because she wanted to return to work. She felt that this would not have been possible without the backing of her parents. During her interview she discussed the importance of the familial support that she received and acknowledged that it was key to her participation in the labour market. 'If something happened to Mum and Dad tomorrow I would have to give up work, I would not be able to work until Jack was in senior school. If it wasn't for them I would have no life at all.' The childcare her parents provide was crucial not only in that Cynthia worked shift work and therefore could not rely on more formal childcare, but also because she did not earn enough for paid childcare to be appropriate and the nearest childminder was eight miles away in the local town. In a similar respect, Carol, a working-class mother of one child who worked 20 hours per week claimed that she was only able to work because her mother looked after her daughter. 'I only really need childcare in the summer holidays or other school holidays in which I rely on my mother and friends. If childcare were cheaper I might consider using it.' Similarly Jess, who worked over 30 hours comments 'I have found childcare very difficult to find in this area. I am only able to work myself due to the high level of support from family'.

What was perhaps most striking was the fact that lone parents who had lived in their local area all their lives were able to rely heavily on the encouragement, support and practical assistance of their local social networks which were often located close by. Without falling into the working-class 'local', middle-class 'newcomer' dichotomy (see Cloke and Thrift 1987), it is clear that these (quite literal) 'relational' assets play a crucial enabling role in terms of lone parents' ability to combine their caring roles and their participation in waged labour. This was especially the case for (working-class) women who would find it very difficult to secure employment that paid enough for them to return to work while at the same time paying for resultant costs of work, such as childcare. Indeed, as Duncan and Edwards (1999) note in their research, many (working-class) women draw on moral rationalities which prioritize informal childcare, particularly that provided by grandmothers, aunts and sisters as the most acceptable form of childcare for their children (Wheelock and Jones 2002). As a result, if childcare provided by family and friends was not available they may have felt that it was inappropriate to look for paid employment outside the home. Conversely middle-class women, who are more likely to rely on more formal childcare arrangements such as nurseries and childminders, were struggling to secure appropriate professional employment and/or identify suitable child minding services that would facilitate their working practices. In this way, the boundaries between middle-class 'worker' and working-class mother becomes blurred in these types of rural locales.

Human Capital

The human capital acquired by lone parents also plays an important role in mediating their ability to combine paid employment with caring for their families. Human capital is defined by the Organization for Economic Cooperation and Development (1998: 9) as 'the knowledge, skills and competences and other attributes embodied in individuals that are relevant to economic activity'. Levels of educational qualification are the standard measures used, but it is widely acknowledged that these are inadequate in capturing the extent of human capital. In this chapter, I am referring to the store of competences, knowledge and personality attributes embodied in the individual parent which influence their ability to undertake waged labour. I argue that although these attributes are linked to education and experience; they also include traits such as health; both mental and physical. These also intersect with the relational assets discussed in the previous section as the social networks provided by extended family, community and organizations inform lone parents' participation in the labour market. Clearly, social and geographical contexts can act to nullify the utilization of human capital in certain circumstances. These competences relate to class in extremely complex ways. Following the work of Bourdieu (1986), it is clear that different class forms are negotiated through a multifaceted web of capitals (economic, cultural and social).

In this study, educational attainment was found to be significantly related to participation in paid employment. Lone parents with lower educational qualifications are less likely to be in paid employment. For example, Louise had not worked since she had her first child at the age of 22. She has no educational qualifications and struggled to find employment. She comments 'When I go to see the Lone Parent Advisor they take all this into consideration. It is quite good because they give you a printout of how much better off that you are in work … I would be 5 pounds better off if I worked part-time. If I worked full-time then I would be better off but that is what I have to weigh up. Do I want to leave my kids with someone else?' Clearly paid work does not offer her a much better quality of life unless she works full-time and claims the appropriate tax credits. However, with the cost of childcare and transportation, she felt she may well be 'out of pocket'. In addition to their higher salaries better educated lone parents were more likely to be involved in employment which includes work benefits such as paid annual leave and sickness related benefits. Moreover, an educated mother is far more able to negotiate the complex labyrinth of 'family friendly' legislation to secure the flexibility in their employment contract that they are entitled.

Undoubtedly educational qualifications have their roots in class based relations. For example, cultural capital which in some cases can be converted into economic capital may also be institutionalized in the form of educational qualifications (Bourdieu 1986). However, for some lone parents these (class based) competences can be nullified, at least in the short-term, by other factors such as their familial structure or ill health which may prevent them from successfully negotiating paid work. For example, there were several middle-class lone parents in the survey educated to degree level who were not working and living on benefit. A lack of childcare, and indeed, a lack of employment opportunities in the rural labour market impeded their participation in employment; highlighting the fact that for rural lone parents, education alone does not necessarily enable engagement in waged labour.

Notwithstanding the above, it is clear that the long term prospects for well educated lone parents in far more optimistic. Barbara, whose story is discussed above, was upbeat about her future. She saw her inability to work as temporary and, as a trained teacher knew she was capable of earning a reasonable wage. With income boosters in the form of tax credits and the maintenance that she receives from her ex-partner, she will be able to provide sufficiently for her family and as she says 'get on with giving my children decent prospects for the future'. The way that Barbara's classed historical biography positioned her very differently from other lone parents was obvious when talking to participants who had not been in paid employment prior to becoming a lone parent. This is because employment histories of lone parents were found to have a profound impact on their relationship with paid work, and these histories are, of course, classed. If a lone parent has been in paid employment before they became a lone parent, they typically continued to work, albeit often with reduced hours. However, if a lone parent had a very limited employment history or had been out of the labour market for a long period prior to becoming a lone parent then it was often a more significant challenge to return to work. These individuals often lacked confidence in their skills and abilities and would often not find it easy to secure such well paid employment. Again, there are clear class based connections here. Working-class women tended to have more fragmented career histories; opting for casual jobs, commonly on the minimum wage.

Further to employment history, the health of the lone parent was also identified as having a significant influence on labour market entry, and again, this was connected to class in complex ways. Roslyn a middle-class lone mother living in a large village in Somerset has a severe long-term illness and receives Disability Living Allowance. She felt that if there were job opportunities locally, she may work part-time. However, the majority of job opportunities were slightly further afield and she felt that she was not well enough to commute. 'The job availability in [village] is almost nil. There are no factories anymore … if you want to work you have to go to Chard or Yeovil. But I am just not well enough to do that.' While poor health can often leave both middle-class and working-class lone parents out of the workforce, highly educated middle-class lone parents possess the credentials and competences which bolstered their financial and social position. For example, Roslyn's Disability Allowance had been cut several times and after each reduction, she successfully launched an appeal, a process she comments which is 'not for the faint hearted'. She talked of 40 page documents which have to be completed and cross referenced with doctors' certificates and hospital notes. In addition to this, Roslyn has ensured that her own quality of life has not impacted on her children's life chances, using her own knowledge of the education system to secure a scholarship for her daughter at a local boarding school. In this way, Roslyn's cultural capital is transferred to her child through securing a privileged place for her child in the education system.

The psychological health of the lone parent is also important in terms of their decisions about paid employment. In many circumstances, lone parents do not have the emotional or physical capacity to engage in paid employment directly after a separation. Again, in this context psychological health could not be directly reduced to class associations. This was the case for both working-class and middle-class parents. Lorna, a working-class mother of two children, stated:

> I had to get my self-esteem back before I could work. When I was separating from my husband my self-esteem plummeted hugely ... At the time you can only think day to day. You can't think long-term. Once you get over that initial shock that you are on your won you can plan ahead and you start to do something ... then you begin to realize that you are not thick like he used to call me [her ex-husband]. I have got a brain. Once you have got your self-esteem back [you can think about employment]. I am proud of the job that I am doing.

Cybil reiterates this sentiment arguing 'when he decided to leave I had to start to build my confidence up ... it was very difficult cos I had had it all knocked out of me completely'. Women who had left abusive relationships felt that undertaking paid employment directly after becoming a lone parent would have been detrimental to themselves but also their children. Emma, a middle-class employed mother of two living in Cumbria, who left her husband after severe emotional abuse stated 'they [the children] need security having just left one home. You just have to be here for them'.

The health of a lone parent is clearly dynamic. Lone parents who have participated in the labour market commonly have to leave paid work after their health deteriorates. The research pointed to several cases where the stress of combining employment and a sole parenting role resulted in the deterioration of the parents' mental and physical well-being. Anita, living in Somerset wrote in her questionnaire 'I tried running a home, being a mum and working full-time with three young children. I had no quality time with children I was always tired and doing housework ... I became very ill and after being sick for six months I gave up my job. It is impossible to do both jobs well'. Indeed, in many ways it was the middle-class professional lone parents who talked most vehemently about the psychological stress of their dual role. This, may, of course be related to the tendency of the middle-classes to shout the loudest; projecting their agenda as the priority.

Although not directly related to the human capital of the lone parent it is important to note that any ill health or disability amongst children also has a profound effect on lone parents' decisions to participate in paid work. Some of the reasons for this were enumerated by Erin, a lone mother living in Cumbria who commented on her questionnaire, 'My eldest daughter has a severe learning difficulty. Although living in a rural area is ideal it creates a lot of stress for me as I have to drive back and forwards to our local town so frequently. This makes me tired and unable to relax'. Further to the issues raised by Erin are the fact that it is often difficult to access childcare when a child is either disabled or 'often sick'. In addition, childcare for disabled children is very difficult to find and often more expensive than for an able-bodied child. Finally, many lone parents and their disabled children receive a combination of Disability Living Allowance and Carers' Allowance which often means it is financially more advantageous to claim benefits than paid employment.

Conclusion

This chapter has examined the multiple connections between lone parents, class and rurality as they relate to engagement with paid work. The importance of exploring lone parents' relationship with paid work has become ever more salient given the acceleration in workfare policies across a range of neo-liberal democracies (Daguerre 2007). Indeed, the United Kingdom government's welfare reform programme has significantly increased the pressure on lone parents to look for work. Since October 2010, lone parents whose youngest child is seven have no longer been eligible to claim income support. Instead they have to actively seek employment. The message is clear; even lone parents with relatively young children are not now legitimately outside the workforce. As welfare reform gains pace and successive governments continue to shift risk and responsibility on to individuals in an attempt to promote self-sufficiency and personal responsibility, the importance of examining the differential impacts of social policies on rural areas must be a priority for rural researchers (Milbourne and Marsden 2010, Weber, Duncan and Whitener 2002).

While class consciousness is clearly less potent in contemporary Britain (e.g., Reay 1997, Skeggs 1997) and lone parents in the survey did not actively talk about themselves as belonging to a particular class, class based relations are clearly bound up with their experiences. However, this chapter has argued that the 'middle-class worker'; 'working-class mother' dichotomy preferred by Duncan (2005) is too simplistic. While recognizing that (non)participation in the labour market is not simply about choice (Hakim 2000a), it is clear that lone parents' relationships with paid work cannot simply be mapped onto traditional class based conceptions of mothering and attitudes to paid work. Instead it is argued that two key sets of factors, which in themselves relate to class in complex ways, are central in mediating lone parents' relationship with waged employment. The first concerns what I have termed 'relational assets' and the second focuses on the lone parents' human capital. Clearly many aspects of these relational assets and human capital have significant connections with aspects of class relations such as income and education; but many are less easily plotted and can, in fact, define the decisions of lone parents about their involvement in paid work.

This research highlights how the relationship between lone parents and paid work is shaped by a combination of choices and preferences on the one hand (Hakim 2000a, 2000b), and constraints on the other (McRae 2003). However, for most rural lone parents, family and work are inevitably interwoven with the majority combining their caring responsibilities with part-time work. As a result, paid work and unpaid caring responsibilities should not necessarily be viewed as contradictory (Driver and Martell 2002). However, there was little evidence of 'the work centred women' (Hakim 2000a) for whom employment was their priority in life; even amongst the well educated middle-class lone mothers.

Clearly, the spatial relations of rurality play a significant role in mediating the ways in which class and gender are being reconstituted in terms of lone parents' entry into waged employment. It is insufficient to explore the relationships between lone parents and their participation in paid employment without taking account of the complex interplays which are intrinsically bound up with 'place', and more specifically the type of communities and local labour markets in which they live. This reiterates McDowell's (2006: 843) argument concerning the need to investigate the 'spatial variations in the ways in which class and gender relations are being reconfigured'.

Finally this chapter raises fundamental questions about the validity of the expression 'lone' parent in academic, policy and practical terms. The parents surveyed here were self-selecting; they defined themselves as lone parents; and certainly all lived without traditional spousal partnerships. However many were far from being 'alone'. As a result, the term 'lone' parent is indeed profoundly misleading. In many cases it was their relational assets; their relationships with others whether ex-partners, family, friends or employers, that played a salient role in lone parents' ability to undertake paid employment, and more broadly facilitated their sense of well-being and efficacy. In terms of participation in the labour market, practical support procured from their (often local) social networks and personal relationships was critical; particularly the provision of no cost or low cost informal childcare. However, more generally, the emotional and financial support and encouragement received by lone parents through a multitude of different social and personal relationships were crucial factors in their coping strategies.

Acknowledgements

Thanks to Dr Corinne Nativel who undertook the fieldwork for this project and who worked with me in developing the ideas presented in this paper. This research was funded by the Economic and Social Research Council (ESRC) (Award No. R000223778). Our thanks go to the ESRC for funding this project and to the participants who gave of their time so generously.

References

Atkinson, K., Oerton, S. and Burns, D. 1998. Happy families: single mothers, the press and the politicians. *Capital and Class*, 22(1), 1–11.

Bourdieu, P. 1986. The forms of capital, in *Handbook of Theory of Research for the Sociology of Education*, edited by J.E. Richardson. Westport: Greenwood Publishing, 46–58.

Brown, J. and Lichter, D. 2001. Poverty, welfare and the livelihood strategies of nonmetropolitan single mothers. *Rural Sociology*, 69(2), 282–301.

Bullock, H., Wyche, K. and Williams, W. 2001. Media images of the poor. *Journal of Social Issues*, 57(2), 229–46.

Cloke, P. and Thrift, N. 1987. Intra-class conflict in rural areas. *Journal of Rural Studies*, 3(4), 321–33.

Daguerre, A. 2007. *Active Labour Market Policies and Welfare Reform: Europe and the US in Comparative Perspective*. Basingstoke: Palgrave Macmillan.

Driver, S. and Martell, L. 2002. New labour, work and the family. *Social Policy and Administration*, 36(1), 46–61.

Duncan, S. 2005. Mothering, class and rationality. *The Sociological Review*, 53(1), 50–76.

Duncan, S. and Edwards, R. 1999. *Lone Mothers, Paid Work and Gendered Moral Rationalities*. London: St Martins Press.

Duncan, S., Edwards, R., Reynolds, T. and Alldred, P. 2003. Motherhood, paid work and partnering: values and theories. *Work Employment Society*, 17(2), 309–30.

Gingerbread. 2010. *Factsheet for Single Parents in England and Wales June 2010: Help Moving from Benefits to Work*. [Online: Gingerbread]. Available at: http://www.gingerbread.org.uk/uploads/media/17/6877.pdf [accessed: 3 October 2010].

Gloster, R., Casebourne, J., Culshaw, S., Mavra, L., O'Donnell, A. and Purvis, A. 2010. *Lone Parent Obligations: Early Findings of Implementation as well as Experiences of the Income Support and Jobseeker's Allowance Regimes*. Research Report 645. Norwich, England: Department of Work and Pensions.

Gregson, N. and Lowe, M .1995. *Servicing the Middle Classes: Class, Gender and Waged Domestic Labour in Contemporary Britain*. London: Routledge.

Hakim, C. 2000a. *Preference Theory*. Cambridge: Cambridge University Press.

Hakim, C. 2000b. *Work-Lifestyle Choices in the 21st Century: Preference Theory*. Oxford: Oxford University Press.

Hughes, A. 1997. Rurality and 'cultures of womanhood': domestic identities and the moral order in village life, in *Contested Countryside Cultures*, edited by P. Cloke and J. Little. London: Routledge, 123–37.

Hughes, A. 2004. Geographies of invisibility: the 'hidden' lives of rural lone parents, in *Geographies of Rural Cultures and Societies*, edited by L. Holloway and M. Kneafsey. Aldershot: Ashgate, 126–44.

Hughes, A. and Nativel, C. 2005. Lone parents and paid work, in *Critical Studies in Rural Gender Relations*, edited by J. Little and C. Morris. Aldershot: Ashgate, 27–44.

Land, H. 2002. Spheres of care in the UK: separate and unequal. *Critical Social Policy*, 22(1), 13–32.

Little, J. and Austin, P. 1996. Women and the rural idyll. *Journal of Rural Studies*, 12(2), 101–11.

Little, M. 2001. A litmus test for democracy: the impact of Ontario welfare changes on single mothers. *Studies in Political Economy*, 66, 9–36.

Marchant, J. 2009. *Off the Beaten Mummy Track: Enabling Employment for Rural Single Mothers*. Paper to the Australian Association for Research in Education (AARE) International Education Research Conference 2009, Canberra Australia, 29 November to 3 December 2009.

McDowell, L. 2006. Reconfigurations of gender and class relations: class differences, class condescension and the changing place of class relations. *Antipode*, 38(4), 825–50.

McDowell, L., Ray, K., Perron, D., Fagand, C. and Warde, K. 2005. Women's paid work and moral economies of care. *Social and Cultural Geography*, 6(2), 219–35.

McRae, S. 2003. Constraints and choices in mother's employment careers: a consideration of Hakim's preference theory. *British Journal of Sociology*, 54(3), 317–38.

McRobbie, A. 2004. Notes on 'what not to wear' and post-feminist symbolic violence, in *Feminism after Bourdieu*, edited by L. Adkins and B. Skeggs. Oxford: Blackwell, 99–109.

Milbourne, P. and Marsden, T. 2010. *Welfare Reform in Rural Places Comparative Perspectives*. Brighton: Emerald Group Publishing Limited.

Murray, C. 1990. *The Emerging British Underclass*. London: IEA Health and Welfare Unit.

Murray, C. 1994. *Underclass: The Crisis Deepens*. London: IEA Health and Welfare Unit.

Nelson, M. 2005. *The Social Economy of Single Motherhood: Raising Children in Rural America*. New York: Routledge.

Organisation for Economic Cooperation and Development. 1998. *Human Capital Investment: An International Comparison*. Paris: Organisation for Economic Cooperation and Development.

Pitt, K. 2002. Being a new capitalist mother. *Discourse and Society*, 13(2), 251–67.

Powell, S. 2005. *Overcoming Stereotypes About Poor Appalachian Single Mothers: Understanding Their Actual Lived Experiences*. Masters Thesis, Faculty of the College of Arts and Sciences. Athens: Ohio University.

Rake, K. 2001. Gender and new labour's social policies. *Journal of Social Policy*, 30(2), 209–31.

Reay, D. 1997. Feminist theory, habitus, and social class: disrupting notions of classlessness. *Women's Studies International Forum*, 20(2), 225–33.

Rodriguez Sumaza, C. 2001. Lone parent families within new labour welfare reform. *Contemporary Politics*, 7(3), 231–47.

Roseneil, S. and Mann, K. 1996. Unpalatable choices and inadequate families: lone mothers and the under-class debate, in *Good Enough Mothering: Feminist Perspectives on Lone Motherhood*, edited by E. Silva. London: Routledge, 191–210.

Rowlingston, K. and McKay, S. 2002. *Lone Parent Families: Gender, Class and State*. Pearson: Harlow.

Skeggs, T. 1997. *Formations of Class and Gender: Becoming Respectable*. London: Sage.

Smith, S. 1999. Arguing against cuts in lone parent benefits: reclaiming the desert ground in the UK. *Critical Social Policy*, 19(3), 313–34.

Son, S. and Bauer, J. 2010. Employed Rural, Low-Income, Single Mothers' Family and Work Over Time. *Journal of Family and Economic Issues*, 31(1), 107–20

Song, M. 1996. Changing conceptualisations of lone parenthood in Britain. *European Journal of Women's Studies*, 3, 377–97.

Van Acker, E. 2005. The Howard Government's budgets: stay-at-home mothers good. Single mothers bad. *Hecate*, 31(2), 90–102.

Wallbank, J. 2001. *Challenging Motherhood*. Pearson: Harlow.

Ward, S. and Turner, H. 2007. Work and welfare strategies among single mothers in rural New England: the role of social networks and social support. *Community Development*, 38(1), 43–58.

Weber, B., Duncan, G. and Whitener, L. 2002. *Rural Dimensions of Welfare Reform*. Michigan: W.E. Upjohn Institute.

Wheelock, J. and Jones, K. 2002. 'Grandparents are the next best thing': informal childcare for working parents in urban Britain. *Journal of Social Policy*, 31(3), 441–63.

Wimberly, C. 2000. Deadbeat dads, welfare moms, and Uncle Sam: how the Child Support Recovery Act punishes single-mother families. *Standford Law Review*, 53(3), 729–66.

Chapter 10
Not all Bright Lights, Big City? Classed Intersections in Urban and Rural Sexual Geographies

Yvette Taylor

Many studies of lesbian and gay men map the lives of white, middle-class, urban dwellers, where 'others' are rendered out of place, arguably reinscribing intersecting inequalities of class and sexuality (Taylor 2007a, 2009). Indeed 'the city' still predominates in most analyses of lesbian and gay lives, where there has been critique of regenerated, 'rebranded' commercialized space, and the way in which this has led to the co-construction of queer sexualities and queer exclusions (Binnie 2004, Taylor 2010a). Yet the urban centric literature on gay and lesbian identities has also constructed 'the city' in highly positive terms, a positioning which itself has relied upon highlighting the connection between the urban, consumption and movement in queer lives. Attention directed towards such urban spaces frequently perpetuates exclusion by focusing on the more visible and open spatial expressions of sexual identity, rather than the diverse, even 'hidden' places outside of *and* inside the city (Bell and Valentine 1995, Binnie and Valentine 1999).

Many researchers now acknowledge spatial diversity, refocusing attention on the possibilities and benefits for separate explorations of differently situated lesbian and gay subjects. This chapter seeks to add to such research in further disrupting the bifurcated view of 'the rural' as either a space which queers do not inhabit, as a space of discrimination and intolerance, or as a rural ideal 'preferred' and 'chosen', against the city. Such a dichotomy between city and country, has relied upon socially constructing 'the urban' in specific ways which present it as the imagined opposite of 'the rural'. This dominant reading of the urban is taken up by many lesbians and gay men in my studies who characterize rurality as backward and homophobic, in contrast to *specific* forms of (middle-class) urbanity. Here I seek to add class, and particularly a working-class perspective, to the discussion, furthering the argument that there is a more complicated map of belonging and inclusion for queers than one simply based on a rural urban continuum.

Drawing on research with lesbian and gay interviewees across two research projects (Taylor 2007a, 2009) this chapter will look at the subjective figuring, and material constitution, of 'the urban' and 'the rural' in interviewees' subjective and material (mis)placements. 'Working class' and 'rural' were frequently collapsed as similarly 'unaccepting' and 'unacceptable', while 'middle class' and 'urban' were centred as 'cosmopolitan' and 'tolerant', dispositions which were coded in people and in place. These spaces are, however, rejected, resisted *and* invested in, troubling the singular, sexualized geographical outness and 'escape' routes in getting 'to a big city' (Weston 1995, Binnie 2004). This interrupts constructions of 'the urban' as utopic where commercialized scene space in not a singular, comfortable, utopia for all lesbians. Rather, it is experienced as exclusive by working-class women living *in* the city. In contrast, middle-class interviewees spoke of moving to more 'mixed' cosmopolitan inner city territory, where the benefits of city life could be accumulated beyond sexual 'potential', enhancing classed parental identities and realities. Articulated notions of an 'good (urban) mix' reinscribe classed and sexualized division around liberal 'tolerance', encoded as middle class, as against an urban working-class 'excess', troubling the opposition between 'urban' and 'rural' as (un)desirable sexual terrains.

In critiquing rural space as *dystopian* lesbian space I again signal the importance of class (Waitt and Gorman-Murray 2007), where class necessarily mediates opportunities for 'escape', while the rural as *utopian* queer space is also problematic, when considering how middle class the literature on rural sexualities has been (Kirkey and Fortsyth 2001, Smith and Holt 2005). While Bell and Valentine (1995: 120) have highlighted that 'the relationship between sexuality and rurality has been shown to be ambivalent, contextual and malleable' what I reveal is that class is potentially key to understanding such ambivalence, contextuality and malleability. Geographers have questioned the aspatiality of arguments that distinguish homonormative privileged middle class, white lesbians and gay men from queer classed and racialized 'others'; yet geographers of sexuality whilst occasionally signalling the importance of class, have been reticent in exploring and fully examining it. Class, as with sexualities, is geographically produced and privilege, as well as marginalization, needs to be explored in recognition of spatial nuance and contingency between people and places (Elder 2002, 2008, Taylor 2010a). This chapter will probe the classed and sexualized intersections between 'the urban' and 'the rural', where lesbians and gay men are frequently misplaced in academic and everyday space, eliding such complex geographical positionings.

(Re)setting the Scene: Classed Interruptions to 'the Urban' and 'the Rural'

Many studies of lesbian and gay life have been conducted in cosmopolitan, progressive urban areas for example New York City and San Francisco in the United States of America and London, Brighton and Manchester in the United Kingdom (eg., Browne, Lim and Brown 2007). Within such literature, commercial venues, from pubs, clubs and cafes (referred to as 'scene spaces') and community events have been conceptualized as sanctuaries, as places of refuge and tolerance and as spaces of consuming and consumable identities, identifications and disidentifications (Skeggs 1999, 2001, Hennessey 2000, Binnie 2004).

Increasingly such spaces are positioned as 'niche' markets for development and exploitation. The pleasures and problems of scene spaces are sharply highlighted in the idea of 'buying into' commercialized leisure space and therefore, by choice or by default, ultimately 'selling out' politicized identity credentials for market based, purchasable ones (Chasin 2000). Identity becomes branded, commodified, consumed and, it would seem, depoliticized, in the move into 'big city' (Hennessy 2000, Evans 1993, Warner 1993). The acceptance offered to the consumer is rather precarious and limited serving to consolidate some spaces while preventing and eroding the creation of other scene spaces not dependent upon cash, consumption and credit (Field 1997).

nice!

Despite such critique it now seems that scene spaces are also gaining a certain desirability and even 'respectability', with the increasing existence of them in city centres across, for example, the United Kingdom, the United States of America and Australia. Such spaces are seen as symbolizing cultural ascendancy, regeneration and gentrification and are consequently actively promoted as indictors of city cosmopolitanism and urban development (Casey 2007, Taylor 2007a, 2007b, 2008). Such spatialized mainstreaming may be seen to produce a new homonormativity, whereby spending lesbians and gay men are afforded a certain presence, visibility and acceptability (Binnie 2004, Duggan 2002). In contrast to arguments that appear to transcend spatial differentiation, I argue that there are differential classed effects within such processes. The 'queer unwanted' encompass those excluded 'others' who are disqualified from homonormative status, for whom movement into lesbian and gay commercial spaces is becoming more restricted (Binnie 2004). Alongside the 'commercial hijacking of gayness', it is important to remember that 'not everyone is invited to the party' (Simpson 1999: 213), because class intersects in creating entitlements, investments and exclusions from urban scene space.

In attempting to relocate scene space within a class framework, Binnie (2004) speaks of 'queer cosmopolitanism' with the distinction between cosmopolitanism and provincialism articulated through discourses of 'sophistication' and a certain 'knowingness'. In contrast, working-class and 'provincial' sexualities are marked as being unsophisticated and 'less developed'. Similarly, Weston (1995) reveals the connection between 'coming out', developing a gay identity and becoming a 'sophisticated' city dweller, which ultimately requires access, both culturally and economically, to these spaces and positions. As such, not having the financial capability seriously compromises one's attempts to lead a 'modern gay lifestyle'. It directly impacts upon one's ability to take up space within 'the city' (Binnie 2000: 171). While Weston (1995) has demonstrated the significance of accessing community and support structures in getting to 'a big city', Binnie (2004) seeks to provide a corrective to previous studies of a (singular) 'coming out geography', centred around commercialized urban scene spaces. Such a centring arguably collapses the (in)visibilites and (im)possibilites between and among urban and rural terrains (Bell and Valentine 1995, Binnie and Valentine 1999, Smith and Holt 2005).

Examining the everyday identity strategies deployed by gay men across different spaces, times and places, Brekaus (2003) takes the focus upon gay identity out of city spaces and into the suburbs, again suggesting a more complicated map of belonging, inclusion and (in)attention. The continual struggle to find a stable, 'ordinary' sense of home, place and identity can be positioned against the emphasis on a queer transgressive global mobility, where aspects of the everyday, the ordinary, the invisible and the mundane are recentred. However, the 'ordinariness' or 'extraordinariness' of interviewees' desires to be average 'Joe fags' raises some questions. That is: Just how 'ordinary' are the suburbs and its inhabitants, and how might these be distinguished from other (un)desirable city spaces? Brekaus' (2003) suburban inhabitants often mixed aspects of their unmarked characteristics, such as their whiteness, masculinity and middle classness with their marked status of being gay, to create a more diffused, balanced 'self'. They contrasted this with the extreme outliers, or gay 'lifestylers', situated in commercialized city scene space. While the 'ordinary' unseen spaces of the suburbs are made visible, a greater exploration is needed of the materiality constructing movements and strategies across place. Esteem frequently accrues to the mobile, reflexive, chooser, often marked with a queer transformative potential in the ability to change space (Ahmed 2004, Byrne 2006). What then are the limitations and opportunities for differently classed queers in occupying 'everyday' urban and rural spaces and scenarios? Lesbians and gay men may indeed be 'everywhere' and in the 'everyday' rather in special, queer enclaves, yet the ability to reconcile, inhabit and spatialize sexual identities, also varies according to classed resources (Ahmed 2004, Taylor 2007a, 2009).

There are many contradictions faced in navigating heteronormative spaces, where privileges may be mobilized to mediate misplacement. Ahmed (2004: 152) writes:

> The care work of lesbian parents may involve 'having' to live in close proximity to heterosexual cultures (in the negotiation with schools, other mothers, local communities), whilst not being able to inhabit the heterosexual ideal. The gap between the script and the body, including the bodily form of 'the family', may involve discomfort and hence may 'rework' the script. The reworking is not inevitable, as it is dependent or contingent on other social factors (especially class).

Ahmed is attentive to the structuring of social space as heterosexual, but, at the same time, her account considers the potential resistance and complicity in such spaces as well as highlighting the intersections between sexuality and class in relation to advantage and disadvantage. Classed *and* sexual misreadings complicate acts of visibility yet, in appreciation of the complexities of coming out, including how spatial practices and preferences intersect with other social divisions, it is possible to think of middle-class queers as exercising more mobility and choice in some contexts and some spaces (Taylor 2010a). Ahmed (2004) also points to differing classed strategies and abilities and the (dis)comforts of 'fitting in'. She notes:

> Some working-class lesbian parents, for example, might not be able to afford being placed outside the kinship networks within local neighbourhoods: being recognized as "like any other family" might not simply be strategic, but necessary for survival. Other working-class lesbian parents might not wish to be "like other families": what might feel necessary for some, could be impossible for others. (Ahmed 2004: 153)

Necessities and impossibilities suggest both complexities and complications in exploring interconnections between class and sexuality in the reproduction of (dis)advantage, across and within urban and rural spaces.

Class and sexuality are mutually materialized across space, where certain bodies, appearances and identities are rendered unentitled to occupy heteronormative space (Bourdieu 1984, Skeggs 1999, 2001). Individuals do not 'arrive', completely dislocated from space, but rather inhabit and rework space on the basis of 'past' dispositions, knowingness and capitals. Classed (dis)comforts and resources are significant to the uptake of, inclusion into and exclusion from space, whether than be commercialized queer space, everyday home space or institutional spaces, such as schools, welfare and services. Speaking of the 'search for home' as individuals negotiate the hazards of everyday life, Weeks, Heaphy and Donovan (2001) claim that access to imagined and physical lesbian, gay, bisexual and transgender (LGBT) 'community' generates emotional well-being, providing a form of 'social capital'. Strategic movements and locations amongst lesbians and gay men, residing in and constructing mostly urban based communities that support diversity have been widely evidenced (eg., Weston 1995, Weeks, Heaphy and Donovan 2001). Relocations offer a potential comfort and ease, an ability to 'fit in', or indeed 'stand out', communally disrupting the heterosexualization of public spaces. Agentic capacity or even transformative abilities are often foregrounded here, where respondents are credited with sophisticated spatial strategies in negotiating 'safe' space (eg., Binnie 2000). Yet spatialized (dis)comforts and the sense of being 'out of place' continues, where classed 'others' cannot access, locate or embody a positive 'diversity', or inhabit a 'good mix', where social capitals generate and multiply (Weeks, Heaphy and Donovan 2001, Byrne 2006, Taylor 2007a, 2009). Thus, sexuality may not be the starting point for the spatialized generation of social capital, or an 'alternative habitus', but may well be a continuation, or transformation, of other (classed) capitals, which enable such geographies of choice, difference and distinction (Bourdieu 1984). This also applies to the constructions of a well educated, middle-class 'rural habitus' (Bourdieu 1984), identified by Smith and Holt (2005) in the movements and comforts of lesbian gentrifies in the rural terrain of Hebden Bridge, United Kingdom.

In considering 'other' rural geographies, Smith and Holt (2005) focus attention on non-metropolitan sexualities, attempting to rewrite geographies of gentrification to take account of sexualized rural – as well as urban – gentrification. Lesbian respondents are situated as rural gentrifies via their residential and cultural consumption practices; that they exercise cultural and economic capitals in doing so is barely attended to (even as the classed consequences of a middle-class influx arementioned). Like the rural 'men in the valley' interviewed by Kirkey and Forsyth (2001), participants valued diversity, but this was safely coded as 'middle class', where the educated, alternative and knowing were (re)situated from the cosmopolitan to the interestingly, if not idyllically, rural. Indeed, as Bell (2001: 99) notes, 'the rural' may figure as a utopian escape from the 'big city':

> The rural may offer the best site to escape the patriarchal and hetronormative strictures embodied in the urban fabric; add to this contemporary spiritual and ecological trends in some quarters of queer culture, plus a general societal orientation towards forms of rural recreation and pleasure, and the country begins to exert a powerful pull on some people.

In (re)producing queer rural spaces, through investments and activities (including gay male 'pot luck' events or lesbian rounders) it can be argued that specifically *classed* ruralities are also (re)produced, culturally, materially and spatially (Kirkey and Forsyth 2001, Smith and Holt 2005). Where 'highly educated' people are accredited with gentrifying capacities and 'alternative lifestyles' the analysis should not stop at emphasizing non-urban sexualities, but rather should then begin to think what other (im)mobilities, (mis)positioning and 'mixes' are compelled and brought into effect. Here, I argue that class and sexuality intertwine in the construction and negotiation of both urban and rural terrain, where class intervenes in and interrupts notions of sexual utopian/dystopian space; such interruptions are apparent also in methodological endeavours.

Working-Class Lesbian Life and Lesbian and Gay Parents: An Overview

Working-Class Lesbian Life: Classed Outsiders (Taylor 2007a) involved one to one interviews, paired and group interviews with 53 women, who identified themselves as working class and lesbian, from Scotland (the Highlands, Glasgow and Edinburgh) and England (Yorkshire and Manchester).[1] Lesbians are a 'hard to reach' group and working-class lesbians may be even harder to locate, given their marginality if not absence from academic agendas and from urban commercial scene spaces (2004b). As such, it is inevitable that the women I interviewed are not representative of all who may fit this categorization, nor are they one internally

---

1   I conducted four focus groups with the following pre-established groups: Young Lesbian Group (Edinburgh), Manchester Lesbian Group, Older Lesbian Group (Glasgow) and the Rural Lesbian Group (the Highlands). For a more thorough discussion of methodological issues see Taylor (2004, 2005).

cohesive group. Respondents ranged from 16–64 years. Notably all respondents, except one British Asian interviewee, were white.[2] Most interviewees were from cities, while ten lived in rural areas, and others were originally from more rural locales. The significance of sexuality and class was explored in relation to their biographies, everyday lives and identities, including their views, experiences and access to commercial scene spaces and/or alternative community space, as well as notions of 'home' space (Taylor 2004). Elsewhere I have discussed the (in) effectiveness and (dis)comfort of my own repeated visits to commercialized and community scene spaces to conduct observations and elicit interview respondents, as I too negotiated urban trendiness, front and backstreet locations and, even, 'dirty wee dives'. As the following will demonstrate such discomforts did not disappear in escaping city space and entering rural lesbian terrain.

Finding Lesbian Space in the Rural

Initial conversation with Margaret, the organizer of the Rural Lesbian Group, indicated the difficulties of conducting research into a sensitive issue with a 'hard to reach', 'out of place' rural group. The group venue, in a small, affluent town centre, was chosen as a location so far free from homophobic violence and as the most 'central' point for women travelling from distant locales. As one of the very few regular groups in the Highlands respondents spoke of the significance of such a meeting, where the problems and pleasures of rural living were also discussed. Conceptualizations and experiences of 'the rural' were mediated through access to transport and the geographical and emotional 'distances' differently negotiated, underlying the fact that inhabiting rural space can be variously freeing or 'fixing', depending on financial resources. Moreover, the challenges of navigating heteronormative space are likely to be intensified in such a context because of what Bell and Valentine (1995: 116) observe are the 'intense hetronormative pressures of rural life with reproduction underpinning the future of family farming and rural communities'. Thus, the Rural Lesbian Group can then be thought of as a refuge and a space of community building, within an otherwise hostile zone. But safety and comfort in this environment were not felt by all. Instead classed discomforts were generated in this 'posh' setting, which suggests a more complicated map of belonging, where rural terrain is stratified and shaped by class. Margaret believed that location and environment contributed to the absence of working-class lesbians from the monthly meetings of the group:

---

2 A significant absence in my own study is the way that ethnicity also structures the participants' classed experiences, though such an absence is not only in terms of the research cohort but rather in the place of ethnicity in the study as a whole. This is intended as acknowledgement of the ways that whiteness, for the majority of respondents, is a valued form of ethnicity, where whiteness can also be seen to be lived differently through the modalities of class.

> The venue for our monthly meetings has been described as "posh." It's also safe, which is the main thing, but it can be a bit of a culture shock … I am concerned about working-class lesbians in [the Highlands], I know there have been homophobic assaults on them and I have heard that some women are getting into prostitution, but some working-class lesbians are scared to come out in their lives and to the group.

Margaret, who established, organized and ran the group voluntarily, highlights not only the difficulty in reaching certain people but also the near impossibility of doing so when there is no viable, long-term infrastructure and no apparent spaces to 'come out'. The situation described by Margaret is a very difficult one. When presented with the idea of taking part in my research, via Margaret, many women in the group were reluctant, leading Margaret to be concerned about the usefulness of such a meeting:

> There were nine women at the meeting last month and they didn't say very much about the idea of having a working-class lesbian focus group. Four of them are very new to the group. Someone else was asking how are you defining working class … I don't want you to have a wasted journey …

'Working class' is not a category around which lesbian groups form and organize and rather than meeting a pre-existing group of potential respondents I was often meeting disparate individuals who only occasionally, and often disappointedly, attended lesbian venues and networks, not least because of material, emotional and geographical constraints and distances. When women had travelled long distances, with often poor or variable transport infrastructure, there was perhaps a prioritization of the social aspects of meeting, a getting to know 'insiders' (other Highlanders, for example) rather than accommodation to an urban 'outside' researcher.

This is completely understandable particularly when some 'rural' spaces continue to be areas from which young queers seek to escape because of overt hostility and threats of written, verbal and physical violence. Some participants expressed a sense of being 'stuck' in their (rural) place. This often worked in subjective, spatial and material tension with desires to find more comfortable locations. Here Jill recounted the 'writing on the wall' as a sign that she should move on and beyond her rural home:

> … I suppose the defining moment for me was when I went to go down the village … and all the way down on every single wall and every single thing I could see was "Jill Walker is gay" [laughs]. I was just like "Fuck! This is where I fucking live!", you know. My mum's got really bad eye sight so luckily she never read any of these things. But the thing was it was all the way down the path that my mum walked down to the pub … then a couple of months later I was walking through the woods, like the middle of the woods and came to the

wee bridge and all over the fucking bridge was the same, I was like "I really need to go." (Jill, 29)

Very differently, the more rural Yorkshire town of Hebden Bridge also featured in some women's accounts though less often, as an area of lesbian concentration (eg., Smith and Holt 2005) It was often not a place where they had actually been even as it was recognized and named as a place 'for lesbians'; this is perhaps because it is seen as 'rural' but it is also because it is seen as a middle-class territory. In this gentrified area, like other gentrified areas of rural Britain, class is a critical factor. Indeed, residing in this space as *middle class* may render it more like urban LGBT friendly scene space. As the Hebden Bridge Times (2001) opines:

> Hebden Bridge far outstrips the gay metropolitan mating grounds of London, Brighton and Manchester, and has established the town as a sort of Sapphic centre serviced by pubs, clubs and cafes with over sexual credentials (Hebden Bridge Times 2001 quoted in Smith and Holt 2005: 316).

The messiness of the rural (and the urban) as neither completely dystopian or utopian queer space which emerges from the above accounts was articulated by Lauren as she expressed some of the 'provincial paradoxes' highlighted by Waitt and Gorman-Murray (2007). She tells of feeling more 'rural' than 'urban' in relating where she is from – and who she is – even as she had 'escaped' the rural home to live in a youth hostel following her mother's adverse reaction to her sexuality:

> I don't know, I've just been brought up in like the countryside and I mean being out and doing things on my own. I mean my family's all out in the country, my mum doesn't come to Edinburgh all that often. There's none of my family or personal friends that live in Edinburgh so I've sort of had to find my own way about Edinburgh and stuff. I feel more comfortable here but I've not been brought up to feel comfortable here. I've just had to find it myself, you know. It's been a bit hard for me ... I've moved from having friends in the country and living in the country all the time and never seeing anything else to like, being in Edinburgh most of the time and seeing, it's just a totally different place. I mean it's not a better place it's just totally different 'cause there's things about Edinburgh that I like more than the country, there's things where I'll say "Oh but I'm not used to that", you know. (Lauren, 18)

Acknowledgment of spatial diversity, discomfort and distinction, including such 'provincial paradoxes', potentially refocuses attention on the possibilities and benefits for separate explorations of differently situated lesbian and gay subjects, challenging dichotomized positioning of the 'urban' against the 'rural'.

Finding Lesbian Space in the 'Scene Spaces' of the Urban

The multiple dimensions of class, sexuality and locale were revealed in interviewees' comments about their (dis)satisfactions with urban scene spaces. Their (di)satisfactions illuminate the construction and negotiation of working-class lesbian identities in and even against urban commercialized scene space. While many interviewees viewed 'the rural' as 'backward' and 'homophobic', they did not necessarily experience 'urban' lesbian space and specifically commercialized scene space as a singular utopian space for all lesbians. Rather, it is experienced as exclusive by working-class lesbian women living in the city. Such geographies provide an interruption to dominant understandings of 'the urban' as desirable terrain.

Even though many of the urban scene spaces had achieved a celebrity status as the gay 'places to be' and/or as 'redevelopment showpieces' (Casey 2007) interviewees spoke of very real financial barriers against entry, and the tensions in accessing a space where only certain embodied presentations and ways of being were recognized and affirmed. As gay urban areas chase the younger, wealthier gay male pound, lesbians are deemed to be 'other' and 'unwanted' (Casey 2007); yet lesbians also invest and disinvest in scene spaces as class intersect with sexuality to produce a sense of being in and out of place. May speaks of the financial restrictions even in 'grubby pubs', while noting that Manchester and Leeds attract more middle-class lesbians, a simple matter of bigger choices and bigger places:

> They've got the dives and you get some strange people over in Manchester as well, you know, particularly the pretentious ones … Even the grubby pubs charge you, they should be paying you, do you know what I mean, but they exploit the fact that not every gay person would be comfortable going to a straight pub. I don't think you should have to be paying through the nose to go to a place where you feel comfortable with your partner, there shouldn't be financial restrictions, but there are. Most of the people that we know that go down to the local are working class, you tend to get more of the middle class, what I'd call middle-class lesbians, in Leeds or Manchester. I think that's purely because they are bigger places. (May, 23)

Leeds, like Manchester, is successfully reworking its image from de-industrial 'grim and grit' to urban glam, gaining recognition as one of the fastest growing cities in the United Kingdom and as Yorkshire's commercial capital and opening up new spaces for engagement. However, May articulates a sense that it is middle-class lesbians who are now able to move and take up more space. Speaking of the climate within gay and lesbian venues in Leeds, Kim (22) relates her frustration in the polarization between 'normal pubs', 'old men's pubs' and those places for 'pretty little boys', conveying a sense of not belonging anywhere, of having no accessible 'niche' within revamped urban leisure venues. Kim's critique of urban scene space relates the prevailing aesthetic, encompassing visual and musical styles and features, to her own discomfort pointing to the gendering of such space and to the relevance of age within this.

In Scotland, the women's choices of lesbian and gay venues tended to be a matter of choosing which city, Glasgow or Edinburgh, to visit. Women from the Highlands particularly lacked social space although monthly discos in temporary accommodation were sometimes hosted by the Rural Lesbian Group. Notably there was an assertion that this was 'real' working-class space, rather different from the 'posh' venue where the group organizers and established members (named as 'middle class') met. Conveying the difficulty in occupying rural space as queer, Elaine compared the rural 'closet' with urban 'outness', suggesting a less than straightforward opposition between intolerance and liberation:

> Geographically you're isolated a lot of the time, as well as socially. In a way if you're in Edinburgh or Glasgow you can just go out onto the gay scene but if you're in the Highlands and you come to the point where you identify as a lesbian, that gives you strength as well. In a way you've got to confront it even more because it's not so easy to just pop in and out of a scene. I've met, I'm thinking of a particular woman I met in Edinburgh, she went out onto the scene as much as she wanted to yet she said she was in the closet. People at her work didn't know, her family. She said she'd been on holiday in Gidley which is a small Christian village on the east coast and stayed in this hotel and the manageress of the hotel came onto her. She said "I really, really fancied her but I couldn't do it because it was in Gidley, I just felt like everybody would know." So in a way it was more difficult but if you manage to get through all that and you manage to identify it makes you stronger because it's more difficult. That doesn't mean that just because you're from the city, because it's easier there's still things you might find harder, like coming out to yourself. (Elaine, 37)

Most, if not all, interviewees had to negotiate physical and emotional journeys when attempting to enter scene space, to gain recognition and affirmation of identity, and that was often just to get through the front door. Access into the scene necessitated geographical travel but it also represented a movement between classed localities (Valentine 1993, Taylor 2004). Lamenting the expense incurred when first 'coming out' and then going out in Glasgow, Tracey (23) states that she just 'couldn't have gone out' in her home town as there was 'no gay clubs or pubs or anything like that, the only place is Glasgow so I needed to come through here... I was 16 or 17 when I first came through to go out, under age drinking!' The move away from home space into commercialized urban scene space in initial 'coming outs' was often experienced as far from comfortable or seamless; instead continued classed struggles affected access and belonging in 'lesbian spaces' (Taylor 2007b). Ultimately there was a sense that commercialized scene space was not really *their* space, whether they lived within the city or not.

In situating themselves beyond the scene, respondents spoke about growing up and belonging to certain families and communities, with a sense of pride in their locations, redrawing binaries of 'urban' and 'rural' through being simply 'at home' (Waitt and Gorman-Murray 2007). Yet this was often matched by understandings that who they were, including and *beyond* sexual status, as well as where they lived, were not valued, meaning 'home' was rarely a simple assertion of presence in place. Moreover, these locations were often the most immediate places where daily inequalities, projected onto imagined futures and (im)mobilities, were experienced, as Cathy demonstrates, in 'owning' a certain city postcode:

> Em, realising at a very young age how restricted my choices were because of that, what you're going to do with your life and what your choices are going to be according to where you're from, the minute you say you're from Maple Grove. (Cathy, 37)

In *Working-Class Lesbians* 'middle class' 'cosmopolitan' scene space was both aspired to and refused, as was rural terrain, situated alongside classed geographies. Such subjective figuring, and material constitutions, of the 'urban' and the 'rural' continued in interviewees' (mis)placements evident in *Lesbian and Gay Parents* where, for middle-class interviewees, 'the urban' and 'the middle class' were seen, as epitomizing cosmopolitanism and diversity, and were actively contrasted with 'working class' and 'rural' places. This theme is explored further in the following section.

Lesbian and Gay Parents: Finding Space in the Urban and/or Rural

Lesbian and Gay Parents details the experiences and views of 60 white parents (46 lesbian mothers and 14 gay dads) from working-class and middle-class backgrounds across a range of localities in the United Kingdom, ranging in age from 18 to 63 (Taylor 2010b). Lesbian and gay families have been depicted as carving out new spaces and communities, building and advancing social capitals with creative, even revolutionary, glee. While such portrayals are indeed positive they contrast somewhat with tales of communal decline, a depiction which variously combines classed and sexual 'failure' in the lack of social capital (Weeks, Heaphy, Donovan 2001). Clearly, geographical distances and proximities are relevant in the urban *and* rural mapping out of families, friends and networks, where supports can be sought in new places and hardships and failures left in 'no go' zones. Interviewees' journeys into space, involve the mobilization of *classed* capitals, resources and demarcations. This is not to say working-class parents exist in some no go landscape, marked by exclusion and absence. This was not, primarily, how working-class lesbian and gay parents expressed and experienced their sense of place. Significantly, the sense of being unable to move, and coping with such limitations, contrasted with another sentiment, articulated by middle-class parents, that limitations could be challenged, movements could be made and, ultimately relocations could secure a safety, even as these remained costly. Classed distance and proximity was negotiated in ways that ultimately served to distinguish and resource middle-class subjects in moving across and into space. The classed boundaries of (un)acceptability can be expanded – or indeed contracted – by a focus of the relevance of class and sexuality in the constructions of (un)desirable urban 'difference' (see Lindsay et al. 2006).

In my research middle-class parents articulated a desire for a 'good (urban) mix' in their immediate localities and neighbourhoods, again expressing that diverse settings would sit alongside and enhance their own difference; clearly though, not all spaces or all inhabitants, were equally desirable, different or diverse. Classed distances were mobilized in desiring a 'good mix', where middle-class parents articulated such 'mix' as a sometimes obvious marker of the degree of cosmopolitan 'tolerance', as against a working-class and 'rural' 'backwardness'. Working-class parental experiences contrasted to the extent that urban 'mix' was described as an everyday reality, a 'mix and match' of circumstances, compelling an everyday 'getting on with it', rather than a measure of 'diversity' in and of itself. Such classed experiences and articulations lead to a consideration of spatialized 'difference' as facilitative or impeditive; sexual difference was often invoked as requiring access to a *different* space, encompassing more than sexual difference. Sexuality was situated 'in-place' in such mixed territories, while working classness was decidedly marked as 'out of place', as an excessive threat.

Extending notions of 'mix', Peter spoke of living in a city centre 'bohemian' area, with the right politics, values and deviation of difference. For Peter, this 'bohemian' atmosphere mostly centred around London, and was lost in his relocation to Scotland where apparently 'there's a narrower band of standard deviation in Easter Hill and it's much more white, it's much more, the area we're in, middle-class and just a little more conservative'. It is interesting to consider how willing Peter is to situate himself on the margins, given that he is still seeking a ('like-minded', 'open-minded') 'sameness', and access to mainstreamed 'good' space with a 'good school'. His fatherhood compounds his networks, rather than negating these, while parental considerations, such as schooling, also make it harder to 'start again' in a new less (less 'urban') place:

> Even before I became a parent, I was already building up a community of like-minded people. Again, not necessarily queer, but just alternative, open-minded, arty, interesting people. That was kind of my peer group. So Cassie was then born into that community so there was a ready-made family, as it were … And when I did start working, the people I met were nice but they were much straighter, they seemed to be, and again, I'm using that in a much wider sense, not just sexuality. Just the standard deviation of deviance in Easter Hill, it's, [laughter], it's much narrower … which is part of the reason why we're thinking of moving because Cassie's now finished school and I'm meeting people here that are much more my kind of person. And it just feels a much more conducive environment. I think

> that's one of the reasons, Easter Hill is quite a conservative city. I mean, I've met the Gay Fathers group, and you know, there's some nice guys there, but again, nothing has really taken off and maybe that's also to do with my engagement in Easter Hill and I'm a bit ambivalent about being here. (Peter, 43)

Peter foregrounds Cassie's needs in his current location, while still being geographically mobile and able to access networks across spaces. Parental and children's needs were constructed from personal and parental roles and preferences, with many pointing to the relevance of resources and amenities in the creation of 'nice', 'safe', 'child-friendly' space where children could go out to play and 'explore' in, for example, a 'nice little cul-de-sac'. Middle-class parents frequently spoke of 'good areas' as encompassing a good school, good transportation links and networks to other places. All such facilities and resources do, as Nigel claims, make parenting life much easier:

> We've worked hard to get this house. Cotton Hill, this area, is a very good area. It makes it easier being a parent. There's not a drink or drugs problem, there's not teenage pregnancies, there's not hooligans etc. The area is quiet … it has made being a parent easier than living somewhere like, say, Windy Rise or somewhere like that. I don't say that from any point of being elitist, but it has made it easier. There are good schools, there's good amenities, swimming pool, the shopping centres. It is actually quite a good place to bring a child up in. One down side is, lack of interaction. It's actually quite cold in that way … We, I've been in the street for 15 years and I'd say that even now I'd be hard pushed to name you two of the houses that have got kids. It's very cold like that in respect that the people don't interact much. That's a little downside and I think it's probably just snobbery, I think it is. But yes, it makes it easier being a parent, living round here. (Nigel, 43)

Nigel mobilizes a classed comparison between the 'good' suburban area and the somewhat infamous council house estate, where 'teenage pregnancies' and 'drugs' are situated by comparison. The lack of human interactions in the suburban area, is replaced by the material resources and amenities, adding to a sense of safety and ease. Yet the variety of middle classness is hinted at here, where city cosmopolitanism may be seen to contrast with suburban frostiness and a lack of interaction (Brekaus 2003).

The difficulties in being a parent are multiplied manifold by the addition of a sexual spatial dimension. However, these difficulties are not always cross class constants with many middle-class interviewees frequently attributing homophobia to working-class others, apparently separating such structuring features in individualizing these to a certain sector of society (Moran 2000, Taylor 2004). A more complex tale depicted the variously classed forms of homophobia, from a subtle silence to a strident scream, complicated in the geographic structuring of rural/urban divides, where more cosmopolitan places were thought of as 'streets ahead' in their diverse 'tolerance' – such places were both protective and privileged locales, structured through classed inclusions and exclusions. Middle-class respondents frequently attributed more obvious homophobia and generally 'backward', 'traditional' values to working-class areas and inhabitants; 'I don't like reverting to stereotypes but maybe the South Yorkshire Neanderthal man still dominates the household, family life, you know, northern values and attitudes' (Jess, 42).

The classed comparison which Nigel invokes between suburbia and a block of flats in Park Row hints this time at what might be better in working-class areas:

> If we lived in a block of flats or somewhere like Park Row it might be a bit different, but because it's somewhere … As I say, it's a bit cold and people don't interact but it's really public and … I wouldn't say it was difficult but there's an element of freezing out a little bit. (Nigel, 43)

The 'freezing out' which Nigel highlights was also negotiated by those living in more rural locales, where city anonymity was contrasted with compelled knowingness. Sarah (42), for example, reported that her next door neighbour wasn't quite able to meet her eye, even as a polite 'good morning' was exchanged, while shared child activities offered associations with others in the neighbourhood, bringing connections and eventual ease. This sentiment is mirrored in Sandra's (50) experience where 'fairly traditional country ladies' in her holiday home now 'adored' her little girl, and Sandra received their seal of approval as a 'good parent'. Kevin struggles to describe the particular form of homophobia, which has changed over the years, whereby his family, once a spectacle, is now welcomed and no one needs to worry:

> In a very quiet way, they've acknowledged that this is a different type of family, because the school is around the village, and the village, you know, you can't hide these things in a village really. And I think people kind of looked upon the whole experience as a kind of spectacle in a strange kind of way … 14 years later, the children are fine and everybody thinks now that there was nothing to worry about and that it's gone really well. But at that time, 14 or 15 years ago, especially in Wales, nobody else had done it in Wales, and it was a real sense of, "Oh, you shouldn't be doing this" and there was, and it was very difficult to get that whole sense of support. (Kevin, 36)

Silences were often equated with a 'small town mentality' existing in some rural areas, where '… everybody sort of knows everyone else's business' (Harriet, 38) contrasted with (correctly) 'mixed' city spaces. Harriet lives in a rural community, and although generally happy with this, she notes the lack of information about any possible lesbian and gay parenting groups. Lynn (39) also remarks that there was just nothing really to comment on – or find controversial about – a previous, rural location, similar to Elizabeth's (52) sense of the 'respectable' 'retirement town' where she lives. Diane laughs that herself and her partner are most likely to be the only gays in the village:

> We're obviously the only two erm you know the only two women [laughs].
>
> Yvette: In the village.
>
> Right. It is a bit like that. (Diane, 37)

Single parent status was often discussed as a negative 'difference' or deficit, something neighbours were curious about rendering it the most significant feature (rather than sexual status) in being in or out of place. The story of the single mother council house dweller is relocated in this rural context, but the curiosity and hostility seem no less real:

> … it's mostly straight community that I'm aware of here that I mix with and obviously the parents as well and erm they usually have a problem with the whole single parenthood regardless of sort of sexuality which wouldn't come into it anyway. But they sort of say, "Oh, did you know you were going to have a child?" And, you know, as if it's sort of like a choice you know, the choice to be a single parent sort of thing so … and they ask really out rightly, "oh will you have any more children then?" which it's such a very sensitive question when you don't know somebody. I'm always very sort of open I just say you know "I'm not with, I'm not with Martha's father", at that first meeting that's what I would say because I don't want any more questions of that nature and I think it's quite sort of over familiar really. (Jenny, 29)

Even as the urban/rural divide was invoked as a significant difference, variations between and within urban and rural areas, disrupt this binary (Bell and Valentine 1995, Binnie and Valentine 1999). Differently classed – or euphemistically 'mixed' – urban locales were placed as welcoming, cosmopolitan and accepting, in contrast with backward, homophobic and differently resourced places (combining, for example, urban working-class 'council estates' and rural middle-class 'country ladies').

Conclusion: Classed Interruptions in Utopian-Dystopian Urban and Rural Locales

Interviewees in *Working-Class Lesbians* and *Lesbian and Gay Parents* negotiate, avoid, recreate and circumvent the boundaries of inclusion and exclusion, in leisure spaces and in 'everyday' space. Their accounts disrupt the bifurcated view of 'the rural' as a space of non-existence or hostility, against 'the urban' as imagined utopia. Urban centric literature on queer identities (from which classed subjects and lesbian and gay parents have typically been excluded) have constructed 'the urban' in positive terms, while recognizing the uneasy connection between the urban and the market in lesbian and gay lives (Chasin 2000). While Binnie (2004) classes scene space, his distinction between (un)sophisticated places perhaps elides the multiple ambivalences and intersections felt and reproduced within 'cosmopolitan' and 'provincial' spaces. Commercialized scene spaces are variously and vividly classed spaces, apparent in the location of such venues, the marketing of these as upmarket venues and in the (classed) individuals who occupy, critique and depart from these places. Dominant readings of 'the urban' are taken up by many lesbians and gay men across the research projects discussed here, who characterize rurality as backward and homophobic. By including classed complications in such designations, I suggest a more complicated map of belonging and inclusion than simply one based on a rural urban continuum, where the ability to take up space – and be 'everywhere' or simply 'everyday' – is a classed and sexual 'choice'.

There are classed interruptions to constructions of 'the urban' as utopian queer space and respondents frequently see 'the rural' as 'backward' and 'homophobic' (such as Jess in her depiction of the 'South Yorkshire Neanderthal man'). However, 'urban' queer space is not a singular utopian space for all lesbians; it is frequently experienced as exclusionary, as expressed by May (23) and Sharon (47) in their depictions of inaccessible urban scenes. To add to this complexity, 'working class' was negatively characterized – especially by middle-class respondents – in much the same way as 'the rural' (as deficient and devoid). 'The urban' and 'the middle class', by contrast, were seen as epitomizing spatialized and embodied 'diversity'. What this chapter hopes to provide is an interruption to such dominant understandings of 'the (middle class) urban', as a true contrast with the rural and working class undesirable 'other'.

To acknowledge this is not to efface the problems within rural and working-class locales, or the 'dystopian' aspects of these. Indeed, some 'rural' spaces continue to be areas from which young queers in particular seek 'escape' from (for example, Jill (29) and Jenny's (29) accounts of getting away from and feeling 'fixed' in rural terrain). That some 'rural' spaces continue to be conflated with heterosexuality and heteronormativity will embed, though not ensure, the performance of heterosexuality, as the (precarious) existence of the Rural Lesbian Group suggests (Bell and Valentine 1995). Yet, consequently, lesbian and gay men entering such spaces will be subject to visibility, surveillance and potential sanction (as conveyed in Kevin (36) and Sandra's (50) experiences of rural objections), where there is a lack of scene spaces for rural queers. Class necessarily mediates sexualized movements and 'escapes'; witness, for example, the fact that Tracey could not go out in her home town where the lack of resources made 'going out' in nearby Glasgow also problematic. This highlights the issue of access to other capitals that may assist movement out of the rural including, for example, social capital, networks, family and friends who have moved to the city, where the city becomes 'knowable' (if not 'sophisticated').

Some rural spaces may well be open to lesbians and provide 'scene spaces' of sorts (witness, for example, the proliferation of lesbian walking groups, rural retreats and so on) but these are likely to be classed, as highlighted by the Rural Lesbian Group. While analysis of 'other geographies' have complicated the focus on the urban, such studies themselves arguable recentre the experiences of the privileged, in neglecting class form their analyses (Smith and Holt 2005), where the 'objective' numeration of samples serves to simplify – and stand for – the role of class, missing out the spatial nuance which is sought. This chapter therefore puts class back into the analysis of lesbian and gay geographies, arguing that there is a more complicated map of belonging and inclusion for queers than one simply based on a rural urban continuum.

Bibliography

Ahmed, S. 2004. *The Cultural Politics of Emotion.* Edinburgh: Edinburgh University Press.

Bell, D. 2001. Fragments of a queer city, in *Pleasure Zones*, edited by D. Bell, J. Binnie, R. Holiday, R. Longhurst and R. Peace. New York: Syracuse University Press, 84–102.

Bell, D. and Valentine, G. (ed.) 1995. *Mapping Desire.* London: Routledge.

Binnie, J. 2000. Cosmopolitanism and the sexed city, in *City Vision*, edited by D. Bell and A. Haddour. Harlow: Prentice Hall.

Binnie, J. 2004. *The Globalization of Sexuality.* London: Sage.

Binnie, J. and Valentine, G. 1999. Geographies of sexuality – a review of progress. *Progress in Human Geography*, 23(2), 175–87.

Bourdieu, P. 1984. *Distinction: A Social Critique of the Judgement of Taste.* London: Routledge.

Brekhaus, W.H. 2003. *Peacock, Chameleons and Centaurs. Gay Suburbia and the Grammar of Social Identity.* Chicago: University of Chicago Press

Browne, K., Lim, J. and Brown, G. 2007. *Geographies of Sexualities: Theories, Practices and Politics.* Aldershot: Ashgate.

Byrne, B. 2006. *White Lives: The Interplay of 'Race', Class and Gender in Everyday Life.* London and New York: Routledge.

Casey, M. 2004. De-dying queer space(s): heterosexual female visibility on gay and lesbian space. *Sexualities*, 7(4), 446–61.

Casey, M. 2007. The queer unwanted and their undesirable otherness, in *Geographies of Sexualities: Theory, Practices and Politics* edited by K. Bowne, J. Lim and G. Brown. Aldershot: Ashgate, 125–35.

Chasin, A. 2000. *Selling Out: The Gay And Lesbian Movement Goes To Market.* Basingstoke: Palgrave.

Duggan, L. 2002. The new homonormativity: the sexual politics of neoliberalism, in *Materializing Democracy: Towards a Revitalized Cultural Politics*, edited by R. Castonovo and D. Nelson. Durham: Duke University Press, 175–94.

Elder, G. 2002. Response to "queer patriarchies, queer racisms, international." *Antipode*, 34(5), 988–91.

Evans, D. 1993. *Sexual Citizenship: The Material Construction of Sexualities.* London: Routledge.

Field, N. 1997. Identity and Lifestyle Market, in *Materialist Feminism: a Reader in Class, Difference, and Women's Lives*, edited by R. Hennessy and C. Ingraham. London: Routledge, 259–71.

Hennessy, R. 2000. *Profit and Pleasure: Sexual Identities in Late Capitalism.* London: Taylor and Francis Group.

Kirkey, K. and Forsyth, A. 2001. Men in the valley: gay male life on the suburban-rural fringe. *Journal of Rural Studies*, 17(4), 421–41.

Lindsay, J., Perlesz, A., Brown, R., McNair, R., Vaus, D. and Pitts, M. 2006. Stigma or respect: lesbian-parented families negotiating school settings. *Sociology*, 40(6), 1059–1077.

Oswin, N. 2005. Towards radical geographies of complicit queer futures. *ACME: An International E-Journal for Critical Geographers*, 3(2), 79–86.

Oswin, N. 2008. Critical geographies and the uses of sexuality: deconstructing queer space. *Progress in Human Geography*, 32(1), 89–103.

Simpson, M. 1999. *It's a Queer World: Deviant Adventures in Pop Culture.* New York: Harrington Park Press.

Skeggs, B. 1999. Matter out of place: visibility and sexualities in leisure spaces. *Leisure Studies*, 18(3), 213–32.

Skeggs, B. 2001. The toilet paper: femininity, class and mis-recognition. *Women's Studies International Forum*, 24(3/4), 295–307.

Smith, D.P. and Holt, L. 2005. 'Lesbian migrants in the gentrified valley' and 'other' geographies of rural gentrification. *Journal of Rural Studies*, 21(3), 313–22.

Taylor, Y. 2004. Negotiation and navigation: an exploration of the spaces/places of working-class lesbians. *Sociological Research Online*, 9(1), 1–24.

Taylor, Y. 2005. Real Politik or Real Politics? Working-class lesbians' political 'awareness' and activism. *Women's Studies International Forum*, 28(6), 484–94.

Taylor, Y. 2007a. *Working-class Lesbian Life: Classed Outsiders.* Palgrave: Macmillan.

Taylor, Y. 2007b. 'If your face doesn't fit...': the misrecognition of working-class lesbians in scene space. *Leisure Studies*, 27(2), 161–78.

Taylor, Y. 2008. 'That's not really my scene': working-class lesbians in (and out of) place. *Sexualities*, 11(5), 523–46.

Taylor, Y. 2009. *Lesbian and Gay Parenting: Securing Social and Educational Capital.* Palgrave: Macmillan.

Taylor, Y. 2010a. Privileged locations? Class, sexuality and parenting, in *Classed Intersections: Spaces, Selves, Knowledges* edited by Y. Taylor. Farnham: Ashgate, 159–77.

Taylor, Y. 2010b. The 'outness' of queer: class and sexual intersections, in *Queer Methodologies*, edited by K. Browne and C. Nash. Farnham: Ashgate, 69–83.

Valentine, G. 1993. Hetero-sexing space: lesbian perceptions and experiences of everyday spaces. *Environment and Planning D – Society and Space*, 9(3), 395–41.

Waitt, G. and Gorman-Murray, A. 2007. *Provincial paradoxes: 'at home' with older gay men in a provincial town of the Antipodes*. Paper to the Queer Spaces: Centres and Peripheries Conference, University of Technology Sydney, 22–3 February 2007.

Warner, M. 1993. *Fear of a Queer Planet: Queer Politics and Social Theory*. London: University of Minnesota Press.

Weeks, J., Heaphy, B. and Donovan, C. 2001. *Same Sex Intimacies: Families of Choice and Other life Experiments*. London and New York: Routledge.

Weston, K. 1995. Get thee to a big city: sexual imaginary and the great gay migration. *GLQ: A Journal of Lesbian and Gay Studies*, 2(3), 253–77.

Chapter 11

Terms of Engagement: The Intersections Among Gender, Class and Race in Canadian Sustainable Forest Management

Maureen G. Reed and Debra Davidson

This chapter is born out of an interest in improving rural community engagement with government and industry in sustainable forest management across Canada, because doing so enhances prospects for effective and durable management practices. Many of the enduring constraints to inclusive participatory community engagement are deeply entrenched aspects of community and institutional culture that are frequently overlooked. Gender is one such construct that has significant implications for participation. Gender is not expressed in isolation, however, but rather in conjunction with other aspects of social structure, such as class and racialized identities. We respond to the question: How does gender intersect with class and racialized identities, and with local forestry culture, to influence how some rural people gain influence in forest management decision-making to the exclusion of others? In doing so, we seek to address the observation of Panelli (2006: 74) that 'future class-specific analyses could more critically re-engage with the continuing struggles over labour, resources ... and decision making as rural cultures and spaces change' as she suggests that it is still relevant to examine how power and resources are unevenly distributed and mobilized by different groups, classes, or interests.

We argue that the creation and operation of 'community based' forums are informed by invisible, taken for granted assumptions about class, gender, and racialized identities[1] that form part of a rural forestry culture. This culture is not

---

[1] We use the term 'racialized identity' to describe an identity that goes beyond 'race' or 'ethnicity', by examining how a social group becomes identified with certain attributes at birth and/or because of the socialization and social location of that group within the power structures of the dominant society (Hill Collins 2000, Fairclough 2003). Aboriginal people in Canada have been accorded a marginalized social identity since contact with Europeans who have sought to annihilate, assimilate, or integrate Aboriginal people into 'Euro-Canadian' society. Identity models are racial when they describe reactions to societal oppression based on race and are ethnic when they describe the acquisition and maintenance of cultural characteristics such as religious expression and language (Helms 1996). Clearly both identity models are relevant to Aboriginal people in Canada, suggesting the need for a merged concept. We have chosen the term 'racialized identity' to emphasize the ongoing marginalization of Aboriginal peoples in Euro-Canadian society and to respect

solely imposed on rural women or men, but rather is co-created by them and by outsiders, establishing norms, values, and expectations for rural residents. Recent attempts to involve local people in forest management decision-making become articulated within this culture; they do not supplant it. Consequently, participatory mechanisms are both shaped by and reinforce local norms, values, and expectations. These mechanisms establish patterns of representation and engagement that privilege particular forms of rural masculinity as expressed in membership, agendas, and participatory styles, for example, to the general disadvantage of those who do not affiliate with these rural norms. Examination of gender, class, and racialized identity suggests that these three elements work together in rural places and they remain salient in explaining the differential opportunities and experiences of rural women and men in relation to sustainable forest management.

Class remains a salient category of rural life, although its identifiers are continually negotiated with other categories such as gender and even place. We adopt the position forwarded by Gibson-Graham (1996) who considered class as a *process* rather than a social position that is negotiated and renegotiated with other relations and axes of identity such as gender and ethnicity. It takes on material and discursive forms; 'it is not a given, but is in continual production' (Skeggs 2004: 3). Many rural residents do not necessarily identify with the notion of class, even though they exhibit the characteristics of particular class positions or processes (Savage 2000, Mills 2007, Bryant and Pini 2009). Despite the fading of class consciousness and/or reluctance to speak of class in rural settings, these places may still inform our understanding of how class is structured and works to organize social relations (Reay 1997).

Bryant and Pini (2009: 55) illustrate how 'gender and class are intricately connected in rural spaces ... actively constructed and reconstructed through daily interactions, the nature of one's work, volunteer activities, leisure choices and memories'. Yet, as community based scholars whose relationship with research subjects is key to our success, we face a dilemma when incorporating 'class' into our analyses. If we speak of class as a fluid process, we risk alienating research partners by offering a category that has limited value for advancing practical, political or policy change; if we try to 'fix' class identity to make it more visible and intelligible outside of academia, we risk damaging relationships with research partners by labeling them with a moniker they may not accept.

The chapter begins by explaining how forestry culture is constituted through interconnecting elements of gender, class, and racialized identity. We then turn to how these elements affect the ways in which rural participants engage in community based forestry planning processes, shaping decisions about who is allowed to participate, what values and knowledge participants can bring to the

---

the perspective of Aboriginal people that they are 'not just another ethnic group'. The term also denotes that social location and identity are perpetuated through racialization; a process characterized by an active and dynamic exertion of power by the dominant white Euro-Canadian society over Aboriginal 'others', even if the 'others' cannot be distinguished by conventional conceptions of 'race'.

table, and how participants are allowed to behave. We draw empirical support from a range of studies of public advisory committees (related to forestry) and community forests across Canada. We draw conclusions from these studies related to how power is exercised in these planning processes and consider the implications for ongoing research.

Creating a Forestry Culture: The Role of Gender, Class, and Racialized Identity

Forestry shares a strong gendered division of labour with other resource dependent occupations (agriculture, fishing, mining). This division has historically been linked to a particular form of masculinity that valorizes hard, dangerous, and physical work, requiring long hours and an ability to adjust to the rough and tumble found in logging camps (Tripp-Knowles 1999, Brandth and Haugen 2000, Brandth, Follow and Haugen 2004). New forms of masculinity associated with managerial proficiency, objectivity, and rationality have become important as forestry has incorporated new technologies and decision-making practices, yet women continue to experience marginality, discrimination and outright exclusion in the forestry sector (Tripp-Knowles 1999, Brandth and Haugen 2000, Reed 2003b). Thus, despite the fact that they typically have higher levels of formal education than their male counterparts, women have often been excluded from many of the well paid forms of forestry employment (Sachs 1996, Tripp-Knowles 1999, Reed 2003a). Women in forestry towns frequently earn less for similar work than women in urban centres (Parkins and Beckley 2001), and during times of economic restructuring women in forestry are more likely than men to lose their job, take a greater cut in pay when they are displaced, or experience significantly more long-term unemployment (Commission on Resources and Environment 1994, Barnes 1999, Hayter 2000). Importantly, this labour market disadvantage mediates women's involvement in community organizing and decision-making. As discussed later, one's employment status shapes the identification of 'stakeholder' and 'stake'; signifies who is deemed 'knowledgeable' and what kinds of knowledge count; and establishes the norms of acceptable behaviour in community based decision-making practices.

Class also operates as a salient category within forestry communities. However, in forestry communities class identity is less tied to property ownership and income than it is in other communities. In Canada, over 90 per cent of the commercial forestry land base is publicly owned. Waged workers have historically been among the highest paid in the country, sometimes earning three or four times the national average salary of a typical Canadian. This wealth allows workers to become multiple property owners, and to engage in activities associated with a middle-class lifestyle (for example, choice of holidays and educational opportunities for children). Furthermore, as with other rural settings (see Bryant and Pini 2009) there is a reluctance of forestry workers to speak of their experiences in class terms (Mills

2007). Nevertheless class positioning in forestry communities can be observed by the way in which workers demonstrate affinity for the company or the collective. Mills's (2007) study of employment diversification noted that unionized women were more likely to present themselves as members of a collective of workers and identify with the union than with the company, even when the union did not support initiatives that would directly benefit women workers (for example part-time work). They also expressed affinity for or used the vocabulary of the union, such as when they described solidarity with workers. Women who worked on salary were more likely to align themselves with the interests of the company than with female waged workers, appearing to describe some degree of autonomy in decisions they made about their work situation. Both waged and salaried workers, however, positioned themselves quite apart from Aboriginal women workers; both reproduced racist discourse, and criticized programs aimed at including Aboriginal workers as unfair to non-Aboriginal people.

Mills's (2007) findings gesture towards a third intersecting social category of importance in rural Canada and of concern to this chapter; namely racialized identity. In Canada, about 80 per cent of Aboriginal communities (First Nations and Métis) are within the nation's forest regions (Gysbers and Lee 2003). In recent years, a range of coalescing factors has seen government and forestry companies seek to increase Aboriginal participation in forestry employment as well as in plant ownership, planning (Parsons and Prest 2003) and management decision-making (Parsons and Prest 2003, Merkel 2007).[2] However, as Mills's (2007) findings illustrate, forestry cultures in Canadian forestry communities are inextricably bound to particular normative assumptions related to racialized identity and thus relatively few Aboriginal people have benefited from recent employment programs. Following up on work by Dunk (1994), Mills (2007) used Census data to compare the employment profiles of Aboriginal and non-Aboriginal men and women within the forestry industry in northern Saskatchewan. She found that both male and female Aboriginal workers were over-represented in seasonal woods based forest industries that offer non-standard and flexible forms of work, while white women were over-represented in clerical occupations. She wrote, 'First Nations people and women were concentrated in lower paying occupations and industries to a greater extent than non-First Nations people and men. First Nations people in particular were concentrated in less stable occupations' (Mills 2006: 161). Furthermore, she noted that First Nations women were not only excluded from male dominated occupations, they were also excluded from the female dominated clerical and secretarial occupations.

---

2   Reasons include the recognition by Canadian courts that Aboriginal people have rights to resources, a legal 'duty to consult' with Aboriginal peoples, the need to maintain a steady workforce in some of the more remote rural areas, and the need for government and industry to address glaring disparities between Aboriginal and settler populations across many social indicators including employment, education, health, and income (Parkins et al. 2006b).

These elements, gender, class, and racialized identity, are significant because they affect who has access to, and control over, local assets; they define suitable local stakeholders or representatives; and they embed social relations and norms that establish a forestry culture that is taken for granted in everyday life. They work together to create a rural culture whereby the norm of the forestry worker is a heterosexual, white, male, hard-working breadwinner who is rightfully a decision maker at both household and community levels. For the remainder of this chapter, we focus on how these elements work to shape public advisory processes related to forest management.

Forestry Culture and the Shaping of Rural Participation

Since the 1990s, as sustainability became a more prevalent theme in public policy around forestry, different forms of engagement among government agencies, companies, and communities emerged to address planning and management issues. Public advisory committees[3] formed as a means of 'community-based public engagement, where local forest users (along with people involved in the forest sector for their livelihood, representatives of other local agencies such as educational establishments and the business community, and elected leaders) participate in discussions about forest management and provide input into local decision-making' (Parkins et al. 2006a: 1). These committees meet regularly (on average eight times per year) and, in some provinces, they are required by provincial regulations and forest management licensing procedures. In some cases, these committees are sponsored by forest companies; in other cases, they are sponsored by government agencies.

The empirical support for this chapter comes from several studies in which we have participated, many of which have been published elsewhere. We refer to a team based project led by John Parkins that surveyed 102 forest advisory committees across the country (Parkins et al. 2006a). Additionally, we discuss results from two other studies that explored some of the themes of the cross-Canada survey using in-depth case studies of three public advisory committees in Alberta (Parkins and Davidson 2008) and two committees in Manitoba and Nova Scotia, respectively (Richardson 2008). We also refer to an analysis of a pilot community forest in British Columbia (BC) (Reed and Mcilveen 2006). The analysis by Reed and McIlveen (2006) specifically addressed the ways in which people were invited to participate and the types of knowledge and values that were introduced to the community forest board in its early stages of operation.

---

3   Also called citizen advisory committees, local level advisory committees, forestry advisory committees, forest sector advisory committees.

Who Gets to Participate

The participatory approach typically used is described as 'interest based'. In this model, participants are nominated by identification of a specific interest, often by affiliation to a specific group that may be significantly or directly affected by management or planning decisions and/or who could impede implementation of decisions made. In many committees, one's economic interest (typically established by one's employment for example as hunter/trapper, logger or municipal councilor) identifies an interest as a stakeholder.

Despite the ubiquity of the interest based model, researchers of environmental management now recognize that it incorporates power imbalances that marginalize and exclude some groups as well as their interests and systems of knowledge (Raish 2000, Hull, Robertson and Kendra 2001, Moote et al. 2001, Skogen 2003). Several studies have noted that committee membership is typically drawn from a pool of male citizens with above average levels of education and income (McComas 2001, McFarlane and Boxall 2002), who have previous forest related training (Jabbour and Balsillie 2003); little effort made to include representation from the lower income levels (Parkins, Stedman and McFarlane 2001). Other literature has demonstrated that migrant labourers engaged in tree planting and harvesting of non-timber forest products in particular are likely to be disenfranchised from planning or management initiatives that affect their interests because of their mobility and marginal status (Fortmann and Roe 1993, Brown et al. 2004). Further inequities emerge around the narrow definition of interest, often only implicitly understood rather than explicitly defined, which leaves out a range of possible voices of concern. For example, organized domains (unionized labour, the forest industry, even some environmental networks) are able to gain influence while less formalized domains, including social interests that are often ascribed to women (who are frequently of low socio-economic status as well), have few, if any, entry points into land use planning.

In contrast to women, Aboriginal people have gained nominal representation as 'stakeholders' in these processes, although their representation has not been granted in proportion to their population in the region. As with other social groups, their interests vary, but many share strong normative concerns regarding industrial impacts to the land base. Aboriginal people are in a unique political position as the Courts have upheld that they are far more than 'stakeholders' but rather they are 'right holders' who have rightful, yet contested, claims to land and resources. Additionally, the Courts have determined that governments have a duty to consult Aboriginal peoples about proposals or policies that may affect their rights to lands and resource. Consequently, some Aboriginal groups refuse to legitimate such processes with their participation because they are concerned that doing so will compromise recognition of their rights and authority. In all cases, however, the absence of 'voices from the periphery' frequently results in the lack of adequate attention and concrete measures to address the socio-cultural and more extensive impacts of land use decisions (Reed 2003b, Turner et al. 2008).

What They Bring to the Table

Gender, class, and racialized identity also shape the types of knowledge and concerns that are brought to the committee table. Research has long demonstrated that women express higher levels of concern than men for environmental issues and for forest protection (Mohai 1992, Davidson and Freudenburg 1996, Tindall, Davies and Mauboules 2003, Reed and Varghese 2007). They also typically express greater aversion to and concern for environmental risks such as climate change than do men (Davidson, Williamson and Parkins 2003, Johnsson-Latham 2007). In Sweden, researchers have observed that women's knowledge about conservation and forest species is different from men's (Uliczka et al. 2004) and they perceive social impacts of forest management differently from men (Arora-Jonsson 2004). Ulickza et al. (2004) found that in Sweden younger women with high formal education showed the most positive attitude towards conservation of all respondents (see also Lidestav and Ekström 2000). Aboriginal peoples, as well, bring a mix of concerns to the table that are unique to this social group, ranging from a desire to increase their access to the wage economy, to protection of traditional lands and greater influence in land-use practices.

What counts as knowledge, on the other hand, is subject to ideological assumptions about appropriate mechanisms for the production and legitimation of knowledge, assumptions that have a tendency to privilege the knowledge borne by particular classes and racialized identities over others. According to Turner et al. (2008), the disjuncture between traditional and western knowledge systems has resulted in "invisible losses" to factors that are important contributors to Aboriginal culture, such as lifestyle, livelihood, knowledge, emotional and psychological well-being, and self-determination. The authors attribute these losses to the failure of western systems of governance to understand or give credibility to other forms of knowledge that might offer alternative processes and outcomes of decision-making practices that can stem the tide of cumulative and interconnected losses of land, culture, and power. They argue:

> One category of invisible loss, described earlier, is the loss of influence or self-determination. For Aboriginal communities, this typically means a loss in the ability to influence decisions about the resources on which they depend and which, based on assertions of Aboriginal title, they rightfully own. This is closely linked to a loss of respect for culturally derived values and wisdom in resource management (Turner et al. 2008: no page).

The knowledge held by certain non-Aboriginal people is excluded as well. Experts in the natural sciences, industry representatives, and government agents have typically had the power to set the agenda and establish norms and rules for adjudicating evidence in environmental decision-making, to the exclusion of individuals who do not have 'expert' status (Richardson, Sherman and Gismondi 1993). As Bäckstrand (2003) points out, 'sound science', as determined by peer reviewed risk assessment, dominates public deliberations of environmental risks. Consequently, alternative discourses and actors are marginalized or excluded.

Democratic governance certainly does not require that local and indigenous knowledge should be necessarily regarded as *better* or *truer* than modern scientific knowledge (Bäckstrand 2003) or that these knowledge claims be free from rules of adjudication and validation (Usher 2000). Yet, Mascarenhas and Scarce (2004: 28) observed 'a palpable tension ... between democratic and technocratic tendencies' in land use planning processes. Their interviews with participants of land use planning in BC revealed an insistence that 'expertise is hard-won and hard-earned' (Mascarenhas and Scarce 2004: 29) and therefore should be influential in local decisions. Thus, the lived and embodied knowledge of those largely outside of the structure of industrial forestry (such as women, Aboriginal people, and non-timber forest users) exemplify a class of users who may find it difficult to challenge the prevailing wisdom of those who have worked within the industrial forestry structure.

How Participants Behave and Share Knowledge

Knowledge is not 'given', but rather is situated within a range of social and cultural practices that shape how knowledge is constituted and legitimated. The authority of people who bring knowledge to the table is linked to expectations regarding knowledge acquisition, documentation, presentation, sharing, and appropriate behaviour. The criteria, tacit or explicit, for accepting these behaviours are subject to institutional factors, local practices and activities, and norms and attitudes; in short, factors described earlier as cultural in character. Both the transmission and the acceptance of information as 'knowledge' is shaped by one's gender, class, and racialized identity. Consequently, even when women, Aboriginal people, and members of other marginalized groups do serve on advisory tables, they may still face cultural norms that determine whether or not the means by which they attempt to share knowledge are considered acceptable. Given the dominance of some forms of knowledge and the social groups who 'hold' it, norms endorsing the acceptability of certain behaviours may be implicit and taken for granted, rather than openly discussed or challenged. Biases can be subtle, almost invisible, and even unintentional. Yet, they form systemic and significant influences on effective participation. They can emerge in procedures that determine criteria for assessment, identify sources and relevance of data, value alternative experiences and knowledge, and provide agency support from government for the process (Alston and Wilkinston 1998, Agarwal 2001).

Interrogating how knowledge and concerns are introduced into decision-making processes illustrates disparities in levels of authority for determining the kinds of knowledge that are relevant to decision-making, and reveals that power relations may constrain deliberations and restrict knowledge claims to fairly narrow domains (see Reed and McIlveen 2006). In the discussion that follows, we examine three aspects that illustrate how gender, class and racialized identity have affected the involvement of rural people in advisory processes by discussing who got invited, what they brought to the discussions, and how they shared knowledge at the committee table.

Findings and Discussion

Who Was Invited

The national survey of public advisory committees revealed that, despite the explicit mandate of forest advisory committees to speak to the issues facing forestry communities, only 17 per cent of committee membership was female. Coincidentally this figure is slightly higher than the percentage of women employed in primary forest industries (15 per cent) or forest manufacturing occupations (14 per cent). About 7 per cent of participants identified as Aboriginal, although only 3.5 per cent stated that they were chosen to *represent* Aboriginal interests. The province with the highest participation of women was British Columbia (BC) (32 per cent) although this province had lower proportions of participation by Aboriginal people (5 per cent). In the Prairies, the participation of women was the lowest (10 per cent), while Aboriginal participation was highest (21 per cent), due to provincial legislation in Saskatchewan requiring Aboriginal involvement in forest management (Table 11.1).

Table 11.1   Respondents by region, gender and aboriginality

Region	Male^	Female^	Self-identified as Aboriginal#
Atlantic*	87.5%	12.5%	6.7%
Québec	81.3%	18.7%	2.9%
Ontario	86.3%	13.7%	4.9%
Prairies~	89.7%	10.3%	20.8%
Alberta	81.3%	18.8%	7.1%
British Columbia	68.4%	31.6%	5.3%
Canada	81.3%	18.7%	7.2%

Notes: ^ Number who responded as male or female=1057, #Number who responded=1040, * Atlantic region comprises New Brunswick, Nova Scotia, and Newfoundland, ~ Prairies region comprises Manitoba and Saskatchewan.

Source: Parkins et al. 2006a.

To understand how people gained access, researchers asked respondents to indicate why they participated. Women were more likely than men to participate because it was required as part of their job. Men were more likely to state that they 'wanted to participate to contribute to planning since the forest is a public resource' and to 'ensure that recreational opportunities are not diminished'. Of those who indicated that they were required to attend as part of their job, more women than men came to these committees as employees of environmental organizations, while men were more likely than women to represent the forest industry. Overall, women, who are more likely to work in social, human, and health services fields, are less likely to get selected. Most individuals were selected by the forest companies or government agencies that sponsored the committees because of their direct interests in renewable natural resource management (for example, forest industry, government regulators, recreation and tourism, trapping); only 7 per cent stated they were selected to represent 'the general public', 5 per cent were selected to represent environmental interests and less than 1 per cent were selected to represent a community or social organization. Furthermore, the total proportion of representatives who identified as Aboriginal was 7.2 per cent, but only 3.5 per cent represented Aboriginal interests. This is important as while Aboriginal people make up about 3.8 per cent of the total population in Canada, they compose a higher proportion of residents living in the boreal forest. In northern Saskatchewan where most forestry takes place in that province, for example, 83 per cent of the population is Aboriginal.

This pattern was described in more depth in a study of three public advisory committees in Alberta. Parkins and Davidson (2008) found that committee members were selected primarily because of their stated interests in environmental issues (for example, through involvement in environmental groups or educational institutions) or because of prior dealings with the company. Although at first blush there appeared to be several interests at the table, a more thorough review of the cultural and demographic composition of participants suggested that membership was highly uniform. That is, the committees consistent of predominantly white, middle-class men. Parkins and Davidson observed that those from lower socio-economic classes, women, and minorities were poorly represented, leading them to conclude that access is often reserved for a narrow range of public interests who share similar fundamental ideological views regarding the appropriateness of industrial activity on the forested land base.

In a study of community forestry in BC's interior, constrictions to membership also emerged. Members of the board were selected by a steering committee because of their business or leadership experience in the community and in forestry. All members of the board had extensive formal and informal forestry experience, formal business expertise, and/or held official leadership (for example, Chief) positions. Thus, they had all the tools of bargaining power and influence. Aboriginal involvement was required as the structure of the forest board required that two seats be held by local First Nations. At the level of Aboriginal involvement, it was the leadership of these organizations, rather than Aboriginal residents in general, who became the members of the community forestry board. It was not clear what/ whose traditional ecological knowledge was included. There were no women on the board. Labour representation was also constrained as mobile contractors or those using forests for small-scale production of non-timber forest products or ecotourism were also left out.

Research across a range of forestry studies demonstrates with empirical regularity that the dominant model of representation restricts access to and participation in forestry decision-making. Accessibility for people living in forestry communities but who are not directly employed in a 'relevant group' is constrained in several ways. For example, due to the gendered division of labour in Canadian rural communities, women continue to bear the burden of home care and their employment status is less secure. Taking time from work or their families, especially without any financial compensation, is simply not an option. Committees typically only covered basic transportation costs; any costs associated with loss of income or childcare expenses while parents attended meetings were not covered (Parkins et al. 2006a). Additionally, in related research, women reported being reluctant to drive the long distances to and from meetings because of the time required and also because of concerns about driving conditions at night and in winter when roads are not well-lit and may be treacherous (Martz et al. 2006, Richardson 2008). While poor conditions obviously affect both men and women it was only women who reported this as a factor which circumscribed their participation.

Many women and some groups of men who are not part of the industrial forestry employment structure also lack the social networks and role models in forestry that give some men greater accessibility to committees (Reed 2003a). For example, private operators in forestry, business associations, unions, and wildlife and hunting organizations from which community members are selected are all male dominated. These associations and networks can be used to gain 'stakeholder status' in advisory committees and advance employment and economic interests, while the networks to which women belong do not usually suggest an immediate interest in forestry jobs or economic development. This narrow consideration of the stakes in forestry communities tends to favour the consideration of men with economic interests as committee members; it is unlikely that women who are not directly employed in forestry or a related resource sector would be asked to participate. Residents employed in the public or community health sectors, for example, were not considered relevant participants. In interviews with members of two forest sector advisory committees, Richardson (2008: 53) learned that 'because we don't have a lot of women in the industry *we don't naturally gravitate towards thinking about or suggesting women* [emphasis added] to be on the committee'. Furthermore, Richardson (2008) found that women employed in forestry described the importance of a role model to build experience and confidence of women. However, interviewees also noted that mentorship had not been extended to women outside the industry who might, with sufficient encouragement, join public advisory committees related to forestry.

In sum, participation on these committees is frequently determined by who holds specific economic interests. In other words, those who derive income from the forest (including occupations such as forestry workers, industry representatives, and tourist operators) and those who are part of well organized domains (such as unions and some environmental networks) are more likely to gain access to forest advisory committees. Those who have social interests in forestry communities (related to issues such as community health and well-being) are unlikely to be considered 'stakeholders' and remain excluded. This gap is reinforced by a relatively narrow range of values expressed at the table and by the concern shared by some participants outside of forestry that they do not have sufficient understanding of forestry issues to contribute effectively. These limitations are described in the next sections.

What They Brought to the Table

Confirming research elsewhere, the national survey of public advisory committees found that women and men had both shared and separate interests and values related to forest management (Reed and Varghese 2007). For example, both women and men strongly agreed that it was important to maintain forests for future generations, but women had stronger support for intrinsic values (that is, they valued the forest for its own sake rather than for its use value), while men rated utilitarian values more highly. Women were more likely to agree that 'humans should have more respect and admiration for the forests' and that 'forests should have the right to exist for their own sake, regardless of human concerns and uses'. By contrast, men rated utilitarian values more highly. For example, men were more likely to agree with the statement 'forests can be improved through management by humans'. Furthermore, women who participated in the survey were more likely than men to belong to natural history or bird watching clubs and environmental organizations, whereas men were more likely than women to belong to hunting or fishing organizations. Thus, the analysis suggested that an over-representation of men on the forestry committees will likely contribute to the prioritization of utilitarian values and may lead to the conflation of the values of this social group with the community as a whole. Perhaps not surprisingly, women who responded to the national survey were less likely than men to believe that all values were represented.

Analysis of community forests in BC confirms how a narrowly constructed committee creates a narrowly conceived set of values and specific interests come to represent general 'community' interests. According to the BC government, community forests were first introduced 'to increase communities' and First Nations' participation in local forest management, to test new and innovative forest management models, to reduce conflict among various stakeholders, and to maintain 'forest-related community lifestyles and values, while providing jobs and revenue that contribute to community stability' (British Columbia Ministry of Forests 1999: 1). Initially five objectives were set for the community forest: to provide a source of revenue and employment for the community, to establish training opportunities, to encourage First Nations to develop and market traditional botanicals testing innovative forest practices and to develop trail systems, and encouraging stakeholder cooperation. Yet the board quickly became focused solely on the first goal – providing revenue and employment (Reed and McIlveen 2006).

In this case, analysis revealed that the industrial forest model and the commercial timber bias retained a strong salience within the community forestry board. This bias was reinforced by regulatory constraints set at higher orders of governance. Reed and McIlveen (2006) concluded that 'community forestry' became more closely allied to 'local industrial forestry' than to the broader ideals that would admit a range of participants, knowledge systems, and cultural values.

Thus, despite a potentially wide range of forest values espoused by a diversity of stakeholders, these values are filtered, or 'funnelled' through several layers of institutional and community culture that function to privilege dominant practices and worldviews. Because such structures are largely uncontested, the exclusion of many voices of concern is also uncontested. Consequently, both the agendas and ensuing discussions characterizing participatory processes have a tendency to become narrowed early in the planning process. This 'funnelling' of legitimate values, concerns, and knowledge forms is demonstrated in the next section through a discussion of how behaviours and acts of knowledge sharing are enacted within group deliberations.

How Participants Behaved and Shared Knowledge

Connected to what participants bring to the table are assumptions about what knowledge they have and how they are expected to behave. This is exemplified in an exchange in a public advisory committee between a provincial spokesperson for the trappers' association and a forest company representative as documented by Parkins and Davidson (2008). The focus of the exchange was concerns with harvest operations including the use of pesticides. Parkins and Davidson (2008: 187) report:

> The representative of the trappers' association began speaking: "there were some fears out there amongst the membership that there are many factors that are not fully known. And we continue to hear articles, some are for and some are against, as ordinary laymen, we don't know where to stand ... So we'd like to err on the side of caution." A forest company representative then asked: "Have there been any papers written that discuss the impact of herbicides on trap lines? Are we bringing science to the table or are we bringing folklore?" To this question, the trappers' representative took exception: "We're bringing laymen experience. It's not folklore." In his defense, and as one of the first public members of the committee to wade into the discussion, a member stated: "The trapper that's out there, and working on the trap line is a professional. And his knowledge, although not well documented, and not necessarily put together scientifically, in his head, collectively is a valuable resource that is difficult to tap into."

This exchange between the trapper and the industry representative suggests that the class position of the trapper as both a participant without formal scientific education and a woods' worker outside of industrial forestry reduced the legitimacy of his concerns to a declaration of 'folklore'. Had the trapper brought with him to the table support from peer reviewed scientific studies, his determination to 'err on the side of caution' would likely have been much more readily accepted.

Women, too, have been validated or criticized according to whether or not they 'fit' norms of appropriate committee conduct or whether they have legitimate knowledge sanctioned by unwritten, although widely-prescribed, rules. In a follow-up study from the national survey involving personal interviews of members from two advisory committees, Kristyn Richardson (2008) found that women believed they were less influential because they did not have formal education or experience in the forest industry (although they typically have higher levels of formal education than rural men). Others expressed the belief that women on the committee were 'exceptionally strong, outspoken women that have the confidence to step into these roles' (Richardson 2008: 78). One male respondent complained that sometimes women are not heard because they are too emotional:

> The emotional approach I have trouble dealing with and I think most guys do when it gets too emotional and it's an emotional argument, as opposed to a rational, science-based as I call it, argument, because it tends to lose credibility in the business. It's a man's business and we don't really want to hear that stuff. (Richardson 2008: 79)

Juxtaposed, these two quotes suggest that women's participation was deemed acceptable or legitimate so long as women overcame stereotypical female behaviours (ie: were described as strong rather than emotional). Taken together, these findings reveal that gender and cultural stereotypes and expectations exist for both women and men. Specific ways of being, working, learning, knowing, and decision-making associated with the dominant culture of forestry (hard work, rational, etc.) were considered the norm, while other experiences and ways of knowing primarily attributed to women, Aboriginal people, and those marginal to industrial forestry were not.

Finally, all committees have a fairly constrained mandate, often restricted to procedural matters (for example, identifying forestry objectives) to the exclusion of normative issues (for example, the legitimacy of large-scale industrial forestry). Parkins and Davidson (2008) analysed the meeting transcripts of three advisory committees and determined that only a small number of substantial discussions had been initiated by committee members, although at many points, substantial discussions had been initiated and sustained by company officials. Within a single meeting of one of the committees, 'where data were recorded on the exact amount of time that each member contributed to committee discussions, committee members contributed approximately 13 minutes of discussion to a meeting that was 102 minutes in length. Company representatives dominated the remaining 89 minutes' (Parkins and Davidson 2008: 185). Interestingly, when asked who had greater influence in setting meeting agendas, women in the national survey saw themselves and other participants as being less influential compared with industry officials, whereas men saw themselves and other participants as the most influential in setting the agenda (Reed and Varghese 2007).

Ultimately, as this chapter has described, the ideals of democratic public deliberation may be distorted by the privileging of certain cultural groups and socio-economic classes and 'a tendency to defer to the hegemonic ideologies of those in power, … whereby the specific interests and values of a privileged few come to be seen as representative of the general interests of all citizens' (Parkins and Davidson 2008: 182). Drawing on Gramsci (1971), Parkins and Davidson (2008: 182) go on to point out that 'the staying power of hegemony derives from the ability to keep internal contradictions associated with privileged ideologies concealed'. This disturbing concealment is possible through the influence of state and corporate interests in committee deliberations. Their pessimistic conclusion is reinforced by Davis (1996: 234) who studied local participation in the East Coast fisheries, concluding that 'investing local user groups with management powers may do little more than entrench the advantages of vested interests, thereby assuring that participation and benefits will be realizable by only a few'. In sum, social identities such as class, gender, and race are not easily accommodated within an interest based model and consequently many potential members are easily excluded or marginalized from planning and management processes.

Conclusions

The overwhelming conclusion of these studies is that community engagement in forest advisory committees is elitist. They are rooted in sexist, class based, and cultural assumptions that shape forestry culture. Dominated by individuals whose stake is largely economic and favourable to industrial forestry, constrained by external priorities and internal dynamics set by government and/or industry, these processes exclude those whose gender, class, and/or racialized identities are not defined by the dominant norms of industrial forestry. Women, Aboriginal people, and those of lower socio-economic status are not only less likely to participate, but also less likely to make substantive contributions when they do take part. Those who had participated in specific committee processes indicate their engagement and influence in decision-making was limited.

The division of labour in forestry employment is important for how it shapes the identification of stakeholders who are asked for representation on interest based public advisory committees. The division of labour may also be a factor in whether people are accepted and treated as equal members. Recall that scientists (according to women) and industry representatives (according to men) held greater legitimacy in the national survey as trusted sources of information about forestry. These two groups (scientists, industry managers) hold particular class (and gendered) positions within the structures of forest based employment. Those with local or indigenous knowledge outside the employment structures of industrial forestry did not have the same influence or legitimacy. The absence of women from forestry employment, and gender norms more broadly, operate to the general disadvantage of women's participation: constraining their likelihood of being selected, reducing their satisfaction with the process, and hampering their effectiveness. The barriers to women's participation are both ideological and logistical. As employment structures change to allow for increased women's participation in the forestry work force, these barriers may change as well.

Racialized and class based inequities are also evident and may be more difficult to transcend than gendered inequities. Aboriginal people, both male and female, are the most marginalized in the current forestry employment structure. This placement is accompanied by prejudices about the appropriate place of Aboriginal people in forestry; and the roles, responsibilities, and rights of Aboriginal and settler populations in settling and meeting the terms of land claims and treaties, and the knowledge Aboriginal people may have of forest resources. These prejudices compound the experience of poverty that marks Aboriginal people as a class that is more difficult to transcend than the conventional markers of 'working' or 'middle' class. These prejudices are not unique to forestry communities, and they will not be erased simply by inviting Aboriginal people to attend the committee meetings.

The recognition by Canadian courts and participants in public advisory committees that Aboriginal people need to be present in planning and decision-making forums is a positive start. Yet, there is a wide chasm in how different groups gain, legitimize, and share knowledge to mutual benefit. As Nancy Turner et al. (2008: no page) explained:

> Researchers often hear claims that a decision-making process did not adequately deal with traditional knowledge, whereas managers and academics, having diligently conducted interviews and collected facts from elders, contend that they are "incorporating" traditional knowledge. The problem is that the definition of knowledge by the scientific community is at variance with knowledge as understood by Aboriginal knowledge holders.

This gap suggests that a cultural shift will be required to ensure adequate representation of Aboriginal people in decision-making related to sustainable forest management.

Thus, 'sustainable forest management' is not a matter of good technique, somehow getting the right balance of participants and finding the correct mechanisms for weighing the options. It is a political exercise wherein the power to set the terms of engagement held by some cultural groups and socio-economic classes shape the debates at the table and the outcomes that arise. A focus on gender, class, and racialized identity helps to sensitize both researchers and practitioners to multiple inequities and helps create opportunities for more inclusive concepts, analyses, and ultimately more inclusive policies and practices that place equal value on the contributions of a wide diversity of people.

Beyond providing ideas about 'sustainable forest management', this chapter also reveals some challenges for academics who seek to integrate gender, race and class into their analyses. Holding these three elements simultaneously is like trying to herd three scorched cats in the dark. Rural studies theorists have often explained one or two of these elements, but rarely all three (e.g., Cloke and Little 1997, Woods 2005, Bryant and Pini 2009). Furthermore, they have not typically turned to environmental practice as a research venue for these interacting elements. Consequently, there is not much guidance about how to conceptualize the three simultaneously and a strong temptation to privilege one element of analysis over others.

Scholars of environmental practice also offer few examples. Although some fields of study in human environment relations have given attention to power relations (for example, political ecology, ecological modernization, environmental justice), research in environmental management and planning has been slow to address the three elements of gender, class, and racialized identity (Agyeman et al. 2009). Part of this gap is due to the applied emphasis of environmental management that privileges the resolution of practical problems over the development of theory. This applied emphasis also challenges researchers who continue to work on issues such as 'class', 'gender' and 'racialized identity' to find ways to communicate these findings to local practitioners in a way that encourages recognition of the gaps, motivates change, and provides recommendations that can easily be implemented. This 'extension' work poses a challenge to academics to find ways to link theoretical advances to real world solutions and to reach beyond their academic borders despite a reward system that favours theory over practice (Martin 2001).

Beyond these practical dilemmas, academics who work within community settings also face ethical dilemmas. Many of us wonder if academic labels serve to reify experiences that some research subjects seek to overcome. For example, the reluctance by local people to describe their experiences in class terms should give academics pause when using this term. Does the continued use of 'class' make academic work on the subject at best irrelevant to the lived experiences of their research subjects or worse, harmful to their research subjects by subjugating them to labels that fix their experiences? We have not resolved these dilemmas, but we hope that by reading and reflecting on the chapters in this collection, readers may consider how a focus on gender, class, and identity can serve rural places as well as the academics who study them.

Acknowledgements

Funding for this research was provided by the Sustainable Forest Management Network and the Social Sciences and Humanities Research Council of Canada. We also thank the participants in the research as well as Belinda Leach and Barbara Pini for their constructive comments and support. We apologise for any errors and omissions that remain.

References

Agarwal, B. 2001. Participatory exclusions, community forestry, and gender: an analysis for South Asia and a conceptual framework. *World Development*, 29(10), 1623–648.

Agyeman, J., Cole, P., Haluza-DeLay, R. and O'Riley, P. 2009. *Speaking for Ourselves: Environmental Justice in Canada*. Vancouver: UBC Press.

Alston, M. and Wilkinson, J. 1998. Australian farm women – shut out or fenced in? The lack of women in agricultural leadership. *Sociologia Ruralis*, 38(3), 391–408.

Arora-Jonsson, S. 2004. Relational dynamics and strategies: men and women in a forest community in Sweden. *Agriculture and Human Values*, 21(4), 355–365.

Bäckstrand, K. 2003. Civic science for sustainability: reframing the role of scientific experts, policy-makers and citizens in environmental governance. *Global Environmental Politics*, 3(4), 24–41.

Barnes, T. 1999. Industrial geography, institutional economics and Innis, in *The New Industrial Geography: Regions, Regulations and Institutions*, edited by T. Barnes and M. Gertler. New York: Routledge, 1–20.

Brandth, B. and Haugen, M. 2000. From lumberjack to business manager: masculinity in the Norwegian forestry press. *Journal of Rural Studies*, 16(3), 343–55.

Brandth, B., Follow, G. and M. Haugen. 2004. Women in forestry: dilemmas of a separate women's organization. *Scandinavian Journal of Forest Research*, 19(5), 466–72.

British Columbia Ministry of Forests. 1999. 27 Communities apply for new tenure under community forest pilot project. [Online: British Columbia Ministry of Forests]. Available at: http://www.for.gov.bc.ca/pscripts/pab/newsrel/mofnews. asp?refnum=1999%3A007 [accessed: 15 December 2001].

Brown, B., Leal-Marino, D., McIlveen, K. and Lee Tan, A. 2004. *Contract Forest Laborers in Canada, The US and Mexico – Land Tenure, Labor, Trade and Community Forestry: The Context For Reforestation Forest Work in the Nafta Region*. California: The Jefferson Center for Education and Research.

Bryant, L. and Pini, B. 2009. Gender, class and rurality: Australian case studies. *Journal of Rural Studies*, 25(1), 48–57.

Cloke, P. and Little, P. 1997. *Contested Countryside Cultures: Otherness, Marginalisation, and Rurality*. London and New York: Routledge.

Commission on Resources and Environment. 1994. *Vancouver Island Land Use Plan*. vol. 1. Victoria, British Columbia: Commission on Resources and Environment.

Davidson, D. and Freudenburg, W. 1996. Gender and environmental risk concerns: a review and analysis of available research. *Environmental Behavior*, 28(3), 302–39.

Davidson, D., Williamson, T. and Parkins, J. 2003. Understanding climate changer risk and vulnerability in northern forest-based communities. *Canadian Journal of Forest Research*, 33(11), 252–61.

Davis, A. 1996. Social research and alternative approaches to fisheries management: an introductory comment. *Society and Natural Resources*, 9(3), 233–5.

Dunk, T. 1994. Talking about trees: environment and society in forest workers' culture. *Canadian Review of Sociology and Anthropology*, 31(1), 14–34.

Fairclough, N. 2003. *Analysing Discourse: Textual Analysis for Social Research*. New York: Routledge.

Fortmann, L. and Roe, E. 1993. On really existing communities-organic or otherwise. *Telos*, 95, 139–146.

Gibson-Graham, J. 1996. *The End of Capitalism (As We Knew It): A Feminist Critique of Political Economy*. Oxford: Blackwell Publishers.

Gramsci, A. 1971. *Selections from the Prison Notebooks of Antonio Gramsci*, edited and translated by Q. Hoare and G. Nowell Smith. New York: International Publishers.

Gysbers, J. and Lee, P. 2003. *Aboriginal Communities in Forest Regions in Canada: Disparities in Socio-economic Conditions*. Edmonton Alberta: Global Forest Watch Canada.

Hayter, R. 2000. *Flexible Crossroads: The Restructuring of British Columbia's Forest Economy*. Vancouver: UBC Press.

Helms, J.E. 1996. Toward a methodology for measuring and assessing racial as distinguished from ethnic identity, in *Multicultural Assessment in Counseling and Clinical Psychology*, edited by G.R. Sodowsky and J.C. Impara. Lincoln: Buros Institute of Mental Measurement, 143–192.

Hill Collins, P. 2000. Gender, black feminism, and black political economy. *Annals of the American Academy of Political and Social Science*, 568(1), 41–53.

Hull, R.B., Robertson, D.P. and Kendra, A. 2001. Public understandings of nature: a case study of local knowledge about 'natural' forest conditions. *Society and Natural Resources*, 14(4), 325–340.

Jabbour, J.R. and Balsillie, D. 2003. The effects of public participation in forest management: a case study analysis of the Morice Innovative Forest Practices Agreement. *The Forestry Chronicle*, 79(2), 1–13.

Johnsson-Latham, G. 2007. *A Study on Gender Equality as a Prerequisite for Sustainable Development*, Report to the Environment Advisory Council, Sweden 2007:2. [Online: GenderCC] Available at: http://www.gendercc. net/fileadmin/inhalte/Dokumente/Actions/ecological_footprint__johnsson-latham.pdf [Accessed: 13 September 2010].

Lidestav, G. and Ekström, M. 2000. Introducing gender in studies on management behaviour among non-industrial private forest owners. *Scandinavian Journal of Forest Research*, 15(3), 378–86.

Martin, R. 2001. Geography and public policy: the case of the missing agenda. *Progress in Human Geography*, 25(2), 189–210.

Martz, D., Reed, M.G., Brueckner, I. and Mills, S. 2006. *Hidden Actors, Muted Voices: The Employment of Rural Women in Canadian Forestry and Agri-food Industries*. Ottawa, Ontario: Research Directorate Status of Women Canada.

Mascarenhas, M. and Scarce, R. 2004. "The intention was good": legitimacy, consensus-based decision making, and the case of forest planning in British Columbia, Canada. *Society and Natural Resources*, 17(1), 17–38.

McComas, K.A. 2001. Public meetings about local waste management problems: Comparing participants and nonparticipants. *Environmental Management*, 27(1), 135–47.

McFarlane, B.L. and Boxall, P.C. 2002. Factors influencing forest values and attitudes of two stakeholder groups: the case of the Foothills Model Forest, Alberta, Canada. *Society and Natural Resources*, 13(7), 649–61.

Merkel, G. 2007. We are all connected: globalization and community sustainability in the boreal forest, an Aboriginal perspective. *The Forestry Chronicle*, 83(3), 362–6.

Mills, S. 2006. Segregation of women and Aboriginal people within Canada's forest sector by industry and Ooccupation. *Canadian Journal of Native Studies*, 26(1), 147–71.

Mills, S. 2007. *Women's experiences and representations of diversity management and organizational restructuring in a multinational forest company*, unpublished PhD Thesis. Saskatoon: University of Saskatchewan.

Mitchell, B. 1997. *Resource and Environmental Management*. Harlow: Wesley Longman.

Mohai, P. 1992. Men, women and the environment: an examination of the gender gap in environmental concern and activism. *Society and Natural Resources*, 5(1), 1–19.

Moote, M., Brown, B., Kingley, E., Lee, S., Voth, D. and Walker, G. 2001. Process: redefining relationships, in *Understanding Community-based Forest Ecosystem Management*, edited by G. Gray, M.J. Enzer and J. Kusel. New York, London and Oxford, United Kingdom: Food Products Press, an imprint of The Haworth Press Inc., 99–116.

Panelli, R. 2006. Rural Society, in *Handbook of Rural Studies*, edited by P. Cloke, T. Marsden and P. Mooney. Thousand Oaks: SAGE Publications.

Parkins, J. and Davidson, D. 2008. Constructing the public sphere in compromised settings: environmental governance in the Alberta forest sector. *Canadian Review of Sociology*, 45(2), 177–196.

Parkins, J., Hunt, L., Nadeau, S., Sinclair, J., Reed, M. and Wallace, S. 2006a. *Public Participation in Forest Management: Results from a National Survey of Advisory Committees*, Northern Forestry Centre Information Report NOR-X-409. Edmonton Alberta: Northern Forestry Centre, Canadian Forest Service, Natural Resources Canada.

Parkins, J., Stedman, R., Patriquin, M. and Burns, M. 2006b. Strong policies, poor outcomes: longitudinal analysis of forest sector contributions to Aboriginal communities in Canada. *Journal of Aboriginal Economic Development*, 5(1), 61–73.

Parkins, J.R. and Beckley, T.M. 2001. *Monitoring Community Sustainability in the Foothills Model Forest. A Social Indicators Approach*, Atlantic Forestry Centre Information Report AFC M-X-211. Fredericton: Canadian Forest Service.

Parkins, J.R. and Mitchell, R.E. 2005. Public participation as public debate: a deliberative turn in natural resource management. *Society and Natural Resources*, 18(6), 529–540.

Parkins, J.R., Stedman, R.C. and McFarlane, B.L. 2001. *Public Involvement in Forest Management and Planning: A Comparative Analysis of Attitudes and Preferences in Alberta*, Northern Forestry Centre Information Report NOR-X-382. Edmonton, Alberta: Northern Forestry Centre, Canadian Forest Service, Natural Resources Canada.

Parsons, R. and Prest, G. 2003. Aboriginal forestry in Canada. *The Forestry Chronicle*, 79(4), 779–784.

Raish, C. 2000. Environmentalism, the Forest Service, and the Hispano Communities of Northern New Mexico. *Society and Natural Resources*, 13(5), 489–508.

Reay, D. 1997. Feminist theory, habitus, and social class: disrupting notions of classlessness. *Women's Studies International Forum*, 20(2), 225–33.

Reed, M. 2003a. Marginality and gender at work in forestry communities of British Columbia, Canada. *Journal of Rural Studies*, 19(3), 373–89.

Reed, M. 2003b. *Taking Stands: Gender and the Sustainability of Rural Communities*. Vancouver: UBC Press.

Reed, M.G. and McIlveen, K. 2006. Toward a pluralistic civic science?: assessing community forestry. *Society and Natural Resources*, 19(7), 591–607.

Reed, M.G. and Varghese, J. 2007. Gender Representation on Canadian Forest Sector Advisory Committees. *Forestry Chronicle*, 83(4), 515–25.

Richardson, K. 2008. *A Gendered Perspective of Learning and Representation on Forest Management Advisory Committees in Canada*, unpublished Master's Thesis. Winnipeg: University of Manitoba.

Richardson, M., Sherman, J., and Gismondi, M. 1993. *Winning Back the Words: Confronting Experts in an Environmental Public Hearing*. Toronto: Garamond Press.

de Saint-Exupéry, A. 1943. *The Little Prince*. Paris: Gallimard.

Sachs, C. 1996. *Gendered Fields: Rural Women, Agriculture and Environment*. Boulder: Westview Press.

Savage, M. 2000. *Class Analysis and Social Transformation*. Buckingham: Open University.

Skeggs, B. 2004. *Class, Self, Culture*. London: Routledge.

Skogen, K. 2003. Adapting adaptive management to a cultural understanding of land use conflicts. *Society and Natural Resources*, 16(5), 435–450.

Tindall, D.B., Davies, S. and Mauboules, C. 2003. Activism and conservation behavior in an environmental movement: the contradictory effects of gender. *Society and Natural Resources*, 16(10), 909–32.

Tripp-Knowles, P. 1999. The feminine face of forestry in Canada, in *Challenging Professions: Historical and Contemporary Perspectives on Women's Work*, edited by S. Smyth, S. Acker, P. Bourne and A. Prentice. Toronto: University of Toronto Press, 194–211.

Turner, N.J., Gregory, R., Brooks, C., Falling, L. and Satterfield, T. 2008. From invisibility to transparency: identifying the implications. *Ecology and Society* [Online], 13(2). Available at: http://www.ecologyandsociety.org/ [accessed: 13 September 2010].

Uliczka, H., Angelstam, P. Jansson, G. and Bro, A. 2004. Non-industrial private forest owners' knowledge of and attitudes towards nature conservation. *Scandinavian Journal of Forest Research*, 19(3), 274–88.

Usher, P. 2000. Traditional ecological knowledge in environmental assessment and management. *Arctic*, 53(2), 183–93.

Woods, M. 2005. *Rural Geography: Processes, Responses and Experiences in Rural Restructuring*. Thousand Oaks: Sage.

Chapter 12

The 'Hidden Injuries' of Class and Gender among Rural Teenagers

Edward W. Morris

In their classic book *The Hidden Injuries of Class* Richard Sennett and Jonathan Cobb write: '[the] fear of being summoned before some hidden bar of judgment and being found inadequate infects the lives of [working-class] people … it is a matter of a hidden weight, a hidden anxiety' (1972: 33). Sennett and Cobb (1972) offer a deep, innovative description of social class as a source of unequal resources, as well as a threat to dignity. In this chapter, I take a similar approach by demonstrating how class-based challenges create hidden anxieties for rural teenagers, prompting them to carve a sense of respect and efficacy. But as I will show, this process is not just about class. The 'hidden injuries' of personal background for these teenagers are refracted through gender and rurality, which shape the particular strategies engaged to heal these injuries.

The data for this chapter come from a one and half year ethnographic study of high school students in a low income rural area of the United States. In the course of this research, I was often struck and personally affected by the stories of the people I came to know. This chapter focuses on two students I interviewed whose life experiences I found poignant and compelling. Although personal, these stories reveal intricate intersections between gender, class and rurality.

Background

A long line of research, including the influential work of Sennett and Cobb (1972), has analysed the emotional dimensions of social class. Recently, researchers have strengthened this approach to emphasize how class is constituted affectively and culturally, through symbolic boundaries and meanings (Bettie 2003, Lamont 2000, Reay 2005, Skeggs 2004). From this perspective, class is experienced and reproduced through people's emotional lives and sense of self, not just through their objective economic standing. Studies in this vein attempt to capture the complex ways that people negotiate, reify and transform class based meanings in their everyday lives.

The early work of Sennett and Cobb (1972) deftly taps this 'hidden' world of class based emotion. The authors plumb an American working-class anxiety in which having less money typically means having less dignity. Although the authors concentrate on adults and employment, their interviewees also recount feeling bored, belittled and unfairly treated in school, similar to other examinations of working-class youth (e.g., MacLeod 1995, Willis 1977). In response, according to Sennett and Cobb (1972: 83–84), 'a counterculture of dignity springs up among these working-class boys' emphasizing 'the breaking of rules', which constitutes 'an attempt to create among themselves badges of dignity that those in authority can't destroy'. Class from this perspective can impugn self-worth and self-efficacy, shaping the means through which working-class youth construct themselves as worthy of respect. However, such constructions can engender resistance to school authority, hindering educational achievement.

Sennett and Cobb's (1972) analysis of class, however prescient, failed to consider intersections with gender. As the above quote implies, such transgressive responses to perceived indignity contain a distinctly masculine edge. Acknowledging such intersections is critical, because class does not stand apart from other identities and modes of inequality such as gender, race and place; it is fundamentally constituted through and interwoven with them. In an evolving, recursive dynamic, gender shapes the experience and understanding of class, and class shapes the experience and understanding of gender. This indicates that the meanings and emotions of class are inextricably gendered, as are the strategies through which people respond to these meanings and emotions.

Research has examined how the interconnections of masculinity and class can result in educational disconnection for working-class boys (Connolly 2004, Keddie 2007, MacLeod 1995, Willis 1977). Recent work on this topic draws from Connell's (1987, 1995) influential theory of hegemonic masculinity. Connell's (1987, 1995) theory emphasizes multiplicity in power relations surrounding the concept of masculinity. Masculinity is constituted through various 'configurations of practice', including those practices deemed hegemonic, which most effectively reflect and promulgate the dominance of men over women (Connell and Messerschmidt 2005). Connell (1987, 1995) argues that such ideals of masculinity are revered by most men (and women) as the embodiment of a 'real man'. He explains that other possible masculinities exist but hold less power. These other masculinities include 'subordinated' and 'marginalized' masculinities (Connell 1995). Subordinated masculinities consist primarily of masculine practices seen as effeminate, especially those embodied by gay men. Marginalized masculinities include practices strongly shaped by modes of inequality such as class and race. It is here that we see applications to some poor and working-class boys in school who may channel their frustration, boredom and marginalization into displays of masculine 'protest' bravado, flouting school rules and conventions in the process (Keddie 2007, Willis 1977).

While useful in examining interconnections of class and gender, the theory of hegemonic masculinity has not eluded critique. As Connell and Messerschmidt (2005) observe, numerous authors have challenged the concept. While I do not have space to review the critiques in full here, I focus on two key concerns raised about the notion of hegemonic masculinity.

First, scholars have disagreed with the static notion of masculinity that can be construed from many deployments of the theory (Hearn 2004, Pascoe 2007). These authors argue that some applications frame masculinities as existing in a wooden typology, where boys and men embody 'hegemonic' 'subordinated' and other forms almost as a set of traits. This reading downplays the fluid, continual and often contradictory process through which gender is constructed. Demetriou (2001) adds to criticism of (Connell 1987, 1995) theoretical framework arguing that too often hegemonic masculinity is constructed as a singular, dominant, monolithic form (Demetriou 2001, Jefferson 2002). As Demetriou (2001) shows, Gramsci's (1971) original formulation theorized hegemony as an ongoing, complex process of forging an historical ruling bloc. This achievement entails consent, legitimization and incorporation of various 'subaltern' as well as dominant groups (Gramsci 1971). This pragmatic, internal and highly variable process was not emphasized in Connell's (1987) early theory, which tended to highlight transnational 'exemplars' of hegemonic masculinity rather than the messy, locally specific means through which different, sometimes contradictory, ideals of masculinity gain pre-eminence.

In responding to these critiques, Connell and Messerschmidt (2005) emphasize that masculinity should not be seen as occurring in pre-set character types, but through sets of practices that can be employed situationally, unevenly, and in a constantly evolving manner. This emphasis aligns with a 'practice' approach, which frames gender as something that is constantly 'done' (achieved, embodied and performed), through interaction (Butler 2006, West and Zimmerman 1987, Yancey Martin 2003). Connell and Messerschmidt (2005) also revise the theory to take greater account of global, regional and local levels in the construction of masculinity. This formulation leaves greater space for considering how 'place' shapes masculinity and power relations surrounding gender.

Indeed, scholars have recently positioned 'place' (rurality in particular) as a crucial factor in the development of class gender identities and discourses (Campbell, Bell and Finney 2006, Corbett 2007, Henderson and Tickamyer 2009, Pini, Price and McDonald 2010). Pini, Price and McDonald (2010) show rurality as a dynamically constructed identity, not simply a geographical location, which intricately molds identities of class and gender. Rurality tends to carry certain blue-collar masculine connotations such as toughness, hardiness and physically active work and recreation (Campbell, Bell and Finney 2006). Bye (2009), for example, finds that young rural men in Norway revere bodily endurance and vitality expressed through outdoor leisure pursuits and interest in pragmatic 'hands-on' skills. At the same time, Bye (2009) emphasizes that notions of rural masculinity are fluid and unsettled, as young men negotiate alternative visions of masculinity such as 'caring' sensitivity. Additional research finds that connections between class, rurality and masculinity create acute challenges for boys in school. Alloway and Gilbert (2004) show that low income rural boys in Australia are more dismissive of higher education than their female counterparts, seeing 'real work' as something that does not occur in school. Keddie (2007: 191) sensitively reveals how rural masculinity can trigger educational apathy, using a longitudinal study of one boy to reflect 'how issues of social class and rurality, in particular, can work to exaggerate investments in harmful enactments of masculinity, and amplify school disengagement'. I have found that disadvantaged boys in Ohio, United States of America, seek empowerment through notions of rural blue-collar masculinity that hinder them academically (Morris 2008). In this chapter I further explore how masculinity (and femininity) are shaped by experiences of class and rurality in ways that influence educational perceptions.

A second major criticism of hegemonic masculinity is that research deploying the concept has almost exclusively focused on men or boys. This focus can result in a tautological cataloguing of masculinity as whatever men or boys do. The concentration on men and boys also fails to consider how women and notions of femininity contribute to the construction of masculinity. As a relational construct, masculinity is constituted vis-à-vis femininity, and hegemonic and dominant masculinities often form through the denigration of femininity (Pascoe 2007). For this reason, Connell and Messerschmidt (2005) urge reviving the corollary notion of 'emphasized femininity' which constitutes idealized practices of femininity that typically encourage being supportive and receptive to men (Connell 1987). Accordingly, the authors encourage greater effort to recognize the complex perceptions of femininity and masculinity among women and girls. They write, 'We consider that research on hegemonic masculinity now needs to give much closer attention to the practices of women and the historical interplay of femininities and masculinities' (Connell and Messerschmidt 2005: 848). This chapter follows this charge by contrasting the construction of femininity and masculinity for two students from low income rural backgrounds.

In documenting the experiences of these two rural teenagers, one boy and one girl, this chapter explores how hegemonic masculinity, as well as emphasized femininity, shape reactions to class based difficulties differently. I examine how class, gender and rurality emerge from individual efforts to represent particular statuses and identities. These representations are not freely produced, but funnelled through constraints of material and symbolic factors stemming from family background, rural location and sex categorization. This chapter underscores how gender, as a situated configuration of practices, provides different means of responding to emotional challenges emanating from class, family and place. I reveal how such constructions produce 'real' impacts, particularly in students' attachment to school.

Methodology

This analysis is based on ethnographic data gathered from a rural high school in Ohio which I call Clayton High School (a pseudonym). The school was located in the centre of a small town I call Clayton, with a population of 1,972. I designate the area as 'rural' primarily because of its sparse population and the fact that its economy historically rested on the extraction of land based resources, specifically coal mining. Although the town emerged as a coal boom town in the early part of the twentieth century, by the later part of the century it had fallen victim to economic restructuring and the loss of virtually all coal related jobs. This created substantial economic decline, along with a sense of isolation in the area. According to 2000 United States Census data, the poverty rate was 25 per cent, the median income was US$24,931, and the median value of owner-occupied housing was US$43,500 (National Center for Educational Statistics 2000).

I conducted interviews and regular field observation at Clayton High School from January 2006 to June 2007. The high school was 98 per cent white and 62 per cent of its students received free or reduced lunch (an indicator of economic disadvantage). I undertook participant observation throughout the school in spaces such as classrooms, hallways, the lunchroom and the library, as well as outside of school at school related events such as sporting events and graduation. I recorded field notes of these observations while on-site and later expanded them as soon as possible off site in a computer file, adding more detail. I had regular conversations with students, school faculty, administrators and a few community members, which I also recorded in field notes. The high school had less than 350 students in total, which allowed me to get to know students and adults fairly well. I formally interviewed 15 students at the school. These interviews followed a semi-structured format and were audio recorded and transcribed. I focus here on two students from this sample. This strategy is meant to convey deeper portraits of these students; it also reflects broader patterns and themes that emerged throughout my data.

Kevin

I first met Kevin (a pseudonym) in a ninth grade English class at Clayton. He had thick, sandy blonde hair and lugubrious, deep-set eyes. He rarely smiled and his brow often furrowed into what approached a scowl. But underneath this foreboding exterior, Kevin was highly personable. He was one of the first students I met and talked to during my fieldwork and he later helped me recruit additional students to interview. Students and teachers seemed to like Kevin, but also viewed him as slightly peculiar. Students occasionally made fun of him, and teachers viewed him as potentially troublesome.

Kevin's Hidden Anxiety: Class, Work and Status

As we walked down the hall to a private room for the interview, I noticed that Kevin's white high-top sneakers squeaked loudly on the concrete floors. Once we sat down for the interview, he told me that he lived in a house with his parents, younger brother, and occasionally his sister and seven year old nephew. Kevin's mother worked as a secretary for an electrician and, as he described it, got 'paid pretty good'. His father was 54 at the time of the interview and disabled. His father dropped out of school in the eleventh grade and was collecting slim federal disability assistance. Kevin vacillated between feelings of pride and shame regarding his father: 'He's said to only have an eighth grade education through IQ tests [pause] I mean but he's a smart guy. He can't really do book work but if you go out and you give him lumber he can build a porch.'

Kevin felt the hidden shame of economic limitations and an unemployed father, and this anxiety expressed itself in everyday life through the peer culture of the high school. For many teenagers, clothing serves as an important emblem of individuality, belonging and status. Although low income in general, the peer culture at Clayton emphasized such outward appearance. Yet, Kevin described the restricted resources he had to achieve such status:

Kevin: Like Meghan [another student], she's got like all kinda money. She's got like name brand clothes, and shoes, and brand new shoes any time she wants to get 'em. And shoppin' all the time [pauses] I don't do that shit. I mean look at these things [looks down, pulls some of the surface off his shoes where it is peeling off, puts finger through holes between upper part of shoe and the sole]. I've had these things since the beginning of the year. I paid like 40 bucks for 'em. That's not a lot for shoes. And they're comfortable. I don't give a shit what they look like. People can call me what they want. I can stand up for myself. But I mean, like, I got good clothes on, I mean I had this shirt since last year [plain gray short sleeve t-shirt]. It's got a little stain on it from where I had lunch, but you know, it's nice.

Edward Morris: So some of it has to do with money and they're sort of trying to be better?

Kevin: [Nods head to indicate 'yes', continues staring down at his shoes. His face has reddened, and he appears upset. Kevin quickly composed himself and continued] I mean these are Loves right here [picks at his shoes again] these are a good brand of shoe. But I got 'em at a discount store, so fake leather, you know, it peels off. But this part up here [points to upper part of the shoe] – I mean it's still white. [pauses] And, I'd probably go out and buy the same pair but just not wear them out as much like I used to. When I got these I was wearin' 'em all over you know? But if I got a pair and didn't wear 'em anywhere but school they'd look brand new every day.

He then described how kids from wealthier backgrounds are not forced to be as careful with clothes and shoes as he was:

I mean, it's just the way people take care of things. Rich kids, and preps and everything – I don't think you see 'em with the same shirt on in a month. I wear this shirt just about once a week. I have like six, seven nice shirts and then I have crappy ones I wear around the house [pauses, slowly] I don't have a lot of nice clothes [pauses] But I wash my own clothes, because I gotta have stuff clean.

Kevin goes on to describe how he had to plan what to wear and when to wash it so he could alternate his few 'nice' shirts and pants every week. He anticipated being ridiculed for wearing the same clothes. He was ashamed of his squeaky, peeling shoes, but appeared to blame himself for being too rough on them.

In the same way that work status and notions of success compromised respectability for adults in Sennett and Cobb's (1972) study, clothing and peer group status created 'hidden injuries' for Kevin. The daily anxiety of this must have been taxing. Kevin responded to these challenges in several positive ways; he established life goals, performed adequately in school, and was socially outgoing albeit not entirely 'popular'. Yet Kevin clearly approached life with a sense of trepidation and distrust. According to him, he had achieved a bad social reputation that inevitably lingered in this rural area: 'I've been outcasted since fifth grade.' Kevin's economic limitations affected his ability to buy new, stylish clothes and, as I will discuss, hindered his participation in school sports, both of which affected his peer status.

Kevin's Response: Physical and Aggressive Masculinity

Kevin earnestly established career goals which gave him the promise of overcoming economic limitations. He wanted to go into construction like his father, but own and operate the business himself: 'Well I like [construction]. I mean it's easy for me. I'm just – you know, cut wood, hook up the gutters, nails, 'cause I helped build our whole entire house the one we live in now.' Kevin aspired to obtain a two year degree beyond high school to help him achieve this career goal. He was a decent student academically with around a B average, but he viewed college as more of a necessary hurdle than something that would provide him with useful knowledge. He preferred to learn from his uncle, also in the construction business: 'I could just learn everything from him. I wouldn't have to go to college or anything.' He described this view as something common to boys and consistent with his understanding of masculinity: 'like most the guys [at Clayton], they're like, well, what's the point [of school]? I can drop out right now and do work with my uncle doing construction and be brought up right underneath his wing.'

Kevin perceived this career plan not only as a way to have 'a big house and a nice wife' but also as a way to demonstrate masculinity through physically vigorous work. In describing his life plans, he underscored bodily attributes:

I have good plans ahead of me and I'm young and I'm in shape pretty much as good as I'm gonna get right now. I mean I have fat, but I mean its muscle underneath there … otherwise I wouldn't be able to box – I'd get wind knocked outta me. And so I'm in good shape, my arms are in good shape, I can run a mile, you know, I can do everything that I'm required to do at my age physically. And I have a good career plan.

As I show elsewhere (Morris 2008), hegemonic masculinity in the rural location of Clayton emphasized physical qualities such as strength, pain management and toughness (see also Bye 2009, Keddie 2007). Historically, the economy of Clayton had been dominated by coal mining, in which men worked arduous physical labour. Although coal industry jobs recently evaporated from the area, boys continued to express a longing for this rural, working-class masculinity through their interest in other forms of manual labour, such as construction. The stable employment and sense of usefulness Kevin and other boys hoped to gain from blue-collar work reinforced the dignity associated with this rural class position. The physical vitality of this work further confirmed their masculinity. Kevin's emphasis on owning his own business echoes findings of a growing interest in business focused masculinity in rural areas (Brandth and Haugen 2006). This reflects somewhat of a diversion from masculinity based in physical vigor, but still maintains the economic power and independence associated with hegemonic masculinity.

It was clear that Kevin crafted such plans in response to his limited economic resources. He did not want to end up like his father, who could not demonstrate his masculinity through physical labour nor through being a primary source of family income. Kevin interpreted his life goals as dependent on his own will power, and contrasted this with other low income kids in the area whom he said were involved in drugs. He stated: 'it just makes me mad that people just want to throw their life away like that and not accomplish anything. Like when I'm 20 and I'm out there runnin' a small business or something, they'll still be on the street rubbin' two quarters together, you know, tryin' to make 75 cent with two.' This sense of will power was a self-efficacious response to depressed economic circumstances in the area and in Kevin's own background.

Sometimes, however, Kevin's response to class and status anxiety was not as positive. He had been suspended from school several times for fighting and other aggressive behaviour and demonstrated a confrontational stance toward school personnel. One day when I was signing in at the school I noticed that the principal was loudly disciplining Kevin in his office. As I turned the corner to walk down the hallway, Kevin emerged from the principal's office and I asked him how he was doing. He responded, 'Pretty shitty. I just got sent to the principal's office for fuckin' talkin' about a test! It's fucked up – for no other reason than talking about a dumb test!'

Kevin admitted that he could let his anger get the better of him in school:

I mean I've cussed out a teacher a couple of times, but that wasn't because I didn't wanna do my work. I mean I was really mad, havin' a bad day and they didn't make it any better by like, one time a [teacher's aide] wouldn't let me use my bathroom pass. And I said no – I have to go to the bathroom, let me go to the bathroom or I'm a walk out. And we got in a big argument about it and I ended up cussin' at 'er and walkin' outta the room.

He described himself as having a problem with his temper:

> I'm a nice guy, but if you piss me off, I can get pretty angry. It runs on both sides of the family – temper problem you know. Yeah, I mean there's really not much to say, I'm a nice guy and I talk nice and I act nice to people and do right most best I can in life.

Although Kevin tried his best to 'do right' he often responded to a sense of being belittled either in classrooms or among peers with aggressive behaviour. This response is consistent with 'protest' practices of marginalized masculinity (Connell and Messerschmidt 2005). Such responses not only alleviated this sense of belittlement, they affirmed masculinity. But they also produced hidden academic costs. Kevin found himself in trouble for insubordination, and also was often in fights at school.

Such academic costs were less salient for Kevin than the necessity of standing up for himself and reconstituting masculinity through fighting. Kevin stated that fighting allowed him to demonstrate his superior toughness over other boys:

> A guy [was] tryin' to think he's tough, takin' food off my tray and sayin' "oh this is mine, you ain't gonna eat this are you?" Well, you know, I took him outside after school and I beat the piss out of him. … And [another day] he goes again. I told him if he didn't quit I was gonna get up and hit him. And he hit me in the head with a spoon. So I got up and I walked over toward 'im, and I told him to stand up. And this was like – from the door to you like where he was standing if he was you and you're him and he didn't stand up so I walked up and, you know, I blasted 'im in the nose [mimics punching motion towards me]. And I hit 'im in the side of the head, and they said I hit him about four or five times, I don't really remember much. I just hit. I just swung. But he had marks all along his head and his eyes were all black and his nose was all busted up. I mean, I beat the piss outta him twice! [laughs].

Kevin viewed fighting as a free social space in which he could demonstrate superiority, unencumbered by the limitations of social status. Fighting allowed Kevin an emotional release in this blue-collar, rural context which demanded emotional stoicism for men. Such a release also aligns with local masculinity because it occurs through physical action: 'I just hit. I just swung.' Fighting confirmed Kevin's masculinity, proving his toughness and superiority over other boys whom he perceived to belittle him.

Another possible outlet to demonstrate physical masculinity at Clayton was through sports. But Kevin perceived that his financial background hindered him from pursuing school sponsored outlets for physical masculinity such as sports:

'I mean the jocks have to have money to buy basketball shoes or baseball cleats. I mean, if a poor parent had a kid that wanted to play football, he would have to almost get a loan to play [laughs].'

Because of the prohibitive cost of school sports,[1] Kevin turned to alternative means of demonstrating masculinity such as fighting, and boxing at a local gym. When I asked him who his role models were, he said his only role model was Tommy, a local man who was once a professional boxer and operated a small boxing gym in town that Kevin frequented. Kevin describes how Tommy used boxing to be successful without higher education: 'I mean, his dad ran a bar. He graduated from high school, but he didn't go to college or anything. ... And I look up to him because I wanna get there someday.' Kevin continued, describing how he used boxing to relieve stress in his home and personal life: 'I get out my stress and I just forget about what went on at the house, or with my girlfriend, if we had an argument. I mean, I just get away from the world – dealing with reality. It's a good get away.'

Aggressive contact sports such as boxing are often seen as a means of stress relief and a way to 'get out your aggression'. But studies find that such activities actually increase the chances of further aggressive behaviour, including physical fights at school (Kreager 2007, Messner 1992). This was the case with Kevin, who (although a good student) was often in trouble for being verbally and physically combative at school. This resulted in suspensions that stunted his educational progress and shaped how teachers and administrators at Clayton viewed him. In the words of one teacher: '[Kevin] has a bad attitude. He's gonna be trouble down the line.'

Kevin's family background and peer status created hidden psychological injuries. Local hegemonic masculinity in this rural community emphasized a stoic independence in managing these emotional tolls, along with the demonstration of physical vitality. This definition of masculinity provided a specific outlet for challenging class based injuries; primarily through aggressive verbal or physical outbursts, often in defiance of school rules. In this way gender itself produced a hidden cost. Kevin felt belittled not only because of his peer status and family financial resources, but also because of limited acceptable paths to display masculinity. In accessing and forming masculinity to challenge and relieve sources of 'stress' in his life, Kevin engaged in aggressive behaviour that limited his attachment to school.

---

    1   Sport funding in public schools varies across the United States. Many states, including Ohio, have recently cut back on public funding for school sports. In order to play American football (considered the most popular and 'manly' sport) at Clayton, for instance, Kevin would have to pay for a copious amount of equipment himself, which he said was too expensive for his family.

Kaycee

Another student at Clayton named Kaycee (a pseudonym) represented the hidden injuries of family background, although in a slightly different way. Kaycee was a vibrant, outgoing girl who always appeared to be in a good mood. She had dark hair, brown eyes and an olive complexion. Her wide, toothy smile was infectious. However, when I interviewed Kaycee I was surprised to find that her bright personality masked some hidden shame regarding her family background.

Kaycee's Hidden Anxiety: Class, Family Reputation and Family Turmoil

Kaycee's parents were no longer together. Her father had long been unemployed and her mother worked as a cashier at a grocery store for over 20 years, but was recently laid off. Kaycee's mother had a high school diploma and her father dropped out of school in the tenth grade. Kaycee's older brother, his girlfriend, and their young child (Kaycee's nephew) lived in Kaycee's house. Like Kaycee's father, her brother also did not have a job. Later in the interview, Kaycee revealed that both her father and brother suffered from addictions to drugs and alcohol.

It soon became clear that Kaycee experienced considerable tension in her home both currently and earlier in her life. When I asked her what she thought about school, she gave an interesting answer:

> Kaycee: I like school. Yeah, I like school. I [pauses] get away from the drama at my house [laughs]. When I come to school I like it. I remember one day last year, like my family is a really disoriented family. Like, we're weird. Like, I'm not, but I'm the only sane one in my family. And one day I walked out of school with a big smile on and looked over and there was my mom sitting in the car and my brother's truck was parked next to her and my brother wasn't in his truck. And I got in the car and my brother was over there and his knuckles were all bloody. And I thought, "great, now I'm out of school" [sarcastically]. Yeah, so school is kind of a place that I like to go to.
>
> Edward Morris: Okay, so what happened to him?
>
> Kaycee: He got in a fight. Like his girlfriend, she hit him with a baseball bat and he just punched the wall 'cause he won't hit her, so [pauses].
>
> Edward Morris: Yeah, well some people would say that school is like too much drama but you [pauses].
>
> Kaycee: Well it is a lot of drama, but like I'd rather have like friend drama than family drama. Like actually going home when my brother's fights with his girlfriend are crazy. Like off and on custody and stuff. It's really weird. And they're not good parents. I just [pauses] hate it [stares down at feet].

Most students I interviewed at Clayton expressed ambivalence or aversion to school. Kaycee, by contrast, perceived school as a welcome respite from a 'dramatic' home life.

The problems experienced by Kaycee's family had resulted in them having a 'bad' reputation in the community. Students at Clayton referred to family reputation as the importance of one's 'last name'. As Kaycee described it, 'I don't have a good last name'. But Kaycee wanted to overcome this reputation through school achievement:

> Like one time I went up to my cousin and her boyfriend said, you're gonna change the McCleary last name. Like you're gonna change what people think about it. 'Cause I'm going to college and I've already planned what I want to do and everything and I don't do drugs or anything, but the rest of my family does. And he's like you're gonna change the McCleary name and I'm like, okay. Because that's what people think about us around here.

Kaycee struggled not only with the tension in her family, but also with the stigma her family had acquired in the community. As in other rural areas, 'family name' and reputation carried heavy weight in Clayton (Batteau 1982, Duncan 1999, Sherman 2006). This was a small, tight-knit community where many families had lived in the area for generations. Students coming from 'bad' families such as Kaycee perceived that they would have to constantly work to overcome this reputation.

Kaycee's Response: Femininity and School Attachment

As Kaycee mentions, drug use and unemployment perpetuated part of her family's negative reputation. They lacked the 'moral capital' often required to achieve status in rural communities (Sherman 2006). Kaycee told me that her father was monitored by local police officers who often searched his car in public. She also poignantly recounted times when she had to manage the repercussions of her father's addictive behaviour:

> Like one time my mom dropped me off like at my dad's house for the day and he was passed out [from drinking] and his head was busted open. I was scared to death. I couldn't wake him up. I thought my dad was dead, and I couldn't get to school. I think I was like ten or eleven. ... But [the next-door neighbour] ended up coming over. It was like a miracle that he just came over and knocked on the door and I just bawled and ran over and gave him a hug and was like, "something happened to my dad!" And he went over and tried to wake him up and couldn't wake him up, so he took me to school, and I went to school squalling.

Astonishingly, Kaycee expresses concern not only with her father, but also with getting to school. One might think that such a troubled family life would hinder

Kaycee's educational progress. But to the contrary, she used school as a space and method for healing her hidden injuries. She described how school comforted her when she was younger:

> My parents were off and on for [pauses] a long time. Like they got in fights and stuff and it sucked. I don't like my childhood, I hated it ... But I thank a lot of my teachers because I would come into school one day and they could see that I was upset and I had my own little cot in a corner where they'd see that my parents had been fighting all night and I hadn't gotten any sleep and I couldn't do anything so they just put me in a cot in the corner and they'd just let me sleep during school. So [school] has been like real good for me [pauses]

> Edward Morris: So you feel like the school has always like cared about you in a sense?

> Kaycee: Yeah. And I told my mom one day, "you know what? Kids my age hate school! I'm not supposed to like school!" But I do.

Instead of frustrations in her family background creating a defiant stance toward school and other people, as they did with Kevin, Kaycee became more attached to school. School did not present a further threat of belittlement, but rather an opportunity to escape: 'I like feel [pauses] protected here. I don't feel like my drama can come here. I just drop it.' Kaycee used this attachment to perform well academically. Teachers described her as an excellent student, and she planned to attend a four year college and eventually become a teacher.

Gender facilitated Kaycee's ability to translate family troubles into concerted school connections. Instead of keeping problems to herself only to have them eventually boil over as Kevin did, Kaycee sought connections to others as a way of mitigating problems. Early in her life, school provided caring adults in the form of teachers that Kaycee could confide in, and consistent with 'emphasized femininity' she interpreted emotional connections to others as acceptable to demonstrating femininity (Connell 1987).

Kaycee's construction of femininity also facilitated her school achievement. Although she performed well academically, she told me that she had trouble reading early in her educational career because her parents did not regularly read to her at home:

> My mom tried, like my mom was a really good mom. Like my mom is my hero. And my mom worked like two jobs when my dad was like an alcoholic and a drug addict. So I mean [pauses] But my mom would try to read to me but she would leave the TV on and I would get up and take off. And she told me half the time she would read to me and I'd stare at the TV and she's be like are you paying attention? And I'd be like "uh-huh" and just stare at the TV!

Perhaps drawing from these early experiences, Kaycee described herself as 'not real smart'. Emphasized femininity in Clayton historically placed women in supportive, dependent roles within the home while men worked in coal mining or other manual labour jobs. Accordingly, girls at Clayton appeared uncomfortable with demonstrating superiority. Conventional views would suggest that this lack of confidence would limit girls' educational progress. But instead of debilitating her, these perceived disadvantages impelled Kaycee to exert more effort: 'I have to like really, really try [in school].' She further described boys as 'naturally' better able to comprehend academic lessons, emphasizing that as a girl, she had to try harder. The local, historical submission of femininity to masculinity provided the guidelines for this view. In framing herself as not smart, Kaycee constructed her gendered identity as consistent with emphasized femininity. Although she excelled academically, she framed herself as subordinate to others. Kaycee accepted herself as not 'real smart' but ironically, instead of stifling her academic self-efficacy, this perception actually encouraged it.

Ostensibly, Kaycee produced femininity in rather conventional ways consistent with the emotional, supportive and submissive tenets of emphasized femininity (as a further example, she discussed her boyfriend and his life through vast portions of the interview). She minimized her academic ability compared to others, especially boys, and she actively sought supportive, caring relationships through the school to protect against family trauma. Yet this very production of gender, although conventional in many ways, provided a school focused pathway that encouraged academic success despite the difficulties of her family background. Some of Kaycee's ability to do this stemmed from personal qualities, but some stemmed from the interactional construction of gender. Femininity in this rural location emphasized being forthcoming with emotions, forging relationships as a means of emotional support, and remaining compliant and subordinate to men. This allowed Kaycee to approach school as a caring, supportive environment. Further, because she lacked confidence in her innate academic ability (something she interpreted as more common for girls than for boys) she put extra effort into schoolwork. Femininity provided Kaycee with unexpected tools that facilitated educational success through positive school attachment and school performance.

Conclusion

This chapter chronicles the stories of two rural teenagers, Kevin and Kaycee. As a focused portrait of two students, this analysis aims for a deep description of personal experience; something large patterns themselves cannot accomplish. I do not suggest that all rural boys and girls from disadvantaged backgrounds produce the same interpretations and strategies shown here. Instead, I use these portraits to highlight how social class can create emotional tolls, and how rural teenagers deploy gender in responding to class based challenges. This shows gender as an ongoing interactional product that interacts with social class and rurality in complex ways. The patterns through which teenagers constitute gender shape how they contend with feelings of shame and how they approach social institutions such as education.

Rurality critically defines these gendered scripts. Both Kevin and Kaycee performed gender in ways socially appropriate to this rural context. Kevin enacted a tough, gritty masculinity. Kaycee exhibited an ebullient, emotive femininity. Such practices were provided and sanctioned by the rural community in which they lived as part of hegemonic masculinity and emphasized femininity. Coal mining economically dominated this community until the late 1980s. The emphasis on tough, physical masculinity expressed by Kevin aligns with the economic relations of the coal industry, in which men historically worked hard labour in the mines to support their families. The emphasis on supportive, deferential femininity revealed by Kaycee is also consistent with this historically based dynamic, as women were tied to domestic labour and economically dependent on men. However, as Kaycee's school effort shows, such ostensibly docile femininity contains hidden routes to achievement through school attachment.

The combination of gender and rurality compelled these teenagers to manage the hidden anxieties of class and family background differently. Kevin's father's unemployment, and his family's inability to buy him 'nice' clothes and fund his participation in school sports, created challenges to his masculinity. He responded by asserting masculinity in overtly dominant ways, such as fighting and boxing. His aggressive behaviour carved an expanding rift between him and the school. Kaycee's low income, tumultuous family background also created hidden injuries. As with Kevin, these were mediated through the construction of gender. However, available patterns of feminine practice provided Kaycee with more useful tools to forge a pro-school orientation. Kaycee approached school as an opportunity to develop supportive relationships. Emphasized femininity encouraged her to disparage her academic skills, but instead of enervating her academic effort, this actually intensified it. Instead of the submission generally implied by 'emphasized femininity', Kaycee channeled local 'feminine' principles to challenge inequalities of class and local family stigma through education.

Previous research has examined class and gender as interconnected sources and outcomes of inequality, but less work has integrated the notion of place. The scripts Kevin and Kaycee used to enact class and gender emanated from their rural location. In addition, rurality can be viewed as a constructed outcome itself, intersecting with class and gender. Kevin's interest in toughness, stoicism and manual labour in areas such as carpentry, represents a working-class masculinity that resonated as a rural, community endorsed version of manhood. Kaycee's fight to change her 'family name' signifies the class and community based constraints of rural Clayton. Her simultaneously humble and ambitious academic intentions to overcome these constraints reflect an innovative, if tenuous, adherence to local emphasized femininity. This chapter demonstrates that by viewing gender, class and place as constructed outcomes interwoven through individuals' personal lives, we learn more about the multifaceted ways people experience and respond to the 'hidden injuries' of inequality.

Acknowledgments

This research was supported by a grant from the Spencer Foundation. I thank the staff and students at Clayton High School for sharing their time and thoughts with me. The views expressed here are solely those of the author.

References

Alloway, N. and Gilbert, P. 2004. Shifting discourses about gender in higher education enrolments: retrieving marginalised voices. *International Journal of Qualitative Studies in Education*, 17(1), 99–112.

Batteau, A. 1982. Mosbys and Broomsedge: the semantics of class in an appalachian kinship system. *American Ethnologist*, 9(3), 445–66.

Bettie, J. 2003. *Women without Class: Girls, Race and Identity*. Berkeley, California: University of California Press.

Brandth, B. and Haugen, M. 2006. Changing masculinity in a changing rural industry: representations in the forestry press, in *Country Boys: Masculinity and Rural Life*, edited by H. Campbell, M. Mayerfeld Bell and M. Finney. University Park: Pennsylvania State University Press, 217–33.

Butler, J. 2006. *Gender Trouble: Feminism and the Subversion of Identity*. Originally published 1990, 10th anniversary edition 1999. New York: Routledge.

Bye, L.M. 2009. How to be a rural man: young men's performances and negotiations of rural masculinities. *Journal of Rural Studies*, 25(3), 278–88.

Campbell, H., Mayerfeld Bell, M. and Finney, M. 2006. Masculinity and rural life: an introduction, in *Country Boys: Masculinity and Rural Life*, edited H. Campbell, M. Mayerfeld Bell and M. Finney. University Park: Pennsylvania State University Press, 1–22.

Connell, R.W. 1987. *Gender and Power*. Stanford: Stanford University Press.

Connell, R.W. 1995. *Masculinities*. Berkeley: University of California Press.

Connell, R.W. and Messerschmidt, J.W. 2005. Hegemonic masculinity: rethinking the concept. *Gender and Society*, 19(6), 829–59.

Connolly, P. 2004. *Boys and Schooling in the Early Years*. London: Routledge Farmer.

Corbett, M. 2007. *Learning to Leave: The Irony of Schooling in a Coastal Community*. Halifax: Fernwood.

Demetriou, D. 2001. Connell's concept of hegemonic masculinity: a critique. *Theory and Society*, 30(3), 337–61.

Duncan, C.M. 1999. *Worlds Apart: Why Poverty Persists in Rural America.* New Havent: Yale University Press.

Gramsci, A. 1971. *Selections from the Prison Notebooks of Antonio Gramsci,* edited and translated by Q. Hoare and G. Nowell Smith. New York: International Publishers.

Hearn, J. 2004. From hegemonic masculinity to the hegemony of men. *Feminist Theory,* 5(1), 49–72.

Henderson, D. and Tickamyer, A. 2009. The intersection of poverty discourses, in *Emerging Intersections: Race, Class and Gender in Theory, Policy and Practice* edited by B. Thornton Dill and R. Zambrana. New Brunswick: Rutgers University Press, 50–72.

Jefferson, T. 2002. Subordinating Hegemonic Masculinity. *Theoretical Criminology,* 6(1), 63–88.

Keddie, A. 2007. Games of subversion and sabotage: issues of power, masculinity, class, rurality and schooling. *British Journal of Sociology of Education,* 28(2), 181–94.

Kreager, D. 2007. Unnecessary roughness? School sports, peer networks and male adolescent violence. *American Sociological Review,* 72(5), 705–24.

Lamont, M. 2000. *The Dignity of Working Men: Morality and the Boundaries of Race, Class and Immigration.* New York: Russell Sage Foundation.

MacLeod, J. 1995. *Ain't No Makin' It: Aspirations and Attainment in a Low Income Neighborhood.* 2nd edition. Boulder: Westview Press.

Messner, M. 1992. *Power at Play: Sports and the Problem of Masculinity.* Boston: Beacon Press.

Morris, E.W. 2008. 'Rednecks', 'rutters' and 'rithmetic: social class, masculinity and schooling in a rural context. *Gender and Society,* 22(6), 728–51.

National Center for Educational Statistics. 2000. *School District Demographic Profile.* [Online: National Center for Educational Statistics] Available at: http://nces.ed.gov [Accessed 20 March 2007].

Pascoe, C.J. 2007. *Dude, You're a Fag: Masculinity and Sexuality in High School.* Berkeley: University of California Press.

Pini, B., Price, R. and McDonald, P. 2010. Teachers and the emotional dimensions of class in resource affected rural Australia. *British Journal of Sociology of Education,* 31(1), 17–30.

Reay, D. 2005. Beyond consciousness? The psychic landscape of social class. *Sociology,* 39(5), 911–28.

Sennett, R. and Cobb, J. 1972. *The Hidden Injuries of Class.* New York: W.W. Norton.

Sherman, J. 2006. Coping with rural poverty: economic survival and moral capital in rural America. *Social Forces,* 85(2), 891–913.

Skeggs, B. 2004. *Class, Self, Culture.* London: Routledge.

West, C. and Zimmerman, D. 1987. Doing gender. *Gender and Society,* 1(2), 125–151.

Willis, P. 1977. *Learning to Labor: How Working Class Kids Get Working Class Jobs.* New York: Columbia University Press.

Yancey Martin, P. 2003. 'Said and done' versus 'saying and doing:' gendering practices, practising gender at work. *Gender and Society*, 17(3), 342–66.

Index

Gender in a Global/Local World